Case Studies and the Dissemination of Knowledge

The case study has proved of enduring interest to all Western societies, particularly in relation to questions of subjectivity and the sexed self. This volume interrogates how case studies have been used by doctors, lawyers, psychoanalysts, and writers to communicate their findings both within the specialist circles of their academic disciplines, and beyond, to wider publics. At the same time, it questions how case studies have been taken up by a range of audiences to refute and dispute academic knowledge. As such, this book engages with case studies as sites of interdisciplinary negotiation, transnational exchange and influence, exploring the effects of forces such as war, migration, and internationalization.

Case Studies and the Dissemination of Knowledge challenges the limits of disciplinary-based research in the humanities. The cases examined serve as a means of passage between disciplines, genres, and publics, from law to psychoanalysis, and from auto/biography to modernist fiction. Its chapters scrutinize the case study in order to sharpen understanding of the genre's dynamic role in the construction and dissemination of knowledge within and across disciplinary, temporal, and national boundaries. In doing so, they position the case at the center of cultural and social understandings of the emergence of modern subjectivities.

Joy Damousi is professor of history in the School of Historical and Philosophical Studies at the University of Melbourne.

Birgit Lang is senior lecturer in German in the School of Languages and Linguistics at the University of Melbourne.

Katie Sutton is lecturer in German and gender studies at the Australian National University.

Routledge Studies in Cultural History

For a full list of titles in this series, please visit www.routledge.com

Case Studies and the Dissemination of Knowledge

Edited by Joy Damousi, Birgit Lang, and Katie Sutton

NEW YORK AND LONDON

First published 2015
by Routledge
711 Third Avenue, New York, NY 10017

and by Routledge
2 Park Square, Milton Park, Abingdon, Oxon OX14 4RN

*Routledge is an imprint of the Taylor & Francis Group,
an informa business*

© 2015 Taylor & Francis

Library of Congress Cataloging-in-Publication Data

A catalog record for this book has been requested

ISBN: 978-1-138-81533-9 (hbk)
ISBN: 978-1-315-74677-7 (ebk)

Typeset in Sabon
by Apex CoVantage, LLC

Printed and bound in the United States of America by Publishers Graphics,
LLC on sustainably sourced paper.

Contents

PART III
Literary Circulations

Foreword

John Forrester

The three great professions of the Western tradition—law, medicine, and theology—developed practices centered on cases, which formed the bedrock of the later efflorescence of case-centered writing examined in this book. In law, the case, alongside the law (statute), developed as the primary unit of legal argument and of record, as the backbone of a legal system of writing and accounting (for example, *Donoghue v. Stevenson* [1932]; *Brown v. Board of Education* [1954], *Wyong v. Shirt* [1980]). The theological case developed entwined with the practice of confession, giving rise to the body of rules and guidance known as casuistry—the application of general moral principles to the particular moral conundrums and oddities of individual action. The permutations of the medical case, through reports, case notes, and case books, developed in the nineteenth century as one, if not the, principal method of record keeping, internal accounting, pedagogy, and dissemination of knowledge. We might conclude that the case was the privileged genre of the professionals, those engaged in "that kind of business which deals primarily with men as men and is thus distinguished from a trade, which provides for the external wants or occasions of men" (F. D. Maurice, *Lectures on the Education of the Middle Classes*, 1839): the case was the form of writing most immediately applicable to difficulties and crises in human relationships over which our professionals preside.

Despite these great and authoritative legal, medical, and theological traditions, novel nineteenth-century developments gave rise to the golden age of the case from the 1850s on. We can point to a series of independent factors that promoted the rise of the case: to the growing maturity and cultural entrenchment of the novel, linked to the rise of new audiences, new classes, new markets, new paths through society (the *Bildungsroman*); the uncomfortable transition by which the moral life, previously regulated by canon law and the Church, became increasingly regulated by criminal law in the secular domain; the development of the first modern speciality of medicine, medical psychology (alienism, psychiatry), with a prominent public face for these struggling new experts giving witness in law courts on the mental condition and standing of parties in both civil and criminal cases; the invention of the detective story, with its first golden era culminating in *The Case-Book of Sherlock Holmes*; the new technologies of many sorts—in publishing, in administration (the invention of the file card amongst many others), in the hospital sciences (the sphygmomanometer and many others) requiring routine inscription and collation in case files. And yet the striking emergence of a flourishing genre of case writing points even beyond these fundamental shifts to something new.

Forty years ago, Michel Foucault proposed that the emergence of this new case was contemporaneous with, maybe even instrumental in, the crystallization of the new concept of the individual "as he may be described, judged, measured, compared with others, in his very individuality; and it is also the individual who has to be trained or corrected, classified, normalized, excluded." Following Foucault's lead, Ian Hacking wrote of "making up people": his work gave historical body to this singular phrase—multiple personalities; autistic children; victims of child abuse; the obese. "Case work" was how singular individuals were generated, recognized, as bearing such distinctive characteristics, increasingly through the plausibility of a narration; how did they come to be as they were? What were the means for understanding how they came to commit a curious act (sexual, criminal, socially transgressive)? At the same time, these singular individuals increasingly participated, with varying levels of enthusiasm, complicity, hope, fear, collusion, resistance, and protest, in the construction of their "case."

This configuration—of new technologies, of new ways of being an individual, of new professional missions, of new scientific programs—undoubtedly contributed to the golden age of case writing. The chapters in this volume aptly direct our attention to the crossroads between the development of sexology and psychiatry, hand in hand; the creation of new "identities"—most famously the homosexual—and new forms of writing, including the extended and internally complex form of the psychoanalytic case history but also, perhaps more fundamentally, the curious sexological form, pioneered by Richard von Krafft-Ebing, of the anonymous autobiography. These contributions are alert to the mutations and variations of the case, from moralizing fable and community-creating autobiographies both modeled on the sexological case, via paradigms, anecdotes, and experimental modernist documentary novel, to the intriguing plasticity of the medical case file and how "the case" still infects apparently very different genres of social psychological experiment and mass questionnaire methods. The range of countries and cultures where the contributors to this book have found their cases goes together with innovative and disciplined attention to publics: the following chapters demonstrate how the case form was—and is—a supple and powerful form for the creation of new publics and the mediation between nonexpert publics, even the mass media, and expert claims to knowledge and authority. Cases so often mediate between singular and general; but this incessant work of mediation is, so the contributions to this volume demonstrate, precisely how considerable ambiguity is introduced into the effects of case writing. The case can be equally a parable or a polemic, an occasion for lascivious denunciation or scientific truth finding, an exploration of the indeterminism of human action and the display of stubborn and unwelcome truths about "human nature"—and any or all of these at once. The case may find its public in millions of newspaper readers or the small circle of embattled individuals in trouble with themselves and their world; subscribers to a professional literature, or a small band of enthusiasts for a new science—in 1908 the very first international meeting of "Freudians" heard Sigmund Freud speak for four hours after dinner on the case of the "Rat Man." Yet this collection shows the case to be as easily a device for the creation of a counterpublic and the fomenting of counterrevolution as it is the flexible vehicle for a revolutionary call to epistemic arms.

John Forrester
July 2014

Acknowledgments

This volume was made possible by the Australian Research Council (ARC), which funded the Discovery Project titled "Making the Case: The Case Study Genre in Sexology, Psychoanalysis, and Literature," led by Birgit Lang and Joy Damousi. The editors acknowledge the importance of the ARC context and subsidy of this project, which began in 2010, and resulted in the appointment of Katie Sutton as ARC Postdoctoral Fellow at the University of Melbourne.

Much of the content of this book has its origins in the conference "Cases and their Publics: Interdisciplinary and Transnational Perspectives on the Case Study Genre," hosted by the University of Melbourne, September 26–28, 2011, with the support of the School of Languages and Linguistics, and the invaluable assistance of Jana Verhoeven. The editors thank all who contributed to this conference, including keynote speakers Warwick Anderson and Laura Doan; those who presented papers, and those who attended. The conference very effectively set the scene for the present volume, demonstrating the richness, variety, and topicality of the case study as a subject for sustained critical enquiry and reflection.

Much more recently, the editors extend warmest thanks to all the contributors to this collection, for their enthusiasm and patience throughout the editorial and publication processes. We are grateful to Warwick Anderson for permission to include (with minor changes) his chapter "The Case of the Archive," previously published under the same title in *Critical Inquiry* 39, no. 3 (2013), 532–47. Warm thanks to John Forrester, who was quick to agree to contribute a foreword to our volume. In the School of Languages and Linguistics at the University of Melbourne, special thanks to Cynthia Troup, who has managed the editorial process, prepared, and polished all aspects of the manuscript with great thoroughness.

We owe much to Max Novick, Commissioning Editor (Research Monographs and Academic Titles) at Routledge; to the anonymous reviewers and editorial board at Routledge, and to Jennifer E. Morrow, Senior Editorial Assistant, Routledge Research, for their expertise, efficiency, and helpfulness. Finally, the editors extend personal thanks to Andrew Schuller for his early assistance in bringing this publication to fruition.

Joy Damousi, Birgit Lang, and Katie Sutton

Acknowledgments

This volume was made possible by the Australian Research Council (ARC)...

...

Joy Damousi, Birgit Lang and Katie Sutton

Introduction
Case Studies and the Dissemination of Knowledge

Joy Damousi, Birgit Lang, and Katie Sutton

The case study has proved of enduring interest to all Western societies, particularly in relation to questions of subjectivity and the sexed self. This volume investigates the means by which the case study genre disseminates knowledge through different publics and audiences, from patients to social reformers, from moral crusaders to literary audiences. More specifically, it interrogates how case studies have been used by doctors, lawyers, psychoanalysts, and writers to communicate their findings both within the specialist circles of their academic disciplines, and beyond, to a wider public. Such an interrogation simultaneously involves asking how case studies have been taken up by a range of audiences to refute and dispute academic knowledge. As such, this book engages with case studies as sites of interdisciplinary negotiation, transnational exchange, and influence, exploring the effects of larger historical and geopolitical forces such as war, migration, and internationalization on a genre pivotal to so many disciplinary and knowledge cultures.

The case study is a central disciplinary apparatus in fields ranging from law and medicine to criminology and psychoanalysis; historically, its "strength of epistemic position" (a phrase coined by Keith DeRose) has depended on its context.[1] From the nineteenth century onwards, cases constituted an increasingly prominent form of knowledge production and dissemination across a range of disciplinary milieus. John Forrester identifies Michel Foucault's analysis of "The Examination" in *Discipline and Punish* as a key starting point for addressing this process, whereby the emergence of the clinical sciences from the late eighteenth century enabled the entry of the individual into the field of knowledge, even as individual cases provided an anchor for new forms of disciplinary authority.[2] As Foucault writes:

The examination, surrounded by all its documentary techniques, makes each individual a "case": a case which at one and the same time constitutes an object for a branch of knowledge and a hold for a branch of power. The case is no longer, as in casuistry or jurisprudence, a set of circumstances defining an act and capable of modifying the application of a rule; it is the individual as he may be described, judged, measured, compared with others, in his very individuality; and it is also the individual who has to be trained or corrected, classified, normalized, excluded, etc.[3]

Yet when it comes to "human cases"—those cases that, whether in legal, medical, or psychoanalytic contexts, involve engaging with individual life experiences and stories, and that are at the heart of our intellectual endeavor—the genre can also furnish and deepen conceptual knowledge about the self, as well as more personal self-knowledge, with all of the tensions this might entail. In line with definitions developed by Michael Warner in *Publics and Counterpublics*, contributors to this volume understand "the" public as a kind of social totality, representing the most common sense of "the people in general," as well as the multiple, text-based publics within any such totality.[4] Our volume focuses on the dynamic interactions between cases, and ways in which their meanings are created and recreated into knowledge about human subjects for a range of publics.

Cases saliently make tangible otherwise complex discourses; due to their readability and specificity, cases forge relations amongst strangers. This specificity creates contextual knowledge through and within specific publics, a fact that accounts for the plurality of terminology now accrued around the case study. Of course the genre of the case study is immensely versatile, and recent decades have seen a surge of interest in the genre, across fields ranging from literary studies to social sciences.[5] Nonetheless, the genre tends to be theorized only within discrete disciplines, remaining undertheorized when it comes to more general, social aspects of inquiry. With a basis in classical rhetoric, case studies have historically risen to prominence during periods of considerable change, and at times of epistemological uncertainty. Clearly, to begin to understand the continued pervasiveness of the case study in the circulation of knowledge, the actual shape and use of any particular case study, or group of case studies, need to be historicized within differing epistemological and social frameworks. The present work takes up this task, scrutinizing the case study from various perspectives in order to sharpen critical understanding of the genre's dynamic role in the definition and redefinition of knowledge for different publics.

Each of the following chapters tests the limits of received interpretations and analyses of the case study within scholarly research. For the key modern theoretician of the genre, André Jolles, cases belong to the very archetypes of narration.[6] Like the investigations of many scholars afterwards, Jolles focused on the case study's normative nature as its main discursive possibility. Introducing one of the most significant contemporary examinations of the case study genre, a special issue of the journal *Critical Inquiry* in 2007, Lauren Berlant states that "as genre, the case hovers about the singular, the general, and the normative." She also touches on an issue vital to our volume, that of the dissemination of knowledge to a range of publics, maintaining that the case "organizes publics, however fleeting. It expresses a relation of expertise to a desire for shared knowledge."[7] The essays in *Critical Inquiry* explore the transformation of norms and distinct professional idioms, as well as questions of personhood and its fragmentation. However, their focus is largely bound to particular disciplinary and national contexts, as is typical for the wider body of literature on cases. The present collection of close studies, on the other hand, highlights the shifting meanings of the case genre for different publics over time and space, and broader questions surrounding the dissemination of knowledge through cases.

THE PLURALITY AND MOBILITY OF CASE KNOWLEDGE

Cases are shaped by traditions and power structures, technologies and typologies—all processes examined in the first part of our collection, "Case Knowledge." Warwick Anderson's opening chapter investigates the development of the hospital case file and its archives in the early twentieth century, when, for the first time, a unitary dossier began to accompany patients along their "illness trajectories" and circulate with them through the modern clinics. Anderson historicizes the medical logics of case-making arising from military contexts in the late nineteenth and early twentieth centuries, linking this to the larger history of the case as genre and archive, which encompasses the modernist case studies of Sigmund Freud. In chapter 2, John Cash compares the "representative anecdotes" of Freud's "Rat Man" case with Stanley Milgram's famous "Obedience to Authority" study, in order to address the complexities of "obedience and its discontents." Cash contrasts the implied publics of these two dissimilar studies with the challenge and fascination they held for their specialist audiences, and rereads Milgram's study through its own case histories.

The multiple typologies and functions of the case for different audiences are also at the center of Birgit Lang's analysis, in chapter 3, of the published work of early twentieth-century German criminologist and sexologist Erich Wulffen. Embracing medical, legal, as well as more popular contexts, Wulffen's collections of cases for educated and professional publics stereotyped criminals, while also educating his readership about court conventions. Meanwhile, his literary cases for the public served to exemplify his political convictions in the turmoil of Germany's Weimar Republic. In chapter 4 Johanna Gehmacher argues that early German radical feminist Käthe Schirmacher made *herself* into a case, so as to epitomize her political viewpoints within a range of feminist and party political contexts. Gehmacher further suggests that historians have much to gain from examining their subjects as "cases," a critical perspective that offers a means of deconstructing the historiographical practice of biography.

The second part of our volume brings the human subject into focus, analyzing the complex bond between the case study genre and the knowledge of modern subjects and subjectivities. A particular strength of this interdisciplinary, transnational, and historically informed section lies in the way it draws into alliance two contradictory strands of post-structuralist scholarship. On the one hand, Foucaultian scholars have identified the case study as a technique of social control, while on the other, the post-structuralist "crisis of the subject" has led—most notably through Pierre Bourdieu—to a critical investigation of the fictions at work in biographical writing.[8] The focus on cases and their dissemination in this section reveals how human subjects have shaped themselves simultaneously in light of and against their own cases, subverting power structures, and sometimes leaving their case writers at a loss. Cases, this section proposes, are part of the reflexive circulation of discourse that constitutes the social space of publics, and of "the" public.

In chapter 5, Katie Sutton shifts the focus from biography to autobiography, examining how cross-dressing individuals in 1920s Germany appropriated the medical language of the sexological case study to construct their own life stories of "transvestite" subjectivity and experience. Sutton observes how these case-like narratives began to assume the shape of a genre within early subcultural periodicals; moreover, they were instrumental in the development of a sense of transvestite "community." The publics and contexts of cases can also stretch far beyond the boundaries of identity or nation, as explored in chapter 6, Timothy Verhoeven's analysis of the case of Polish nun Barbara Ubryk. Afflicted by decades of abuse and imprisonment, this nineteenth-century Galician nun became the subject of one of many tales concerned with so-called convent captivity. Contemporaries viewed Ubryk's case as both extreme and highly topical—characteristics that Verhoeven productively aligns with the fundamental positioning of the case study at the intersection of the singular and general. Following the discovery of Ubryk, her case was reported well outside its immediate Austro-Hungarian context, in newspapers across Europe, in North America, and in Australia. Pandering to a transnational current of anticonvent and anti-Catholic sentiment, Verhoeven's sources combine the suppression or normalization of "perverse" sexualities with widespread anticelibacy arguments.

Chapters 7 and 8 share a concern with the doctor-patient relationship. Lisa Featherstone addresses the medical case from the perspective of social and sexual normativity, as expressed in the record keeping of Australian medical practitioner and eugenicist Victor Wallace. Joy Damousi examines the practice of analyst and political activist Viola Bernard in the United States, delving into the multiple, often unacknowledged publics of the psychoanalytic case. This includes the ways in which the analyst herself or himself functions as a key "public" for the psychoanalytic patient's personal narrative, even as, through the transference relationship, she or he influences its content and direction.

Part three, "Literary Circulations," considers the transnational and interdisciplinary circulation of cases from fields as diverse as medicine, psychoanalysis, and sexology, but concentrates on the role of case writing in literary and cultural realms. This section emphasizes the dependence of cases on their respective publics by highlighting the temporality of their circulation, and in so doing sheds new light on what Warner calls the "poetic world-making" of both publics and cases. These chapters spotlight the twentieth and twenty-first centuries; they represent an innovative approach to literary investigations of the case, which have to date focused primarily on early modern and nineteenth-century Romantic literature.[9]

In chapter 9 Alison Lewis demonstrates how a novella by German modernist writer Alfred Döblin helped to create a new subgenre: that of the over-determined, anxious case. Based on a contemporary murder trial, Döblin's unique literary creation also undermined previous conventions of literary cases. The transgression of disciplinary boundaries enabled by the case study genre is also examined by Jana Verhoeven in chapter 10, which discusses the incorporation of German medical case materials into "pulp fiction" for the French middle classes. Armand Dubarry was a journalist who published a series of "psychopathological novels" from the late 1890s and early 1900s. Through translation and wide distribution, this kind of publication helped to make titillating tales of sexual perversion more acceptable to a respectable middle-class audience. Exchanges between literature and psychoanalysis further help to define the final two chapters: Christiane Weller foregrounds Freud's reliance on interpretations of German literature for his theories of castration, before rereading accounts of castration by both Freud and Jacques Lacan through the lens of E. T. A. Hoffmann's "original" case of the sandman. Lastly, Alex Kurmann uses psychoanalytic theory to explore French migrant writer Linda Lê's fashioning of German writer Ingeborg Bachmann into a literary "Antigone figure." This process, in turn, brings Bachmann to the attention of a range of migrant and wider reading publics.

CASE STUDIES, PSYCHOANALYSIS, AND THE HISTORY OF SEXUALITY

The influence of psychoanalysis on all aspects of the case study is a theme sustained throughout this volume. Psychoanalysis is discussed directly and forms the centerpiece of some chapters, while other chapters are overtly informed by the insights of psychoanalysis as a method, or body of knowledge at a particular historic moment. Freud's theoretical paradigms were shaped through his celebrated case histories, such as those of the "Rat Man," the "Wolf Man," "Little Hans," "Dora," and Fräulein Anna O.—all of which address the formation of subjectivity. While Freud did not invent the case study, his contribution to promoting the genre as a distinctive textual mode in medical, literary, philosophical, and other fields cannot be underestimated; Freud developed the case study as a methodological approach, producing it in an authoritative form that is distinctly interdisciplinary, profound, and enduring.[10]

Anderson positions Freud's case studies at the core of his discussion of the history of the bureaucratic case file. He identifies the transference between patient and analyst, and Freud's presence in the narrative, as points of difference with the bureaucratic case file: in the latter, physicians are far less present in the narrative. As a form, the Freudian case study is akin to the short story—a narrative that builds to a climax—whereas the administrative case file is far more closed, retrospective, much less fluent and creative. The history of the case file in the military and medical context charted by Anderson is framed by Freud's case study as the necessary starting point of reference and defining paradigm.

Cash draws directly on one of Freud's most powerful and insightful cases, that of the "Rat Man," to develop Kenneth Burke's argument about the case study as a source of knowledge, and a genre that constructs various publics. The "Rat Man" case provides the exemplary vehicle, Cash argues, to identify the case study's strengths, which lie in the organization of complex detail, and the simultaneous presentation of a theory or system. Cash shows Freud deftly utilizing the case study to communicate to a public a wider theory in exhilaratingly condensed form.

Damousi's examination of the work of American émigré psychoanalyst Viola Bernard develops the theme of the uses of the psychoanalytic case study, but in the context of sexuality. In comparing the psychoanalytic case study to case studies drawn upon in other discursive domains, such as those in literature (Mary McCarthy), medicine (Alfred Kinsey), science (William Masters and Virginia Johnson), and journalism (Betty Friedan), Damousi explores the uses of case studies during the immediate postwar period. While some of these discussions were conducted in the public arena, analysts like Bernard may not have obtained celebrity status, but her approach quite possibly achieved more explanatory power than the approaches of those theorists who sought media attention in wider forums. Damousi's chapter opens new perspectives on the vital links between the case study form, sexuality, and public culture.

In other contexts discussed in this book, the influence of Freudian ideas and psychoanalytic practice is likewise discernible. Concentrating on mid-twentieth-century medical practice, Featherstone notes the presence of Freudian influences in the work of Australian doctor Victor Wallace. Wallace was supportive of psychoanalysis, and recommended to some of his patients that they undergo psychoanalytic treatment, appreciating its possible benefits for certain individuals.

In this collection, literature is another context where the nexus between psychoanalysis and the case study is plainly in evidence. Lewis's chapter identifies the influence of Freud in Döblin's novella *Die beiden Freundinnen und ihr Giftmord* (Two girlfriends commit murder) that signified a new literary crime genre of the 1920s. Addressing the new connections between female criminality and sexuality—also explored in Lang's chapter—Lewis argues that Döblin includes in his fictional treatment traces of insights from Freud's account of the Oedipus complex. Freud's pathbreaking work on the subject appeared in 1924, the same year as Döblin's novella.[11] Döblin was himself a medical doctor, and Lewis is interested in his transformation of a sensational contemporary murder case involving two female lovers into a literary case; one that pushed at the boundaries of case writing, not least in its inclusion of an appendix of psychoanalytic diagrams. Continuing the theme of literature and psychoanalysis, Weller explores the ways in which Freud and Lacan both formulated their theories in relation to castration and the Oedipus complex. Weller compares approaches and understandings from Freud and Lacan, concluding that literary strategies of reading and writing are embedded within psychoanalytic case studies, and vice versa. The dialogue between the two narrative modes brings together two complex discourses, each indispensable to the other. This intersection is further analyzed in Kurmann's chapter, which points out how writings by Lacan infuse Lê's literary case study of Bachmann—in particular, Lacan's symbolic world of language.

Just as psychoanalysis has been highly influential in shaping the structure, interpretive possibilities, and dissemination of the case study genre in the context of twentieth-century modernity, so too has the discourse at the heart of psychoanalytic explanation from the time of Freud—that of sexuality. Since Foucault's *History of Sexuality* it has become almost impossible to discuss the history of modernity without considering how the development of ideas about "sexuality" and "sexual identity" during the late nineteenth century contributed to understandings of modern subjectivity. Historians of sexuality have consequently described the period immediately prior to and following the fin de siècle in terms of "sexual modernity," or "plastic sexuality."[12] In doing so, they point to a wide range of transformations, all of which occurred well before the widely heralded "sexual revolution" of the latter half of the twentieth century, in areas such as sex research, birth control technologies, law reform, and the emergence of sexual minority cultures.

Sexual modernity, as Harry Oosterhuis writes in a recent article, entailed a "fundamental transformation of the definition and explanation of sexuality and of its meaning in human life," and included a shift away from reproductive demands in favor of pleasure and desire; a growing focus on the psychological rather than physiological aspects of sexual life; a push to classify sexual "perversions" and desires, and a more positive conceptualization of sexuality as a constructive, natural force.[13] Anthony Giddens's articulation of "new mechanisms of self-identity which are shaped by—and yet shape—the institutions of modernity" provides a useful focus for exploring the interactions between discourses of sexuality and the case study genre.[14] From the late nineteenth century onwards, an emerging subgenre of sexual cases constituted an increasingly prominent form of knowledge production and dissemination across a range of disciplinary cultures; scholars have shown that the classification of sexual "perversions" at this period was based almost entirely on patient case histories.[15]

For fin-de-siècle European sexologists such as Richard von Krafft-Ebing, Magnus Hirschfeld, or Havelock Ellis, case histories provided a means of securing the power of their emerging discipline to name and explain a range of conditions, behaviors, and forms of intimate relations rendered increasingly visible by the conditions of urban, industrialized modernity.[16] Often collected from patients in the form of first person autobiographical narratives, these cases offered "proof" of sexual "pathologies" such as homosexuality, fetishism, or masochism, in the absence of the kind of qualitative or experimental data that would be collected by researchers such as Kinsey or Masters and Johnson during the course of the twentieth century. Sexology's dependence on the autobiographical case form, as Oosterhuis observes, helped to accelerate the move away from a sexual science based in physiology and degeneration theory, and toward explanations grounded in "personal history, subjective experience, and inner feelings."[17]

Such foregrounding of the subjective through the sexual case is highlighted in many of the chapters in this collection, from Cash's consideration of the role of childhood sexual experiences in Freud's "Rat Man" case, to Weller's reading of the significance of castration in Freud's interpretation of the "The Sandman." From Bernard's case files, Damousi analyses shifting sexual attitudes and identifications in the United States during the mid-twentieth century. Across the Pacific, Featherstone shows how Dr. Wallace created an archive of sexual cases in which he distinguished himself by sympathetically listening to and treating problems dismissed by other physicians as irrelevant or unsavory. Even though his practice remained constrained by dominant attitudes towards questions such as homosexuality, he productively intervened in his patients' processes of sexual identity formation.

With the professional expansion of sexology, psychiatry, criminology, and psychoanalysis by the turn of the twentieth century, the audiences for case studies addressing sexual questions grew both within disciplinary contexts, and in society and culture more broadly. These new reading publics, or "sexual publics," to borrow Warner and Berlant's term, frequently crossed boundaries of nation, class, gender, and educational or professional background. Thus Jana Verhoeven examines here how Dubarry's middlebrow novels disseminated the material gathered in Krafft-Ebing's pioneering collection of sexual "pathologies," *Psychopathia Sexualis* (1886), to a more general French middle-class readership. With their risqué themes, these novels appealed to readers' voyeurism, while also responding to bourgeois demands for respectability via a "pseudoscientific" discourse that grafted the case studies of sexual science onto literary texts. An aesthetically more sophisticated grafting of medical, legal, and literary discourses around sexuality, meanwhile, can be found in Döblin's modernist case writing. Using the "heterogeneous and flexible space" of literary discourse, fictionalized cases such as Döblin's, argues Lewis, simultaneously drew on and competed with the empirical human sciences in claiming knowledge about the female sexual criminal. In doing so, they began to constitute in their own right a "life science" (*Lebenswissenschaft*)—to use Ottmar Ette's term—"mimicking, copying, and borrowing" from actual cases for a nonscientific readership.

The dissemination of sexual cases across disciplines and reading publics is likewise central to Lang's chapter on Wulffen, who, several decades before Döblin, had already begun to use sensational, real-life criminal cases to explore criminal psychology in ways that would resonate with a broader readership. Lang shows Wulffen using his case writing to shape public opinion on several notorious cases of the Wilhelminian and Weimar eras, including that of "sex criminal" Grete Beier, the last woman executed in Saxony, amidst a climate of widespread discontent with an elitist judicial system. Together with the chapters by Gehmacher and Sutton, those by Lang and Lewis showcase Germany's Weimar Republic—a period frequently described in terms of "crisis" and historical caesurae—as a particularly productive moment in the proliferation of new discourses about sex, and new ways of experimenting with the case study form.[18]

The transnational appeal of sexual cases, on the other hand, is central to Timothy Verhoeven's examination of the case of Sister Ubryk. Verhoeven shows that, in its voyeuristic depiction of graphic sexual abuse and torture, this "sad tale" shared certain features with the erotic medical confessions of late nineteenth-century sexology, in line with Vernon Rosario's characterization of the latter as "liminal narratives" situated in the "shady boundary between scientific documents and licentious popular literature."[19]

That such confessional tropes are key to understanding the cultural workings of the case study genre is strongly emphasized by Foucault, who famously characterized the confession as "the general standard governing the production of the true discourse on sex" in modernity, and one that can take a wide range of forms: "interrogations, consultations, autobiographical narratives, letters."[20] It was on the basis of the ritualistic confessional structure, Foucault argues, that modern Western society developed a sexual science in the first place, in contrast to the more sensuous *ars erotica* of many traditional societies.[21] This argument has been criticized by some for overvaluing the influence of the confessional form. Giddens, for example, finds that even in therapeutic and psychoanalytic contexts the comparison is "too forced to be convincing," with its assumption that "that the individual is readily able to provide the information required," rather than subject to those "emotional blockages" that psychoanalysis insists inhibit individual self-understanding and agency.[22] Nonetheless, the confession remains a powerful model for theorizing the historical interconnections between ideas about sexuality and identity, and for viewing these against the decidedly modern urge to uncover the "truth" about oneself.[23]

In Damousi's account of Bernard's analysis of "Grace Hamilton," for instance, the confidential, confessional framework of the analytic encounter provides a space for Hamilton's nonheteronormative sexual explorations, which are read here in terms of a "fluid engagement with the self and the social—with internal and external experience" in the United States of the 1940s. Although psychoanalysis as a therapeutic discipline might be understood, at least on the surface, as directed towards curing neurosis, its "specific significance," according to Giddens, "is that it provides a setting, and a rich fund of theoretical and conceptual resources, for the creation of a reflexively ordered narrative of self."[24]

Sutton's analysis of "transvestite" magazines and columns in 1920s Germany, meanwhile, exemplifies what Dagmar Herzog describes as the "dialectical interaction" between an increasingly professionalized field of sex research and the self-representation of sexual minorities, at a time when "ordinary" people came to view themselves as possessing not just a sexual identity, but also sexual rights.[25] Several decades before the Stonewall riots, these publications bear witness to the role of the case study form in helping to initiate such a discursive shift—which can also be seen, albeit in more subtle ways, in the motives driving Dr. Wallace's (mostly heterosexual) patients to seek treatment in 1950s Melbourne; or leading Hamilton to Bernard's consulting rooms in 1940s New York City; or enabling the individuals interviewed by Kinsey and his team during the 1940s and 1950s to disclose the most intimate details of their sexual histories. At the level of content as well as genre, the case study played a fundamental role in this move towards recognizing the sexual self as a locus of agency and civil rights.

No other genre expresses the social dimensions of knowledge as succinctly as the case; no other genre continues to be at the center of knowledge production in medicine, sciences, humanities, social sciences, and the law. *Case Studies and the Dissemination of Knowledge* challenges the limits of disciplinary-based research in the humanities. The cases examined serve as means of transmission or passage between disciplines, genres, and reading publics, from law to psychoanalysis, and from auto/biography to modernist fiction. The following chapters scrutinize the case study in order to sharpen critical understanding of the genre's dynamic role in the construction and dissemination of knowledge within and across disciplinary, temporal, and national boundaries. In doing so, they seek to position the case at the center of cultural and social understandings of the emergence of modern subjectivities.

NOTES

1. Keith DeRose, *The Case for Contextualism: Knowledge, Skepticism and Context*, vol. 1 (Oxford: Oxford University Press, 2009), 8.
2. John Forrester, "If *p*, then what? Thinking in Cases," *History of the Human Sciences* 9 (1996): 1–25, at 11–12.
3. Michel Foucault, *Discipline and Punish: The Birth of the Prison* (London: Penguin, 1991), 191; emphasis in original.

4. Michael Warner, *Publics and Counterpublics* (New York: Zone Books, 2002).
5. See, for example, Jason Tougaw, *Strange Cases: The Medical Case History and the British Novel* (London: Routledge, 2006); Johannes Süßmann, ed., *Fallstudien: Theorie—Geschichte—Methode* (Berlin: Trafo, 2007).
6. André Jolles, *Einfache Formen: Legende, Sage, Mythe, Rätsel, Spruch, Kasus, Memorabile, Märchen, Witz* (Tübingen: Niemeyer, 1968).
7. Lauren Berlant, "On the Case," *Critical Inquiry* 33 (2007): 663–72, at 664f.
8. See Pierre Bourdieu, "The Biographical Illusion," trans. Yves Winkin and Wendy Leeds-Hurwitz, *Working Papers and Proceedings of the Center for Psychosocial Studies (Chicago)* 14 (1987): 1–7.
9. See, for example, James Chandler, *England in 1819: The Politics of Literary Culture and the Case of Historic Romanticism* (Chicago: Chicago University Press, 1998), and, more recently, Tougaw, *Strange Cases*. A notable exception in this context is Todd Herzog's *Crime Stories: Criminalistic Fantasy and the Culture of Crisis in Weimar Germany* (New York: Berghahn, 2009).
10. On psychoanalytic case writing see Joy Damousi, "Viola Bernard and the Analysis of 'Alice Conrad': A Case Study in the History of Intimacy," *Journal of the History of Sexuality* 22 (2013): 474–500; John Forrester, "On Kuhn's Case: Psychoanalysis and the Paradigm," *Critical Inquiry* 33 (2007): 792–819; Ulrich Stuhr, "Die Bedeutung der Fallgeschichte für die Entwicklung der Psychoanalyse und heutige Schlußfolgerungen," *Psyche. Zeitschrift für Psychoanalyse und ihre Anwendungen* 61 (2007): 943–65.
11. See Sigmund Freud, "The Dissolution of the Oedipus Complex (1924)," *The Standard Edition of the Complete Works of Sigmund Freud*, vol. 19 (London: Hogarth Press, 1961), 173–79.
12. See Harry Oosterhuis, "Sexual Modernity in the Works of Richard von Krafft-Ebing and Albert Moll," *Medical History* 56 (2012): 133–55, and Anthony Giddens, *The Transformation of Intimacy: Sexuality, Love and Eroticism in Modern Societies* (Stanford: Stanford University Press, 1992).
13. Oosterhuis, "Sexual Modernity," 140; Giddens, *Intimacy*, 2, also 27; see also Arnold I. Davidson, *The Emergence of Sexuality: Historical Epistemology and the Formation of Concepts* (Cambridge MA: Harvard University Press, 2001).
14. Anthony Giddens, *Modernity and Self-Identity: Self and Society in the Late Modern Age* (Stanford: Stanford University Press, 1991), 2.
15. Michel Foucault, "Scientia Sexualis," in his *The History of Sexuality*, trans. Robert Hurley, vol. 1, *The Will to Knowledge* (London: Penguin, 1998), 53–73; Forrester, "If *p*, then what?"; Ivan Crozier, "Pillow Talk: Credibility, Trust and the Sexological Case History," *History of Science* 46 (2008): 375–404.
16. On the impact of modern capitalist relations in enabling new forms of social and political organization, particularly for sexual minorities, see e.g. John D'Emilio, "Capitalism and Gay Identity," in *Powers of Desire: The Politics of Sexuality*, ed. Ann Snitow, Christine Stansell, and Sharon Thompson (New York: Monthly Review Press, 1983), 100–13.
17. Harry Oosterhuis, *Stepchildren of Nature: Krafft-Ebing, Psychiatry, and the Making of Sexual Identity* (Chicago: Chicago University Press, 2000), 149–50.
18. There is a considerable body of scholarship devoted to the influence of sexual discourses on Weimar modernity—significant contributions include Atina Grossman, *Reforming Sex: The German Movement for Birth Control and Abortion Reform, 1920–1950* (New York: Oxford University Press, 1995); Richard McCormick, *Gender and Sexuality in Weimar Modernity* (New York: Palgrave, 2001); and several essays in the recent collection Scott

Spector, Helmut Puff, and Dagmar Herzog, ed., *After* The History of Sexuality: *German Genealogies with and beyond Foucault* (New York: Berghahn Books, 2012). For critical discussions of the language of "crisis" as applied to the Weimar Republic see e.g. Rüdiger Graf and Moritz Föllmer, "The Culture of 'Crisis' in the Weimar Republic," *Thesis Eleven* 111 (2012): 36–47.

19. Vernon A. Rosario, *The Erotic Imagination: French Histories of Perversity* (New York: Oxford University Press, 1997), 10, as cited by Timothy Verhoeven (this volume).

20. Foucault, *History of Sexuality*, 63.

21. Foucault, *History of Sexuality*, 58–64.

22. Giddens, *Intimacy*, 30.

23. A recent example of scholarship informed by this model is Geertje Mak, *Doubting Sex: Inscriptions, Bodies and Selves in Nineteenth-Century Hermaphrodite Case Histories* (Manchester: Manchester University Press, 2012), 11.

24. Giddens, *Intimacy*, 31.

25. Dagmar Herzog, *Sexuality in Europe: A Twentieth-Century History* (Cambridge: Cambridge University Press, 2011), 2–3.

Part I
Case Knowledge

1   The Case of the Archive

Warwick Anderson

As medical students during the late 1970s, we routinely searched the hospital wards for cases, for the "good cases" of some particular disease. By early morning, rumors spread about which cases had come in overnight, and their disposition. We clustered around the good cases, trying to avoid the bad and routine ones. Even around 1980 our clinical teachers were insisting we should not regard patients simply as cases of whatever it is that afflicts them, as medical or administrative objects. But we continued to do so; indeed, the creeping sense of misconduct just seemed to make more tantalizing our quest for the case. We wanted exemplary cases of some disease, not sick people. It made us feel like grown-up doctors, whatever our instructors might say.[1] But what makes someone a case? How does one authorize a case? Does the case boast a genealogy? What are the consequences of becoming a case, or making cases? These are not the questions that medical students ordinarily ask, but they began to trouble me as I drifted away from the profession.

This chapter primarily concerns the case file, the administrative dossier, not the long case study, which is a distinct modernist genre—though the two are not unrelated. Michel Foucault connected the emergence of clinical sciences toward the end of the eighteenth century with the "problem of the entry of the individual (and no longer the species) into the field of knowledge; the problem of the entry of the individual description, of the cross-examination, of anamnesis, of the 'file' into the general functioning of scientific discourse." In closed institutions like prisons, asylums, barracks, schools, and hospitals, "the examination, surrounded by all its documentary techniques, makes each individual a 'case': a case which at one and the same time constitutes an object for a branch of knowledge and a hold for a branch of power." The case becomes the "individual as he may be described, judged, measured, compared with others, in his very individuality; and it is also the individual who has to be trained or corrected, classified, normalized, excluded, etc."[2] Here I want to focus on one of these documentary techniques: the development of the hospital case file and its archive in the early twentieth century, more than one hundred years after the clinical sciences, according to Foucault, began making cases. For the first time, a unitary dossier necessarily accompanied patients along their "illness trajectories," circulating with them through the modern clinics, waiting in the hospital records department for their return, available to turn them again into serviceable individuals within the bureaucratic matrix.[3]

Despite Foucault's discovery of the disciplined individual in the clinical case, we still know remarkably little about the documentary techniques that came to stabilize this identity. The bureaucratic entailments of making a diagnosis, fixing someone as a case, remain frustratingly obscure.[4] We know that during the nineteenth century the medical record assumed a more standard form, almost ritualized, with more emphasis on "objective" physical examination and laboratory results, and a tendency to discount the patient's own impressions of the illness. Mostly, these accounts consisted of brief notes, accumulating piecemeal in casebooks and bundles, usually arranged chronologically, but sometimes according to diagnostic category. Not until the early twentieth century were the patient's records commonly collated in a unitary file, organizing and consolidating the ordinary concatenation of medical events and interventions into an individual life.[5] The hospital record then comes to resemble the dossier, yet another example of the bureaucratic mode that produced during this period the police file, the military record and service number, and the anthropometric data card in physical anthropology. In the unitary administrative file, the individual case finally takes form in serial order, accompanied by rules of accessibility.

CASE STUDIES

The bureaucratic case file, which usually required secrecy, should be distinguished from the contemporary genre of the case study, which demanded full disclosure. Lauren Berlant wryly observes, "case history tends to be what physicians *take*, while case study is what academics and psychoanalysts *write*."[6] At the beginning of the twentieth century, Sigmund Freud wrote five long case studies that served as exemplars of psychoanalytic technique and literary style: "Dora" (1905), the "Rat Man" (1909), "Little Hans" (1909), Daniel Paul Schreber (1911), and the "Wolf Man" (1918). These narratives artfully described in each case a continuity of experience, suturing together apparent disjuncture, eventually revealing the hidden cause of the individual's distress. Unlike hospital case files, these studies emphasized the interaction of patient and analyst, dramatizing the transference implicated in the clinical encounter, thereby providing examples of how to perform psychoanalysis. Freud makes himself self-consciously present in his narratives in ways forbidden to ordinary physicians in their hospital case notes.[7] Indeed, these ideographic case studies convey the impression of resisting, perhaps even subverting, the bureaucratically serviceable, and hence nomothetic, case file. Thus Freud's strategy of avoidance and denial parallels the concurrent rise of photographic modernism in opposition to the Bertillon system of photographic realism, then a common means of criminal identification.[8]

"It still strikes me myself as strange," Freud observed as early as 1895, "that the case histories I write should read like short stories and that, one might say, they lack the serious stamp of science."[9] In the study of the Wolf Man, his last major case, Freud proclaimed: "I am unable to give either a purely historical or a purely thematic account of my patient's story; I can write a history neither of the treatment nor of the illness."[10] Instead, he wrote a modernist short story in which the author became the central character. At least since the 1960s, Freud's case studies usually have been taken as evidence of his literary bent, not read as scientific reports.[11] To be sure, historians have traced the genealogy of the Freudian case study—its family romance, perhaps—and noted legal, philosophical, and clinical antecedents to reasoning in cases.[12] But the Freudian literary style obviously is distinct from the bureaucratic dossier, which gained form about the same time. Although sharing a focus on the case, they boast different functionality. Still, their potential relations are intriguing. How, one wants to know, did Freud organize his own case notes? In the Freud archive there are numerous patient files from his days at the Allgemeines Krankenhaus, Vienna (1881–1883), and from the Bellevue Sanatorium, Kreuzlingen, in the early twentieth century.[13] Those from the 1880s seem to have been bound together in a larger journal or case book, while the later ones are bound individually, with the patient's name on the cover. In each case, Freud filled out two pages of pre-printed physical examination sheets, then wrote ten to twenty pages of progress notes. The file's progress notes—exceptionally extensive, yet clinically detached—surely represent the first draft of the modernist case study, which soon diverged in style, scope, and mandate. In 1904, Freud gave his last lecture to a medical audience; in 1905, he stopped publishing in medical journals.[14]

The modernist case study and administrative case file, both pedagogic instruments, accumulate dissimilar collectives or publics.[15] The exemplary psychoanalytic case is addressed to a bourgeois readership interested in new explanations of their mental constitution and the nature of psychological and sexual individuality. Through the process of interpretation of such closed, retrospective narratives, modern subjects can self-consciously reframe their complex selves, entering into the field of psychoanalytic interiority. In contrast, the case file becomes part of the machinery for making individuals into normative collectives, for rendering them bureaucratically knowable and serviceable.[16] Case files are interoceptive, evolving, often heteroglossic documents, oriented toward the future, shaping the prognosis. Sometimes, as a form of closure, the file can be written up and published as a case report, perhaps even turned into a psychoanalytic case study. Although related, locating identity in a case study and finding it in a case file are distinct disciplinary maneuvers, one promiscuously generating subjectivities, the other serializing clinical objects.[17]

THE UNIT SYSTEM

Since Hippocrates, European medicine has used exemplary cases to structure and inform clinical reasoning. Explaining cases proved an especially
powerful pedagogical technique, a conceptual tool demonstrating the natural course of disease, the means of diagnosis, and the effects of therapeutic intervention. But the case record did not become a bureaucratic
instrument until the nineteenth century. Even then, most hospitals failed
to keep systematic records. The Massachusetts General Hospital, established in 1821, appears to have been unusually rigorous initially in reg-
istering and documenting the histories of the patients on its wards. From
1837, a daily progress report was required for each patient, noted in the
hospital casebook, which was ordered chronologically. Physicians sought
to simplify and standardize accounts of the presenting complaint and the
personal history, to make them brief, pithy, and comparable. The tally of
findings on physical examination also became more succinct and coded,
less impressionistic, and more evidential or "objective." By the 1870s, the
record contained charts for respiratory rate, pulse, and temperature. Later
still, standard forms for new laboratory tests, for biochemical, bacteriolog-
ical, and radiological results, became available. Photographs might even
appear in its pages. The hospital appointed its first custodian of records
in 1897, but only after 1904 were records kept systematically for outpa-
tients.[18] These changes in the patient record represent, according to medical historian John Harley Warner, "the emergence and consolidation of
a new epistemological and aesthetic sensibility, expressed as a narrative
preference for what was universal and precise over what was individual
and discursive."[19]

At the beginning of the twentieth century, the case report emerged as a
recurrent motif in medical training.[20] In the 1870s, Christopher C. Langdell
had introduced the case method of teaching to the Harvard Law School.
Its success inspired a rising Harvard medical student, Walter B. Cannon,
to promote around 1900 the use of clinical cases as exemplars in the medical school too. These illustrative cases, expressed in standard and exact
form, offered guidance in diagnosis and therapeutics to medical students
and young physicians. Cannon extolled the power of cases to "rouse
enthusiasm" and their "great value drilling the mind of the student."[21] A
few years later, Richard Cabot began setting up clinicopathological case
conferences at the Massachusetts General Hospital. These turned into
gripping performances, where physicians contended with one another in
determining correct diagnosis and treatment, learning of their success or
failure only when pathologists dramatically provided the answer at the end
of proceedings. The record of such case conferences became a regular feature of the *Boston Medical and Surgical Journal*, later the *New England
Journal of Medicine*. They helped generations of physicians to reason in
cases.[22]

The transformation of hospitals in the early twentieth century into large, complex institutions with proliferating bureaucracies spurred efforts to reform and systematize record keeping.[23] Gradually, flexible individual case files replaced cumbersome casebooks and bundles. In 1907, the Mayo brothers started a trial of singular records, or unitary files, at St. Mary's Hospital in Rochester, Minnesota. Presbyterian Hospital in New York City made the first major investment in individual records around 1916, as the United States entered armed conflict in Europe. It was the first hospital to demand that information from all clinical encounters in every division be inscribed in a single file, assigned a serial number, which could be supplemented on further admissions.[24] Unlike the casebook, the "unit system" exerted considerable influence on clinical work, aiding the coordination of multiple specialists in the bureaucratic hospital and clarifying the illness trajectory of their patients. Although physicians remained the primary authors, other groups within the hospital, including nurses, could contribute to limited parts of the file. The unit record collated the patient's history, examination, test results, clinical progress, through multiple admissions; correspondence and administrative forms, some in typescript, soon attached to it; and it came to serve both as aide-memoire and prognostic indicator for the doctors managing the case. (Particularly thick case files, and multiple volumes, did not augur well.) Before long, other hospitals were following Presbyterian's lead—and not just in the United States.[25] We know that Canadian, British, and Dutch hospitals took up the unit record system in the 1920s. "The explicit discussion and implementation of novel record-keeping methods occurred first in the United States, and then spread to Europe," according to Stefan Timmermans and Marc Berg. "Hospitals in Europe followed suit in remarkably similar ways."[26]

The new paper technology not only defined more coherently the case, thereby regularizing and mobilizing the individual patient; it also enhanced standardization and efficiency within the hospital.[27] It was, crucially, a record *system*. According to Stanley Joel Reiser, the unit record system "would become an organ for measuring success and failure and for fixing responsibility" within the modern medical institution.[28] Serialized case files were flexible, standard, portable, accessible—and readily available for comparison and audit. The record system therefore appealed to the rising cohort of hospital administrators, a group that tended to praise efficiency and order, to admire the "business ethic." E. A. Codman at Massachusetts General Hospital was one of the more strident promoters of efficiency in medical practice during this period. From 1910 he sought, with little success, to monitor and reform his medical colleagues, urging upon them the unitary case record, since it allowed more rigorous scrutiny and audit. Codman's "end-result system" demanded "accurate, available, immediate records for scientific, efficient analysis"; for him, the ideal record was the "complete description of the individual from his conception to his grave."[29] But the new American College of Surgeons, deploying its accreditation authority, proved more effective than any nagging Boston physician. After World War I, it took its recent experience assessing military hospitals into the civil sphere, establishing a committee on hospital standardization, which focused on the medical record.[30] Few doubted that paper technology, as Steve Sturdy suggests, made it "possible to divide up or conceptualize populations and their environment in ways that permitted more economical forms of medical management."[31]

THE MILITARY RECORD

The military has long provided a model for the management of collective space, especially in the United States.[32] Early in the twentieth century, it became an administrative guide and resource for growing civil bureaucracies, which found that many of its modes of surveillance and discipline could be readily transferred across to the body politic. Its management of fatigue and morale, for example, formed the basis of the medical specialties of industrial hygiene and occupational health.[33] The US military also proved adroit during this period in the development of paper technologies, such as unit records, for the identification, monitoring, and deployment of soldiers.

After the debacle of the American Civil War, when medical officers became too burdened with the care and transport of the sick to properly document their patients and communicate effectively with their colleagues, the surgeon general of the US Army decided to implement a new records system. In 1863, an investigating board recommended a series of registers as the most efficient means to secure accurate information. The register books linked individual cases from the battlefield to the general hospital, and then to the medical department through separate reports based on registered information. An expanded clerical staff in the medical department ensured no duplication of information on individual soldiers.[34] Between wars, decisions about the allocation of pensions became the major stimulant for paperwork in the surgeon general's office. In 1886, when surgeon Fred C. Ainsworth took charge of the records and pensions division, he calculated that each case was taking almost three months to process, causing a backlog of over nine thousand cases. He therefore introduced a system of numbered index cards, which allowed his clerks to collate all cards referring to a single soldier. Before long, most cases could be decided within a day, and only 350 or so were in arrears.[35] Army authorities were so impressed they moved thirteen sections of the adjutant-general's office over to Ainsworth's division— the adjutant-general was failing to muster the military records as quickly as Ainsworth was compiling the medical cases. Later, they made Ainsworth adjutant-general.[36]

In the 1890s, the identification of soldiers continued to preoccupy the US military. The attempts of "deserters, bounty-jumpers, and other undesirable characters" to join the army, or to re-enlist, caused serious embarrassment.[37] During the American Civil War there had been a makeshift effort to tattoo anyone dishonorably discharged; later, vaccination on the left leg, leaving a distinctive mark, was tried, although this often led to infection. In the 1890s, the army shifted from branding the bodies of miscreants to putting their bodies in its archive. Surgeons Charles R. Greenleaf and Charles Smart devised a method of identification based on the Bertillon system, which was already proving popular in prisons and police departments across the United States. A Paris police officer, Alphonse Bertillon, had developed in the 1880s a system of criminal identification consisting of a photographic portrait, anthropometric description, and standardized notes on a single fiche or card. The cards were classified according to the length of the head, then by its width, then by the length of the left middle finger, and so on. The measurements thus served not only as a means of identification but also as an index of potential recidivists. Comparing the measurements of the suspect with those in the card file, as well as with the photograph and any distinguishing marks, would enable efficient detection of any criminal or degenerates trying to rejoin the army.[38]

From 1889, for every man that enlisted or re-enlisted, the medical officer filled in an outline figure on a card bearing the individual's name and organization, age, height, color of hair and eyes, and marks or scars on the skin. This constituted a shortcut of the Bertillon system, since detailed anthropometry and photography was too complicated and time-consuming for mobile recruiting parties. Each completed card was maintained in alphabetical order in the surgeon general's office, until a report of desertion or dishonorable discharge, when copies of the original card were transferred to files organized according to body color, features, and dimensions. By 1896, the surgeon general kept almost sixty thousand cards identifying recruits and re-enlisted men. That year, his office made over one hundred identifications of miscreants and undesirables. Although some officers had objected at first that *Bertillonage* was too closely associated with the detection of criminals to become a routine practice in recruitment, the army soon became accustomed to it. As observed by assistant surgeon-general C. H. Alden in 1896, "it is now relied on as an indispensable agency in maintaining discipline and in improving the standard of character in the ranks of the army."[39] Mobilization for the Spanish-American War after 1898 served to amplify these processes of serial individuation.[40]

After 1905, due to the success of the identification cards in enlistment and pension allocation, these cards replaced the old medical register system, and the composite report of the sick and wounded listings.[41] Each medical card showed the individual soldier's name, rank, organization, age, race, birthplace, and date of recruitment, along with a brief description of his disease, his treatment, and the outcome. For complicated or repeat admissions, the case record accumulated additional sheets of paper, clipped together and placed inside an envelope for filing. Before being archived, these records were used to chart daily the patient's response to treatment; they included temperature, pulse and respiration forms, progress notes, operation description, medication list, and pathology results.[42] The surgeon general instructed medical officers "to exercise the greatest care and thoroughness in preparing the clinical histories of medical and surgical cases. . . . Whenever possible the text should be illustrated by sketches, drawings, or photographs, which should accompany the clinical report. . . . On the termination of the case, the report should be promptly made out and forwarded to the surgeon general."[43] In 1918, the individual's new military service number (or serial number) could be emblazoned on each file.

The unitary medical record, or individual case file, was commonplace in the surgeon general's office of the US Army before World War I. After the war, the military's medical record system became a model for the American College of Surgeons in its campaign to reform civil hospital administration. In particular, Cleveland surgeon George W. Crile, chief of the US Army's Base Hospital No. 4 in France, returned dedicated to the systematic reform of patient records along military lines, working relentlessly through the college's standardization committee. Experience of war convinced him that "mediocrity well organized is more efficient than brilliancy combined with strife and discord."[44] Crile deplored armed conflict but he recognized that wars "bring order and discipline to men," and "military training is a valuable preparation for any civil career."[45] According to the director of the college, John G. Bowman, systematic individual case records had become a crucial test of "medical patriotism." Like his colleagues, Bowman believed that "history of hospitals is a series of waves of advancement, stimulated by war."[46] Thus the military mode of tracking disabled or otherwise pensionable soldiers and identifying criminals, degenerates and undesirables led, perhaps irresistibly, to the development of standard unitary medical records—to the proliferation of modern cases—first in army hospitals, then in burgeoning civilian clinics.[47]

CONCLUSION: ARCHIVED CASES

In the clinic, case files shape and monitor work routines, direct and coordinate medical activities, and create alliances between experts. Flexible, transferable unitary records discipline the behavior of those caring for the patient, the multiple authors of the file, training them to think about the sick person as both a singular object, a case to be worked over, and an example of a nosological category, a case of something. As a modern knowledge practice, the case file allows efficient and productive management of patients at the same time as it produces the individual as an object of medical procedure, organized around an ontological impression of disease.[48] Of course, inscribing someone as a case, and even practicing on cases, does not necessarily transform patients' sense of themselves. Most sick people continue to resist experiencing themselves as cases, and their friends and family rarely imagine them as such.[49] Nonetheless, even if it is not hegemonic, paper technology has made visible the individual or case as a serviceable object in medical work.

The case file requires an archive in order to appear functional once the clinical encounter ends. In the records department, the file gains authority, and sometimes permanence, or at least greater longevity than its referent. Once a case is assigned a hospital record number—which functions like the army service number—it gives the patient a retrievable identity, a file available for clinical and administrative correlation. Access to the institutional archive is limited, circulation of the file is restricted, and personal information is regarded as confidential. But what can the archived file *do*? Many years ago, when I roamed the hospital wards, clinical staff members examined obsessively the fresh record of the current admission, held in a separate folder, while the battered volume of past admission notes was usually piled up with others on a table in some dark office. We might look briefly at its contents, trying to find traces and fragments of the current complaint, searching for origins and antecedents. The absences in the record usually were more striking than what was there: the question not asked; the sign missed; the test not done, or lost. That is, it was just like any other archival document—except in this case it rarely mattered.

Jacques Derrida claimed that the principle of the archive "is in the order of commencement as well as in the order of commandment."[50] In the cases I treated, the issue of origins and antecedents generally was trivial. The authority of the clinical archive seems to depend more on its organization of paper technology, its serial disposition of individual cases, than on the retrievable contents of any file.[51] Derrida suggested something of the sort when he wrote: "the technical structure of the *archiving* archive also determines the structure of the *archivable* content even in its very coming into existence and its relationship to the future. The archivization produces as much as it records the event."[52] Certainly in the hospital the archived file did not do much, but the presence of an archive meant a lot. It provided a sort of authorization. In a different context, Ann Laura Stoler also points out that archiving as a process is at least as revealing as the archive, "as a thing." According to Stoler, colonial archives "were both transparencies on which power relations were inscribed and intricate technologies of rule in themselves." She urges us to treat the archive, regardless of its contents, "as a force field that animates political energies and expertise, that pulls on some 'social facts' and converts them into qualified knowledge, that attends to some ways of knowing while repelling and refusing others."[53]

Derrida provocatively noted the resemblance of psychological "repositories" to archival collections. Like inscriptions, traces of experience are archived and later recollected or mentally suppressed. According to Derrida, we are involved in a feverish, and ultimately futile, effort to recover what the mind, or the institution, has buried in its archive.[54] But the hospital archive does not operate like Derrida's imagined Freudian or psychoanalytic archive. In the clinic, the mechanism of making an individual file and adding to an archive is more significant than the actual contents of the repository. It is easier to get access to a file than to recover experience, but there is little more indexed in the file than indexicality, a practice of writing. There is no real injunction to remember, only to order. The creation of serial objects, operationalized within a medical bureaucracy, distinguishes the unitary hospital record from the modernist genre of the Freudian case study. Indeed, one might argue that Freud's exemplary cases ultimately act as a counter-discourse, opening up new possibilities for framing subjectivity, just as the objectifying hospital case archive was closing them down, or limiting them, becoming "clinical." For centuries, the case, whether written up or taken down, has been an important part of our cognitive equipment, but there is more than one way to think in a case.

NOTES

1. For an analysis of what constitutes a good case in the hospital, see Michel Wieviorka, "Case Studies: History or Sociology?," in *What Is a Case? Exploring the Foundations of Social Inquiry*, ed. Charles C. Ragin and Howard S. Becker (Cambridge: Cambridge University Press, 1992), 159–72. Around 1994, Homi K. Bhabha asked me about the history of the case, a question that at the time I found intriguing and unanswerable. I would like to thank Joy Damousi, Birgit Lang, and Alison Lewis for encouraging me to reflect again—belatedly perhaps—on case-making. Laura Doan, Volker Hess, Sarah Igo, Hans Pols, Charles E. Rosenberg, Huan Saussy, John Harley Warner, and Alice Wexler also gave helpful advice. Cecily Hunter provided extensive research assistance. For guidance through the Freud archive, I thank Leonard C. Bruno at the Manuscript Division, Library of Congress, Washington DC. An earlier version of this chapter was published in *Critical Inquiry* 39, no. 3 (2013), 532–47.
2. Michel Foucault, *Discipline and Punish: The Birth of the Prison*, trans. Alan Sheridan (London: Allen Lane, 1977), 190, 191. See also Stanton Wheeler, ed., *On Record: Files and Dossiers in American Life* (New York: Russell Sage Foundation, 1969), and John Forrester, "If *p*, then what? Thinking in Cases," *History of the Human Sciences* 9 (1996): 1–25.
3. On illness trajectories and the work of patients, see Anselm Strauss, Shizuko Fagerhaugh, Barbara Suczek, and Carolyn Wieder, *The Social Organization of Medical Work* (Chicago: University of Chicago Press, 1985).
4. Charles E. Rosenberg's plea for a "careful study of the hospital record as a genre" is still pertinent (*The Care of Strangers: The Rise of America's Hospital System* [New York: Basic Books, 1987], 382 n37). See also Charles E. Rosenberg, "The Tyranny of Diagnosis: Specific Entities and Individual Experience," *Milbank Quarterly* 80 (2002): 237–60.
5. Although individual case files occasionally circulated in hospitals in the nineteenth century—as medical student souvenirs, exceptional examples of pathology, or for legal and accountancy purposes—this did not constitute a unit medical record *system*. The continuing research of Volker Hess and colleagues in the records of the Berlin Charité Hospital suggests a more complex history, at least at that exceptional institution. See Volker Hess and Sophie Ledebur,

"Taking and Keeping: A Note on the Emergence and Function of Hospital Patient Records," *Journal of the Society of Archivists* 32, no. 1 (2011): 21–32; and Volker Hess, "Formalisierte Beobachtung: Die Genese der modernen Krankenakte am Beispiel der Berliner und Pariser Medizin (1725–1830)," *Medizinhistorisches Journal* 45 (2010): 293–340.

6. Lauren Berlant, "On the Case," *Critical Inquiry* 33 (2007): 663–72, at 663 n2 (emphasis in original).

7. Charles Bernheimer and Claire Kahane, eds., *In Dora's Case: Freud-Hysteria-Feminism* (New York: Columbia University Press, 1985); Julia Epstein, "Historiography, Diagnosis, and Poetics," *Literature and Medicine* 11 (1992): 23–44; Susan Wells, "Freud's Rat Man and the Case Study: A Genre in Three Keys," *New Literary History* 34 (2003): 353–66; and Anne Sealey, "The Strange Case of the Freudian Case History: The Role of Case Histories in the Development of Psychoanalysis," *History of the Human Sciences* 24 (2011): 36–50. While Freud's case studies are iconic, others contributed to this literary genre, especially Pierre Janet, who published in the 1890s a series of studies of hysterics from the Salpêtrière hospital, Paris. For example, see Pierre Janet, "Histoire d'une idée fixe," *Revue Philosophique* 37 (1894): 121–63. The relative obscurity of the journals in which Janet published diminished his influence. More generally, Thomas W. Laqueur argues the case report or study, developing along with the novel in the nineteenth century, contributed to the "production of humanitarian sentiment and reform" ("Bodies, Details, and the Humanitarian Narrative," in *The New Cultural History*, ed. Aletta Biersack and Lynn A. Hunt [Berkeley: University of California Press, 1989], 176–204, at 197).

8. Alphonse Bertillon, "The Bertillon System of Classification," *Forum* 11 (1891): 330–41, at 335, and *Identification Anthropométrique; Instructions Signalétiques* (Paris: Melun, 1893). For an extended contrast of photographic modernism and the images in Bertillon's criminal archive, see Allan Sekula, "The Body and the Archive," *October* 39 (1986): 3–64.

9. Sigmund Freud and Josef Breuer, "Studies in Hysteria [1895]," in *The Standard Edition of the Complete Psychological Works of Sigmund Freud*, trans. and ed. James Strachey, 24 vols. (London: Hogarth Press, 1953–74), vol. 2, 160. Freud was referring to the case of Fräulein Elisabeth von R.

10. Sigmund Freud, "From the History of an Infantile Neurosis [1918]," in *The Standard Edition of the Complete Psychological Works of Sigmund Freud*, trans. and ed. James Strachey, 24 vols. (London: Hogarth Press, 1955–74), vol. 17, 13.

11. For example, Steven Marcus, "Freud and Dora: Story, History, Case History," in his *Representations* (New York: Random House, 1975), 247–309; and Peter Brooks, "Fictions of the Wolf-Man: Freud and Narrative Understanding," in his *Reading for the Plot* (Oxford: Blackwell, 1984).

12. Forrester, "If *p*, then what?"

13. Box 45 and OV 1, and box 46, Sigmund Freud Papers, Library of Congress, Washington DC.

14. Ernest Jones, *The Life and Work of Sigmund Freud*, 3 vols. (New York: Basic Books, 1953–57).

15. Michael Warner, "Publics and Counterpublics," *Public Culture* 14, no. 1 (2002): 49–90.

16. Berlant, "On the Case."

17. It is tempting, if reductive, to cast the case file as a form of mechanical objectivity and to discern in the case study or report the exercise of trained judgment, referring to the styles of objectivity described in Lorraine Daston and Peter Galison, *Objectivity* (New York: Zone Books, 2007).

18. Stanley Joel Reiser, "Creating Form out of Mass: The Development of the Medical Record," in *Transformation and Tradition in the Sciences: Essays in Honor of I. Bernard Cohen*, ed. Everett Mendelsohn (Cambridge MA: Harvard University Press, 1984), 303–16. See also Walther Riese, "The Structure of the Clinical History," *Bulletin of the History of Medicine* 16 (1944): 437–49; and Harriet Nowell-Smith, "Nineteenth-Century Narrative Case Histories: An Inquiry into Stylistics and History," *Canadian Bulletin of Medical History* 12 (1995): 47–67.

19. John Harley Warner, "The Uses of Patient Records by Historians—Patterns, Possibilities, and Perplexities," *Health and History* 1 (1999): 183–205, at 109. See also Guenter Risse and John Harley Warner, "Reconstructing Clinical Activities: Patient Records in Medical History," *Social History of Medicine* 5 (1992): 183–205.

20. Reiser, "Creating Form out of Mass"; Forrester, "If *p*, then what?"; see also Stanley J. Reiser, "The Clinical Record in Medicine. Part I: Learning from Cases," *Annals of Internal Medicine* 114 (1991): 902–7.

21. Walter B. Cannon, "The Case Method of Teaching Systematic Medicine," *Boston Medical and Surgical Journal* 142 (1900): 31–36, at 34, 35. On Cannon, see Saul Benison, A. Clifford Barger, and Elin L. Wolfe, *Walter B. Cannon: The Life and Times of a Young Scientist* (Cambridge MA: Harvard University Press, 1987). See also Steve Sturdy, "The Scientific Method for Practitioners: The Case Method of Teaching Pathology in Early Twentieth-Century Edinburgh," *Bulletin of the History of Medicine* 81 (2007): 760–92; and Seth M. Holmes and Maya Ponte, "En-case-ing the Patient: Disciplining Uncertainty in Medical Student Patient Presentations," *Culture, Medicine, and Psychiatry* 35 (2011): 163–82.

22. Christopher Crenner, *Private Practice: In the Early Twentieth-Century Medical Office of Dr. Richard Cabot* (Baltimore: Johns Hopkins University Press, 2005).

23. On the American hospital at the turn of the nineteenth century, see Charles E. Rosenberg, "Inward Vision and Outward Glance: The Shaping of the American Hospital, 1880–1914," *Bulletin of the History of Medicine* 53 (1979): 346–91.

24. Hugh Auchincloss, "Unit History System," *Medical and Surgical Report of the Presbyterian Hospital in the City of New York* 10 (1918): 30–72; and Dorothy L. Kurtz, *Unit Medical Records in Hospital and Clinic* (New York: Columbia University Press, 1943). See also Reiser, "Creating Form out of Mass," and *Medicine and the Reign of Technology* (Cambridge: Cambridge University Press, 1978), 206–10; also Barbara L. Craig, "Hospital Records and Record-Keeping, c. 1850–c. 1950. Part I: The Development of Records in Hospitals," *Archivaria* 29 (1989–90): 57–87.

25. Massachusetts General Hospital did not introduce the unit system until 1937.

26. Stefan Timmermans and Marc Berg, *The Gold Standard: The Challenge of Evidence-Based Medicine and Standardization in Health Care* (Philadelphia: Temple University Press, 2003), 34. For Canada and Britain, see Craig, "Hospital Records." Further study of the globalization of this paper technology is needed.

27. Marc Berg and Geoffrey Bowker claim that the medical record performs not only the patient's body but also the clinic ("The Multiple Bodies of the Medical Record: Toward a Sociology of an Artifact," *Sociological Quarterly* 38 [1997]: 511–35). See also Marc Berg, "Practices of Reading and Writing: The Constitutive Role of the Patient Record in Medical Work," *Sociology of Health and Illness* 18 (1996): 499–524.

28. Reiser, "Creating Form out of Mass," 312. Systematic individual records also made possible the clinical research enterprise: see Harry M. Marks, *The Progress of Experiment: Science and Therapeutic Reform in the United States, 1900–1990* (New York: Cambridge University Press, 2000). The American Society of Clinical Investigation was established in 1909, the same year in which Freud embarked on a lecture tour of the United States.

29. E. A. Codman, *A Study in Hospital Efficiency as Demonstrated by the Case Report of the First Five Years of a Private Hospital* (Boston: Thomas Todd, 1918), 67, 71, and "Case Records and Their Value," *Bulletin of the American College of Surgeons* 3 (1917): 24–27. See also Susan Reverby, "Stealing the Golden Eggs: Ernest Amory Codman and the Science and Management of Medicine," *Bulletin of the History of Medicine* 55 (1981): 156–71; George Rosen, "The Efficiency Criterion in Medical Care, 1900–1920," *Bulletin of the History of Medicine* 50 (1976): 28–44; and Morris Vogel, "Managing Medicine: Creating a Profession of Hospital Administration in the United States, 1895–1915," in *The Hospital in History*, ed. Lindsay Granshaw and Roy Porter (London: Routledge, 1989), 234–60.

30. For example, see Carl E. Black, "Securing, Supervising and Filing of Records," *Bulletin of the American College of Surgeons* 8 (1924): 71–78; and John Wesley Long, "Case Records in Hospitals," *Bulletin of the American College of Surgeons* 8 (1924): 65. See also Paul A. Lembcke, "Evolution of the Medical Audit," *Journal of the American Medical Association* 199 (1967): 543–50; Joseph V. Rees, "The Orderly Use of Experience: Pragmatism and the Development of Hospital Industry Self-Regulation," *Regulation and Governance* 2 (2008): 9–29; Reiser, "Creating Form out of Mass"; and Craig, "Hospital Records."

31. Steve Sturdy, "The Political Economy of Scientific Medicine: Science, Education and the Transformation of Medical Practice in Sheffield, 1890–1920," *Medical History* 36 (1992): 125–59, at 129. In the 1920s, the enhanced administrative reach of the US government generated in parallel "a documentary regime of verification in which documents begat documents to produce official identities verified through the archival memory of the state" (Craig Robertson, "Mechanisms of Exclusion: Historicizing the Archive and the Passport," in *Archive Stories: Facts, Fictions, and the Writing of History*, ed. Antoinette Burton [Durham NC: Duke University Press, 2005], 68–86, at 82). Milton O. Gustafson emphasizes the military origins, through the adjutant-general's office, of the State Department records system in "State Department Records in the National Archives: A Profile," *Prologue: Journal of the National Archives* 2 (1970): 175–84, esp. 179. See also Roger W. Little, "The Dossier in Military Organization," in Wheeler, ed., *On Record*, 255–74; and Stephen Skowronek, *Building a New American State: The Expansion of National Administrative Capacities, 1877–1920* (New York: Cambridge University Press, 1982). The case record also took form in social work during this period: see Karen W. Tice, *Tales of Wayward Girls and Immoral Women: Case Records and the Professionalization of Social Work* (Urbana: University of Illinois Press, 1998).

32. Michel Foucault, "The Eye of Power: A Conversation with Jean-Pierre Barou and Michelle Perrot," in *Michel Foucault, Power/Knowledge: Selected Interviews and Writings, 1972–1977*, ed. Colin Gordon (London, 1980).

33. It is revealing to compare Edward L. Munson, *The Theory and Practice of Military Hygiene* (London: Ballière, Tindall, and Cox, 1902) with his advice to industry in *The Management of Men: A Handbook on the Systematic*

Development of Morale and the Control of Human Behavior (New York: Henry Holt, 1921). See also Warwick Anderson, *Colonial Pathologies: American Tropical Medicine, Race, and Hygiene in the Philippines* (Durham NC: Duke University Press, 2006). For military influences on the development of orthopedics, see Roger Cooter, *Surgery and Society in Peace and War: Orthopaedics and the Organisation of Modern Medicine, 1880–1948* (Manchester: Manchester University Press, 1993). On the emergence of rehabilitation medicine after World War I, see Beth Linker, *War's Waste: Rehabilitation in World War I America* (Chicago: University of Chicago Press, 2011).

34. John H. Brinton, *Personal Memoirs of John H. Brinton, Civil War Surgeon, 1861–1865* (Carbondale: Southern Illinois University Press, 1996), 251. Brinton was a member of the investigating board. See also Mary C. Gillett, *The Army Medical Department, 1865–1917* (Washington DC: Center of Medical History, United States Army, 1995), 23.
35. Gillett, *Army Medical Department*, 23; and P. M. Ashburn, *A History of the Medical Department of the United States Army* (Boston: Houghton Mifflin, 1929), 248, 390.
36. Ashburn, *History of the Medical Department*, 249, 390.
37. C. H. Alden, "The Identification of the Individual, with Special Reference to the System in Use in the Office of the Surgeon General, US Army," *American Anthropologist* 9 (1896): 295–310, at 295.
38. Alden, "Identification of the Individual"; Bertillon, "The Bertillon System of Classification"; and Simon A. Cole, *Suspect Identities: A History of Fingerprinting and Criminal Identification* (Cambridge MA: Harvard University Press, 2001). On the development of physical examination of recruits from the 1880s, which involved Greenleaf, see Anderson, *Colonial Pathologies*, 26–28. For fears of degeneracy in the army, and examples of cases, see Charles E. Woodruff, "Degenerates in the Army," *American Journal of Insanity* 57 (1900): 137–42.
39. Alden, "Identification of the Individual," 310. See also C. H. Alden, "The Identification of the Soldier," *Proceedings of the 7th Annual Meeting of the Association of Military Surgeons* 7 (1897): 209–26; and Paul R. Brown, "Objections to the System of Identification in Use in the United States Army," *Proceedings of the 6th Annual Meeting of the Association of Military Surgeons* 6 (1896): 243–72.
40. Ashburn, *History of the Medical Department*. See also Bobby A. Wintermute, *Public Health and the US Military: A History of the Army Medical Department, 1818–1917* (New York: Routledge, 2011).
41. There is some evidence of scattered efforts to introduce individual medical case files since the 1890s. See Albert G. Love, "The Importance of Adequate Records of the Sick and Wounded in the Military Services in Times of War, and the Best Methods of Obtaining Them," *Military Surgeon* 86 (1939): 461–81.
42. For example, the case records from 1909 in "Medical Case Files of Patients, Walter Reed General Hospital, 1909–1910," box 1, record group 112, National Archives and Records Administration, Washington DC.
43. Instructions, "Clinical History Form—No. 33," n.d., George Miller Sternberg Papers, 1861–1917, MC C 100, National Library of Medicine, Bethesda, Maryland.
44. G. W. Crile, "The Unit Plan of Organization of the Medical Reserve Corps of the USA for Service in Base Hospitals," *Surgery, Gynecology and Obstetrics* 22 (1916): 68–69, at 68; and American College of Surgeons, "Report of the Hospital Conference held at the Clinical Congress of the American College of Surgeons, Chicago, October 23, 1923," *Bulletin of the American College*

of Surgeons 8 (1924): 3–119, at 10. On Crile, a founder of the Cleveland Clinic, see R.E. Hermann, "George Washington Crile (1864–1943)," *Journal of Medical Biography* 2 (1994): 78–83. Codman, Harvey Cushing, and William Mayo were also heavily involved in this project: see F.H. Martin, "Hospital Standardization: Its Inception, Development, and Progress in Five Years," *Bulletin of the American College of Surgeons* 6 (1922): 3–4.

45. George W. Crile, *A Mechanistic View of War and Peace*, ed. Amy F. Rowland (London: T. Wesner Laurie, n.d. [c. 1916]), 43. Crile feared that war led to "race deterioration" (*Mechanistic View*, 41).

46. John G. Bowman, "The Standardization of Hospitals," *Boston Medical and Surgical Journal* 177 (1917): 283–85, at 283. Previously president of Iowa State University (1911–14), Bowman moved on to serve as chancellor of the University of Pittsburgh (1921–45). He was once secretary (1907–11) of the Carnegie Foundation for the Advancement of Teaching, which gave financial support to the hospital standardization movement.

47. Roger Cooter observes more generally that in the early twentieth century "military organization could be seen as providing an administrative ideal for coping with ever-greater problems of perceived social complexity, waste, and inefficiency. The military offered a model for the application of system, uniformity, and expertise to these problems, in a word a model of rationalization" ("Medicine and the Goodness of War," *Canadian Bulletin of Medical History* 7 [1990]: 147–59, at 152).

48. Owsei Temkin, "The Scientific Approach to Disease: Specific Entity and Individual Sickness," in *The Double Face of Janus and Other Essays in the History of Medicine* (Baltimore: Johns Hopkins University Press, 1977), 441–55; and Georges Canguilhem, *The Normal and the Pathological*, trans. Carolyn R. Fawcett with Robert S. Cohen (New York: Zone Books, 1989). It would be interesting to compare the disposition of the "normal" in the case file and the Freudian case study.

49. Anthropologists make careers providing examples of this failure. See Carol A. Heimer, "Concerning Children: How Documents Support Case versus Biographical Analyses," in *Documents: Artifacts of Modern Knowledge*, ed. Annelise Riles (Ann Arbor: University of Michigan Press, 2006), 95–126; and Adam Reed, "Documents Unfolding," in Riles, *Documents*, 158–79.

50. Jacques Derrida, *Archive Fever: A Freudian Impression*, trans. Eric Prenowitz (Chicago: University of Chicago Press, 1996), 2. For a challenge to Derrida's notion of "archival violence" (*Archive Fever*, 7), see Carolyn Steadman, "'Something she called a fever': Michelet, Derrida, and Dust (or In the Archives with Michelet and Derrida)," in *Archives, Documentation, and Institutions of Social Memory: Essays from the Sawyer Seminar*, ed. Francis X. Blouin, Jr., and William G. Rosenberg (Ann Arbor: University of Michigan Press, 2007), 4–19.

51. On the significance of paper technology and seriality in modern science and medicine, see Nick Hopwood, Simon Schaffer, and Jim Secord, "Seriality and Scientific Objects in the Nineteenth Century," *History of Science* 48 (2010): 251–85; and Volker Hess and J. Andrew Mendelsohn, "Cases and Series: Medical Knowledge and Paper Technology, 1600–1900," *History of Science* 48 (2010): 287–314.

52. Derrida, *Archive Fever*, 17 (emphasis in original). Derrida went on to write that we have no fixed concept of the archive, only an impression: "an insistent impression through the unstable feeling of a shifting figure, or of an in-finite or indefinite process" (29).

53. Ann Laura Stoler, *Along the Archival Grain: Epistemic Anxieties and Colonial Common Sense* (Princeton: Princeton University Press, 2009), 20, 22. See also Nicholas B. Dirks, "Annals of the Archive: Ethnographic Notes on the Sources of History," in *From the Margins: Historical Anthropology and its Futures*, ed. Brain Keith Axel (Durham NC: Duke University Press, 2002), 47–65.

54. Derrida, *Archive Fever*.

2 The Case Study as Representative Anecdote

John Cash

Men seek for vocabularies that will be faithful *reflections* of reality. To this end, they must develop vocabularies that are *selections* of reality. And any selection of reality must, in certain circumstances, function as a *deflection* of reality. Insofar as the vocabulary meets the needs of reflection, we can say that it has the necessary scope. In its selectivity, it is a reduction. Its scope and reduction become a deflection when the given terminology, or calculus, is not suited to the subject matter which it is designed to calculate.

Kenneth Burke, *A Grammar of Motives*

In *A Grammar of Motives*, first published in 1945, philosopher and literary critic Kenneth Burke discusses the virtues of selecting a "representative anecdote" in order to address the complexity of some field of "human relations." He writes, for instance, that "one should seek to select, as representative anecdote, something sufficiently demarcated in character to make analysis possible, yet sufficiently complex in character to prevent the use of too few terms in one's description."[1] This précis suggests that the anecdote and the case study are convergent. Certainly, as if to stress the similarity between case study and anecdote, Burke, in outlining why and how state constitutions (such as the Constitution of the United States) serve as excellent representative anecdotes, gives his lead chapter the subheading "Necessity for Representative Case."[2] In the same chapter Burke goes on to draw a distinction between representative anecdotes that are poorly chosen, and hence representative in a bad or reductive manner, and those anecdotes that are well chosen, and thus representative in a manner that condenses yet incorporates complexity. He also issues a warning in the comment, "If you don't select [an anecdote] that is representative in a good sense, it will function as representative in a bad sense." In the terms of the epigraph quoted above, the poorly chosen anecdote will function as a reduction that is also a deflection, due to the inadequacy of its terminology for the purpose at hand. Burke illustrates representative anecdotes that are poorly chosen with the following example: bad anecdotes are "naturalistic or simplist anecdotes of one sort or another, such as laboratory experiments with the conditioning of animals, treated as *point de départ* for the construction of a rudimentary terminology to which complex instances may be 'reduced'." Then comes a delightful turning of the epistemological tables that, I will argue, captures the virtues of the case study, by also asserting the need to adequately address complexity:

> For if much of service has been got by following Occam's law to the effect that "entities should not be multiplied beyond necessity," equally much of disservice has arisen through ignoring a contrary law, which we could phrase correspondingly: "entities should not be reduced beyond necessity."[3]

The two studies considered below can be usefully evaluated against this duality, this dialectic, of law and counterlaw; Occam's razor tempered by Burke's grammar.

Both of the studies that I discuss have achieved marked prominence amongst a range of publics. My intention is to explore the qualities of each that have generated such broad interest. How do they entice or attract the engagement of various publics, from like-minded professionals to the breadth of public cultures? How does such broad appeal relate to their being either "good" or "bad" representative anecdotes? The first of these is a classic case study: Sigmund Freud's "Notes Upon a Case of Obsessional Neurosis"—the case of the "Rat Man."[4] Freud's case study begins, for him, late in 1907 and is completed and published in 1909. It has been discovering new publics ever since. The second study discussed below is more contentious in the present context, both in its status as a good representative anecdote, and in its status as a case study at all. I refer to Stanley Milgram's "Obedience to Authority" study.[5] This series of experiments was formally commenced in August 1961, although a pilot study was conducted with twenty undergraduates at Yale University in 1960. The first report of the research was published in 1963; a longer and fuller article was published in the journal *Human Relations* in 1965, and the book that discussed the full set of experiments, namely *Obedience to Authority*, appeared in 1974.[6] There were several other publications between 1963 and 1974. Since then, Milgram's study has resonated throughout public culture, having captured the attention of various publics and, like Freud's case studies, having generated many reiterations.

An online search using Google Search suffices to reveal the broad public appeal of these two studies, and the appeal of the larger theory of human subjectivity and human relations for which each stands as a representative anecdote. A shared feature of both the "Rat Man" case and the obedience to authority experiments is the mixture of attraction and repulsion that they arouse. Such complex ambivalence arises from the manner in which these studies fascinate by revealing some abject and usually secret or hidden aspects of human subjectivity. Publics congregate around these two cases because they divulge striking features of human subjectivity and, in that process, assault the narcissism of the publics they construct and attract. Their shared focus on struggles with authority, and on the psychic limits of the capacity to take responsibility and act responsibly, renders them particularly apposite and resonant studies for some of the most disturbing features of the twentieth century and its aftereffects.

In particular, the period from 1909 onwards in Europe (to take the date when the "Rat Man" case was first published) was marked by anxiety concerning transformations in the way authority operated within families, societies, and polities; it was marked as well by transformations in what Peter Gay has termed "the cultivation of hatred," or what might also be characterized as new forms of aggressivity.[7] The period after World War II through the 1960s and beyond, especially in the United States, likewise confronted changes in patterns of authority, while reflecting on the horrors of Nazism and Fascism, and the war in Vietnam. The *Authoritarian Personality* study, led by Theodor Adorno and others, and published in 1950, bridges these two periods. With origins in the Frankfurt School's attempt to analyze Nazism, the study's immediate concern was postwar anxieties about the pre-fascist or "potentially fascistic" individual in the United States.[8] As is well known, *The Authoritarian Personality* relies on a mixture of case study material and statistical analyses of responses to the various scales developed—such as the anti-Semitism scale and the ethnocentrism scale. In this research, the case studies were used to generate hypotheses and, interestingly, also to "validate" the scales. Hence, the case studies of "Mack" and "Larry" that are woven throughout *The Authoritarian Personality* appear at the outset of the study and near the end of several sections or parts.[9]

To generalize somewhat, in the postwar period, the slow unfolding of knowledge about individualizing processes, accompanied by marked reversals, created a profound interest in the ways in which human subjects relate to authority, exercise responsibility, and perform or repress aggression—especially after the revelations of the Holocaust. This interest in obedience to authority and its antithesis, the capacity for individual responsibility, was accompanied by a narcissistic illusion that obedience to authority was in retreat, at least in those liberal democratic societies that had resisted Nazism and Fascism. In this context Freud's "Rat Man" case study, and the broader psychoanalytic theory it illustrates and represents, captured a public culture more concerned than ever with the complexities of "authority and its discontents," while Milgram's obedient subjects punctured an array of illusions about liberal democratic societies and their citizens. Milgram, of course, was strongly affected by the ongoing revelations regarding the nature and extent of the Holocaust in wartime Europe and was at first surprised to find apparently similar tendencies to obey authority in the United States.

The trial of Nazi war criminal Adolf Eichmann, beginning in April 1961, virtually coincided with the early stages of the "Obedience to Authority" study. While not an influence on Milgram's conception of his experimental study, the Eichmann trial and the Milgram experiments soon merged in the public imagination. Anticipating this merger, Milgram's famous mentor, the social psychologist Gordon W. Allport, dubbed Milgram's research "the Eichmann Experiment."[10] Milgram himself regarded Hannah Arendt's notion of the "banality of evil," presented in her account of the Eichmann trial, as entirely apposite; it came "closer to the truth than one might dare imagine."[11] In his view, "the most fundamental lesson of our study" is that "ordinary people, simply doing their jobs, and without any particular hostility on their part, can become agents in a terrible destructive process."[12] However, it is important to note that Milgram was confounded by the first results of his research. Amongst the citizens of the democratic United States (as opposed to Germany), he had expected to find a resilient capacity to resist authority. His initial consternation and accompanying fascination is evident in a letter he wrote to Henry Riecken, the head of Social Sciences at the National Science Foundation, on September 21, 1961, just several weeks after his experiments had begun. Milgram wrote,

> In a naïve moment some time ago, I once wondered whether in all of the United States a vicious government could find enough moral imbeciles to meet the personnel requirements of a national system of death camps, of the sort that were maintained in Germany. I am now beginning to think that a full complement could be recruited in New Haven.[13]

Milgram was already recognizing that the self-understanding of the leading postwar liberal democracy was oddly awry, and that any presumed moral superiority could be recharacterized, to use Freud's terms, as "the narcissism of minor differences."

"PUTTING ON A SHOW": CONSTRUCTING PUBLICS AND DISSEMINATING KNOWLEDGE

If a well-chosen representative anecdote has, as a principal virtue, its adequacy as a distillation of complexity without undue reduction, the same virtue also carries implications for the anecdote's capacity to construct public(s), and to disseminate knowledge to such public(s). This is evident in Burke's choice of the Constitution of the United States as a suitable representative anecdote, due to its capacity to construct a public. His principal criterion for this choice is the Constitution's character as "some representative public enactment, to which all members of a given social body variously but commonly subscribe."[14]

In developing his argument that "a public is poetic world making," Michael Warner's account resonates in interesting ways with Burke's own account of a representative anecdote, and with Burke's broader "dramatism" method, with its emphasis on agents, agency, acts, purpose, and scene—Burke's famous "pentad."[15] As Warner writes,

> Public discourse says not only "Let a public exist," but "Let it have this character, speak this way, see the world in this way. It then goes in search of confirmation that such a public exists, with greater or lesser success—success being further attempts to cite, circulate, and realize the world understanding it articulates. Run it up the flagpole and see who salutes. Put on a show and see who shows up.[16]

It is evident that when Freud "put on a show" with his case studies, eventually a variety of publics "showed up" and began to "see the world in this way." Similarly, although not as extensively, when Milgram published his studies of obedience to authority he extended the construction of a public that was already beginning to recognize both the horror of the Holocaust, and the pervasive willingness of people to perform cruel or terrible acts in the name of authority while echoing the refrain "I was only obeying orders." Indeed, Milgram's research design was so dramatic and compelling that it quickly captured the public imagination, and might be regarded as a figure into which the manifold concerns about the modern State, conformity, bureaucracy, and perverse authority were condensed.

In what follows I will explore aspects of these two studies—Freud's case study and Milgram's social psychology experiment—and ask about the relationship between their capacity to construct publics, disseminate knowledge, and create "ways of seeing" on the one hand, and their status as "good" or "bad" representative anecdotes on the other hand. Milgram's research becomes particularly interesting here, as it fails the test of being a good representative anecdote. Yet, in its fullest elaboration at book length, it contains in a marginal form certain case study features that reveal a salient counternarrative.

THE "RAT MAN" CASE

Ernst Lanzer was the name of the patient/analysand whom Freud called the "Rat Man." Freud presents the "Rat Man" case as a sequence of closely related vignettes, each demonstrating the analysand's hectic, yet eventually futile work of thinking and acting—but especially thinking—as a defense against anxiety. The anxiety is generated by the young man's intensely fraught relation to authority. This intense burden has persisted since early childhood, and is organized around the figure of his father: a father who obstructs and prohibits his erotic desires. The vignettes recur as a series of scenes throughout the case history, and they plot, as a series of repetitions, the life as reported by the patient/analysand. For instance, there is the young Lanzer's punishment by his father, ostensibly because he had bitten someone, but perhaps due to one of his erotic adventures with a maid or governess. This punishment prompts a verbal tirade from the young boy, aged about three and a half at the time; he shouts abuse at his cruel father—except that he knows no words of abuse. So he shouts, "You lamp! You towel! You plate! and so on."[17] The father is so shocked by the intensity of the child's hostility that he comments, "The child will be either a great man or a great criminal." This scene of rage against authority, in which the proper words to voice that rage are unavailable, is echoed years later in the psychoanalytic treatment, where Lanzer finds it impossible to acknowledge in speech his continuing hatred and aggression towards his father. Instead, a series of "rat" signifiers insert themselves into his speech—a regular rat currency, as Freud puts it—allowing his rage, now unconscious, to find distorted expression, because he still cannot find the words to speak it plainly.[18] This currency includes terms such as *Spielratte* (colloquial for gambler), *Hofrat* (an honorific title), and the confusion between *Raten* (rate of payment for the psychoanalytic sessions) and *Ratten* (rat). Along with stories about rats, such as the rat torture, these rat signifiers kept recurring in Lanzer's speech within the psychoanalytic sessions. Between the scene at home when Lanzer was a young child, and the scene in Freud's consulting room, repression had intervened. Freud elaborates by commenting that Lanzer's early confrontation with authority and his rage at his father for the punishment inflicted turned him into a coward, but not simply out of fear. Rather, as Freud explains, "out of fear of the violence of his own rage"; a rage that Lanzer was obliged to repress, but that insisted on returning in distorted and distorting form.[19] Already we can see that the manner in which the case is reported condenses some central elements of psychoanalytic theory into a narrative organized by a particular grammar and a corresponding set of concepts. Often these concepts are left largely implicit, while their implications in the grammar and detail of the case study communicate their meaning and their "way of seeing."

The immediate event that prompted Lanzer to seek therapy from Freud occurred when, as a young man, he was training with the army as part of the required annual military service. One of the regulars, an old army sergeant, told him of a torture practiced "in the East" in which "a criminal was tied up . . . a pot was turned upside down on his buttocks . . . some rats were put into it . . . and they . . . *bored their way in.*"[20] Lanzer was both fascinated and appalled by this story. He immediately imagined the torture being performed on the woman he loved, Gisela, and also on his father, even though his father had died some time previously. These thoughts and fantasies also gave rise to feelings of guilt, and he repudiated and disowned them as thoroughly alien to himself. Yet they persisted, and such was his fear of their power—his magical thinking—that he felt obliged to perform a series of actions in order to prevent the torture befalling Gisela and his father, including the coordination of actions by other soldiers in order to repay a debt. These various coordinated actions were so internally contradictory, however, that the repayment of the debt could not be completed. Hence, unconsciously, while imagining that he was protecting Gisela and his father, Lanzer had managed to leave them exposed to the violence of the rats.

This same unresolved ambivalence is evident in the "Glejisamen" prayer that Lanzer recites, in increasingly frenetic spasms, so as to ward off the bad thoughts about harm befalling Gisela and his father. Freud takes pleasure in explaining how the prayer intended to ward off the dangerous thoughts actually manages to represent them unconsciously, through the conjoining of the name Gisela with the German word for semen, or seed.[21]

With analytic material like these vignettes, it is hardly surprising that Freud was delighted and energized by Lanzer's case. From the first few sessions it was clear that Freud had encountered case material that would support the development of an excellent representative anecdote; namely this troubled young man's psychopathology as constructed through the language and grammar of psychoanalysis, and its established and emerging concepts. Here, then, was a tortured psyche whose current obsessionality perfectly matched its childhood original. The significance of childhood desires, phantasies, and experiences was apparent. The young man quickly and readily revealed a history of childhood sexual experiences with sisters, governesses, and maids. There was an iconic episode of punishment by a father whom Lanzer thereafter idealized and detested in equal measure— but the son's aggressivity and hatred were repressed, and unavailable to consciousness, except as uncanny moments that disrupted his self-image as the good son and suitor. Moreover, these momentary illuminations of his hatred, sadism, and aggressivity felt so alien that they were immediately repudiated and disowned. There was the obstruction of his desire by this same father, who had beaten him as a boy and prompted furious abuse via the homely words "lamp," "towel," and "plate." Whether his actual offense had been sexual or merely general naughtiness, in young Lanzer's mind the punishment he received was connected to the father's prohibition of his sexual desire. This sense of prohibition resurfaced in later life, when Ernst's father and whole family opposed his desire to marry Gisela instead of her wealthier and well-connected rival, whom his family preferred. Oedipus was present and accounted for, although as yet not named as such.

The case study of the "Rat Man" is also replete with what can be termed "obsessional-work" as a mode of thought, a complement to the grammar of the dream-work and the joke-work that Freud had addressed in *The Interpretation of Dreams* (first published in 1899), and *Jokes and their Relation to the Unconscious* (first published in 1905). No wonder Freud took the earliest opportunity to present, in a double session over two weeks, his first account of the "Rat Man" case at the weekly meetings of the circle that would become the Vienna Psychoanalytic Society. The speed of this reportage is striking. Freud first met with the "Rat Man" on October 1, 1907, and he presented the case—while still in process—to the incipient Vienna Psychoanalytic Society in the same month, on October 30, following up a week later on November 6. According to minutes of the society's meetings, one of Freud's main points was that "hatred of the father as strong as in this case can arise only if the father has disturbed the child in his sexuality."[22]

Freud also presented the "Rat Man" case to the first meeting of the International Psychoanalytic Congress in Salzburg, in 1908. Ernest Jones's report of this arresting presentation is well known.

> Delivered without any notes . . . it began at eight and at eleven he offered to bring it to a close. We had all been so enthralled, however, at his fascinating exposition that we begged him to go on, and he did so for another hour. I had never before been so oblivious of the passage of time.

This account gives a vivid sense of both Freud's own engagement with the case, and the matching fascination of its first international audience. For this audience it was, Jones writes, "both an intellectual and an artistic feast."[23]

While the burgeoning community of psychoanalysts and like-minded intellectuals and writers was an early public—or audience, at least—for this case study, the "Rat Man" himself was the case's very first audience. The process notes that Freud made throughout the analysis make clear that he took pains to explain to Lanzer the psychoanalytic principles of free association, the unconscious, infantile sexuality, transference, repression, and so forth.[24] The published case study preserves this personalized mode of instruction. While now available to much wider publics, the text retains some of the intimacy of the original setting, notably in "Section D" of the first part of the case study, under the heading "Initiation into the Nature of the Treatment." There, set in relation to the details of the case, we read about the differences between the conscious and the unconscious; the significance of the infantile and its relation to the unconscious ("The unconscious, I explained, *was* the infantile"); the centrality of repression ("every fear corresponded to a former *wish* which was now repressed"), and the positive Oedipus complex (although the latter is not named as such, but characterized as "The Father Complex").[25] It should come as no surprise that this case continues to be routinely used by psychoanalytic training institutes for instructional purposes.

Freud's second session with the "Rat Man" begins with Freud outlining the one and only condition for the treatment—namely, that Lanzer is "to say everything that comes into his head, even if it was *unpleasant* to him, or seemed *unimportant* or *irrelevant* or *senseless*": the rule of free association.[26] In response to Freud's encouragement "to start his communications with any subject he pleased," Lanzer began by telling a story about two friends.[27] Through his interpretations Freud explains how these two very different friendships represent and condense the two poles of Lanzer's transference to Freud, as well as his highly ambivalent relation to Gisela and to his father.

The first friend mentioned is a good object, we might say. When troubled or "tormented" by his sense of himself as a criminal, Lanzer would resort to this friend, who would calmly reassure him that "he (Ernst) was a man of irreproachable conduct, and had probably been in the habit, from his youth onwards, of taking a dark view of his own life."[28] The bad friend—who eventually became his tutor—was a young man five years older than Lanzer who had initially praised his intelligence and radically raised Lanzer's self-esteem. However, after he gained access to the Lanzer household it became clear that this false friend was interested only in Lanzer's sister. He began treating Lanzer "as though he were an idiot."[29]

The true friend is mentioned again at the beginning of Lanzer's fourth session with Freud, and discussion of this theme is developed in "Section D" of the published case study, "Initiation into the Nature of the Treatment." The discussion proceeds as a kind of Socratic dialogue, as does much of the case study. Following the death of an aunt about eighteen months after his father's death, Lanzer's guilt about having been absent when his father died—although he was resting nearby—returned to haunt him, and seriously incapacitated his ability to work. His true friend became a great source of solace by reassuring Lanzer that his self-reproaches were grossly exaggerated. Freud takes this opportunity to give Lanzer "a first glance at the principles of psychoanalytic therapy." He explains that the kind friend is mistaken, and that Lanzer really does have reasons to feel guilty and to reproach himself. However, there is a "mesalliance between the affect and its ideational content." Freud then continues in his tutelary role by carefully explaining,

> A layman will say that the affect is too great for the occasion—that it is exaggerated—and that consequently the inference following from the self-reproach (the inference that the patient is a criminal) is false. On the contrary, the physician says: "No. The affect is justified. The sense of guilt is not in itself open to further criticism. But it belongs to some other content, which is unknown (*unconscious*), and which requires to be looked for. The known ideational content has only got into its actual position owing to a false connection.[30]

Here we see Freud working with an instance that arises early in the treatment, in a manner that respects the patient's strong affect of guilt while explaining its unconscious origin. Although well-intentioned, the kind friend's common sense argument is wrong, while Lanzer is right about his feelings. He is simply mistaken about their true reference, due to the operations of the unconscious. These false connections can be undone. This is a masterful example of the way in which the case study, through a sequence of such scenes or instances, can communicate to its publics an implicit rendering of the fuller theory of which it is a representative anecdote.

OBEDIENCE TO AUTHORITY

Turning to consider the Milgram experiments, do these meet Burke's criterion of bad and poorly selected representative anecdotes, by being merely "naturalistic or simplist anecdotes...such as laboratory experiments" that unduly reduce complexity? Or do they contain features that redress and overcome such unduly reductive tendencies? As explained above, my response to such questions is to argue that the Milgram studies, as originally conceived and as usually reported, are poor representative anecdotes. Their disabling shock effect and their implicit counsel of despair emerge from their undue simplification, and their primary focus on "final scores."[31] However, the book *Obedience to Authority*, and to a lesser extent earlier publications, contain a set of vignettes that resemble case studies; they concern several of the research subjects, and how they experienced and performed in the experimental setting. When reexamined with due attention to the tensions, emotions, and conflicting identifications that are evident in the responses of these subjects to the experimental conditions, a more complex counteranecdote may be discerned.

Milgram's research was initially conceived as a comparative study, one with the ultimate aim of analyzing the German character and its tendencies towards obedience to authority, in contrast with "more democratic" character types, who were presumed capable of taking personal responsibility, even in the face of authority. This framing assumption concerning marked comparative differences soon collapsed in the face of the responses that Milgram's experiments in New Haven were actually eliciting. Milgram had quickly learned that most subjects of his experiment obeyed instructions to administer electric shocks of higher and higher voltage, up to the highest register of 450 volts. Unlike Solomon Asch's experiments with conformity, measured merely by agreement or disagreement about the length of a line, Milgram conceived an experimental design that was dramatic and nontrivial. As he explained in an interview of 1980,

> One of the criticisms that had been made of (Asch's) experiments is that they lack a surface significance, because, after all, an experiment with people making judgements of lines has a manifestly trivial content. So the question I asked myself is: how can this be made a more humanly significant experiment?
>
> It seemed to me that if, instead of having a group exerting pressure on the judgements about lines, the group could somehow induce something more significant from the person, then that might be a

step in giving greater face significance to the behavior induced by the group.[32]

The ingenious experimental mise-en-scène developed by Milgram certainly met this purpose admirably. The setting was a laboratory, with a large and complex shock generator mounted on a table; the true subject of the experiment sat before this table. The characters in the scene were a scientist or experimenter dressed in a lab coat; a "teacher," who was the actual subject of the experiment, and a "learner." This "learner" was actually a confederate of the "experimenter," but was regarded by the "teacher" as another, second subject of the experiment. This illusion was achieved by a contrived drawing of lots, to decide who would be the "teacher" and who the "learner." Having been allocated the role of "teacher," the true subject of the experiment was then administered a sample shock of 45 volts, to acquaint him or her with the experience of that level of shock. He or she was then instructed on how to proceed with the teaching and specifically instructed to administer shocks of ever-increasing voltage in response to each new mistake by the "learner."

In this "theatre of cruelty," as it might be characterized, obedience was far more prevalent than had been anticipated. This high level of obedience necessitated several modifications and additions to the experimental conditions, in order to achieve variations in response. Eventually, there were four experimental conditions. In two of these, the "learner" or victim was located in an adjoining room. In the first condition, called "Remote Feedback," the victim could not be seen or heard, except when he or she pounded on the wall to protest the electric shock of 300 volts, thereafter falling silent. Only 34 percent of the subjects involved under this condition refused to complete the experiment: in other words, 66 percent administered shocks all the way to the level of 450 volts, the level marked "Danger: Severe Shock." Called "Voice Feedback," the second condition varied from the first in one significant respect: the "teacher" could hear protests from the victim at stages along the way to 450 volts. Under this condition, 37.5 percent of the subjects refused to administer shocks of 450 volts, while 62.5 percent obeyed to the bitter end. Under the third and fourth conditions, the victim or "learner" was located near to the teacher-subject, and could be seen and heard. In condition three ("Proximity"), the victim was only 1.5 feet from the "teacher." Such close proximity made a significant difference, and 60 percent refused to increase the shocks to the level of 450 volts. The fourth condition ("Touch-Proximity") pushed the requirements further in the attempt to generate refusals. In this condition when, beyond the level of 150 volt shocks, the learner-victim made a mistake and feigned unwillingness to place his or her hand on the shockplate, the experimenter "ordered" the teacher-subject "to force the victim's hand onto the plate. Thus obedience in this condition required that the subject have physical contact with the victim in order to give him punishment beyond the

150-volt level."[33] Even so, 30 percent of subjects completed the experiment up to the level of 450 volts.

In a postscript to his 1965 article about the experiment, Milgram reflected on the lengths required to generate disobedience.

> What is the limit of such obedience? At many points we attempted to establish a boundary. Cries from the victim were inserted; not good enough. The victim claimed heart trouble; subjects still shocked him on command. The victim pleaded that he be let free, and his answers no longer registered on the signal box; subjects continued to shock him. At the outset we had not conceived that such drastic procedures would be needed to generate disobedience, and each step was added only as the ineffectiveness of the earlier techniques became clear. The final effort to establish a limit was the Touch-Proximity condition. But the very first subject in this condition subdued the victim on command, and pro-ceeded to the highest shock level.[34]

This stark recognition that obedience to authority is commonplace, even when the administration of severe punishment to another is involved, led Milgram to conclude that

> with numbing regularity good people were seen to knuckle under to the demands of authority and perform actions that were callous and severe. Men who are in everyday life responsible and decent were seduced by the trappings of authority, by the control of their perceptions, and by the uncritical acceptance of the experimenter's definition of the situation into performing harsh acts.[35]

As already argued, this is the way in which the Milgram study is typi-cally read and reported. In the public imagination, this is how it is typically understood. It has become a reflexive reference by which social anomie and rampant individualism are rationalized, and in this regard it is a power-ful symbolic figure—"The Milgram Experiment"—into which apathy, dis-illusionment, distrust, and self-justifying narcissism have been condensed. However, across the four experimental conditions outlined above, the varia-tion in obedience ranged from 66 percent to 30 percent. This variation high-lights that aspects of the experiment were not well captured by Milgram's organizing grammar of motives; they demanded a more adequate gram-mar of motives. Such other, marginalized aspects are best recaptured and "released," as it were, by focusing on iterations of the experiment *in process*, as each unfolds—instead of simply counting the outcomes as observed and registered according to the criteria of obedience or disobedience, and shock level at which the punishment was sometimes discontinued. In other words, what extra dimensions can be observed when each iteration is treated more like a case study?

Milgram's subjects found themselves in a situation akin to that explored by Freud in his landmark essay "Group Psychology and the Analysis of the Ego," first published in 1921. So powerful were the experimental conditions that the psyches of those involved in Milgram's experiment were being reorganized in the "here and now" of the experiment in progress. During the course of the experiment, the strain of responsibility became evident, and the case-like features of the research began to open out. Confronted by interpellations both powerful (the scientist-experimenter) and weak (the abject learner-victim), and by processes of identification (with the authority, with the abject), most subjects enacted a passionate struggle between responsibility and obedience. They turned and turned again as the experimenter's demand to inflict more punishment was obeyed or disobeyed. That is, a common response was, literally, to turn towards the experimenter in either a mute or voiced plea for reassurance that the subject, as "teacher," should continue to administer ever more intense shocks—despite cries and demands from the "learner" to be released ("let me out of here!"), or the dreaded silence that followed mistakes made by the "learner" at the point when the shocks were administered near the top of the 450-volt scale. When analyzed with particular attention to the ways in which individuals negotiated the experimental conditions, as reported by Milgram in the brief case study vignettes, the complexity of subjects' responses becomes evident. From this perspective the research results take on the fuller dimensions of a moment by moment struggle between obedience to authority on the one hand, and, on the other, the taking or surrendering of individual responsibility. To catch this complexity, close consideration of the unfolding process is required—and a statistical analysis of ultimate outcomes is inadequate.

Transcripts of some individual iterations of the experiment are available in the book *Obedience to Authority*, although these transcripts are only segments. Rod Dickinson's *The Milgram Re-enactment* (2002), is an artwork in which several separate iterations of the experiment were performed in full at the Centre for Contemporary Art in Glasgow.[36] These performances were based on transcripts of the particular interactions between the teacher-subject, the learner-victim, and the experimenter. They were enacted in an "exact facsimile" of the Social Interaction Laboratory at Yale University, and with an exact replica of Milgram's shock generator. Three iterations of this reenactment were filmed, and they provide an invaluable sense of the course of the experiment, as it unfolded for each subject. The transcripts and filmed reenactments add the complexity of the "case-in-process" to the rigor of Milgram's elegant and dramatic research design. They reveal that the assault on the cultural and individual narcissism of the leading liberal-democratic societies in an age of individualization remains, but now complicated by passionate struggles against authority, as well as frequently troubled collusion with authority.

One example must suffice as illustrative. Heightened emotion was a common experience for many who participated in Milgram's experiments. For instance, most subjects reported their level of tension and nervousness as somewhere between "moderately so" and "extremely tense and nervous."[37] The documentation of Elinor Rosenblum (the name is a pseudonym bestowed by Milgram) provides a good illustration of such heightened emotions and anxieties, showing them coupled with a thoroughgoing acceptance that she must complete the experiment up to the shock level of 450 volts, even as she expresses her reluctance all the way. Throughout, she regularly turned to the experimenter and asked "in a tone of helplessness,"

> Must I go on? Oh I'm worried about him. Are we going all the way up there (pointing to the higher end of the generator)? Can't we stop? I'm shaking. I'm shaking? Do I have to go up there?[38]

Despite such shaking and evident distress, Rosenblum continues to address the "learner" in an "officious tone," and obeys every instruction, to the extent of administering the ultimate shock of 450 volts three times. In the debriefing, like all other subjects, Rosenblum was informed that the "learner" was actually an actor who received no shocks, and that the procedure was all artifice. In response she excused herself in the following way:

> You're an actor, boy. You're marvellous . . . I'm exhausted. I didn't want to go on with it. You don't know what I went through here. A person like me hurting you, my God. I didn't want to do it to you. Forgive me, please. I can't get over this.[39]

A further indicator of Rosenblum's reluctance and distress, coupled with her incapacity to disobey, is the manner in which, from the point of administering a shock of 270 volts, she attempted to guide the "learner" to the correct answer by accentuating her pronunciation of that word as against the other three that were incorrect. In a similar vein, some other subjects, when unobserved, would give a lower shock than the schedule required.

Like the heightened emotional states experienced by most subjects of Milgram's experiments, such "guidance" of the learner to the correct answer, and such opportunistic avoidance of administering high voltage shocks point to the fact that there is evidence throughout the study of fraught and passionate struggles between obedience and the taking on of personal responsibility. Milgram reports this tension in his case study-like vignettes, but fails to capture its full significance. For instance, the discussion of Elinor Rosenblum covers approximately five pages, and exemplifies how Milgram's "grammar of motives" unduly reduces the complexity of Rosenblum's responses, even as it reports them.[40] At the same time, Milgram's general conclusions, as in some of his statements quoted above, emphasize the strong tendency to obey, and the difficulty in finding experimental conditions that promoted disobedience. Moreover, the study has typically been received as confirming the pervasiveness of "the banality of evil" (Hannah

Arendt's term); an interpretation fostered by Milgram's own rendition.[41] As I have argued, the brute fact of obedience is only part of the story, although clearly a highly significant part. In contrast, I have stressed the multidimensionality of Milgram's findings; the complex features that become evident when each iteration is treated as a case in process. Most significantly, resistance to authority is evident not only in the response of those individuals who refused and discontinued the experiment against the commands of the experimenter. The prospect of resistance is also raised in the fitful, often desperate turnings to the experimenter by subjects like Rosenblum, who, importantly, constitute the majority of research subjects. In their passionate pleas to "stop now," their trepidation in the face of increasing shock levels, their attempts at minor collusions with the "learner," and in their willful avoidances when unobserved, these "obedient" subjects also enact the struggle between obedience and the taking of personal responsibility. Such is the virtue of adding a case study method to the rigors of experimental design.

CONCLUSION

Kenneth Burke's argument regarding representative anecdotes assists in specifying the strengths of the case study as a source of knowledge, and as a genre that communicates with and constructs various publics. When a case study operates as a good representative anecdote, its grammar condenses and implicitly reveals the larger theory that informs its organization. This is quite evident in Freud's case study of the "Rat Man," where Freud steers between Occam's law and Burke's counterpoint against undue reduction, as he simultaneously develops and illustrates psychoanalytic theory and practice to a variety of publics. Burke's description of the good representative anecdote matches nicely the grammar of motives generated and deployed by Freud in this and other case studies: "the anecdote is in a sense a summation, containing implicitly what the system that is developed from it contains explicitly."[42] In turn, this summation by implication generates a second summation, which Burke terms "the paradigm or prototype."[43] Surely the very strengths of the case study lie in such an organization of complex case detail by a grammar and terminology that implicitly condense a larger theory or "system" without undue reduction—while presenting that theory or system in ways that are intuitively grasped by a public that has itself been constructed, or further elaborated, by the theory or perspective in question. It is this synecdochic capacity for condensation with summation (and without undue reduction), due to the conceptual resonance of the case study's well-chosen and adequately represented instances, that makes the case study such a suitable form for constructing and developing theory *and* for constructing receptive publics. Of course, not all case studies meet these exacting standards, but all case studies contain this potential.

Clearly Milgram's study was not a case study in its conception. Yet it contains material that can be treated as a case study supplement, so to speak, and that material is particularly instructive. Milgram's own treatment of his evidence reveals an ambivalence between highlighting the shocking revelations and the narcissistic wound delivered by his study, and a more nuanced attention to the tension, nervousness, heightened emotionality, and avoidances that he also observed.[44] My argument has been that by taking this a step further, by paying closer attention to each iteration of the experiment in process, as it unfolds, Milgram's study—hovering between being a good and a bad anecdote—can have its strengths redeemed. As indicated, such a supplement involves an expansion of grammar, in Burke's sense. At the least it involves drawing out Milgram's own discussion of the resistances that he notes. Burke's argument, quoted at the outset of this chapter, warrants repetition: "one should seek to select, as representative anecdote, something sufficiently demarcated in character to make analysis possible, yet sufficiently complex in character to prevent the use of too few terms in one's description."[45] Captured by his own fascination with the distressing spectacle that his experiments revealed and enacted, and by the manner in which the subjects' obedience confounded established self-understandings and garnered notoriety for his research, Milgram was tempted to use "too few terms" in his reporting of the research. Such an emphasis sat in tension with the case study-like vignettes that contained more complexity than Milgram was able to fully integrate into his "grammar of motives." Moreover, as the protocols or transcripts of his experiments reveal, each iteration of the experiment, as it unfolded, demanded supplementary terms that added complexity to the analysis. The public fascination with the obedience to authority study relies on its being "a bad anecdote" from which profoundly pessimistic and one-dimensional conclusions can be drawn. If the case study method and its expansion of a grammar of motives can begin to redeem that somber and dispiriting conclusion, as I have argued it can, then the method will definitely have demonstrated its great strengths. Indeed, through its capacity to handle complexity it can restore a more nuanced understanding of the profound issue that has haunted the twentieth century and beyond; namely, the conflict and tension between the taking of responsibility and obedience to authority.[46]

NOTES

1. Kenneth Burke, *A Grammar of Motives* (Berkeley: University of California Press, 1969), 324.
2. Burke, *A Grammar of Motives*, 323.
3. Burke, *A Grammar of Motives*, 324 (the two quotes).
4. Sigmund Freud, "Notes Upon a Case of Obsessional Neurosis" (1909), in *The Penguin Freud Library*, vol. 9, *Case Histories II*, trans. James Strachey, ed. Angela Richards (London: Penguin Books, 1987), 31–128.

5. Stanley Milgram, *Obedience to Authority: An Experimental View* (London: Tavistock, 1974).

6. See Stanley Milgram, "Behavioral Study of Obedience," *Journal of Abnormal Psychology* 67 (1963): 371–78, and, by the same author, "Some Conditions of Obedience and Disobedience to Authority," *Human Relations* 18, no. 1 (1965): 57–76.

7. Peter Gay, *The Bourgeois Experience: Victoria to Freud*, vol. 3, *The Cultivation of Hatred* (New York: Norton, 1994).

8. Theodor Adorno et al., *The Authoritarian Personality* (New York: Harper, 1950).

9. For instance, Part IV E is headed "Validation By Case Studies: The Responses of Mack and Larry on the E Scale": Adorno, *The Authoritarian Personality*, 143.

10. Milgram, *Obedience to Authority*, 178.

11. Hannah Arendt, *Eichmann in Jerusalem: A Report on the Banality of Evil* (New York: Viking, 1963); Milgram, *Obedience to Authority*, 6.

12. Milgram, *Obedience to Authority*, 6.

13. Thomas Blass, *The Man Who Shocked the World: The Life and Legacy of Stanley Milgram* (New York: Basic Books, 2004), 100.

14. Burke, *A Grammar of Motives*, 323.

15. Michael Warner, *Publics and Counterpublics* (New York: Zone Books, 2002), 114. On Burke's pentad, see Burke, *A Grammar of Motives*, xv, xvi, and 56.

16. Warner, *Publics and Counterpublics*, 114.

17. Freud, "Notes Upon a Case of Obsessional Neurosis," 86.

18. Freud, "Notes Upon a Case of Obsessional Neurosis," 94–96 passim.

19. Freud, "Notes Upon a Case of Obsessional Neurosis," 86.

20. Freud, "Notes Upon a Case of Obsessional Neurosis," 47 (emphasis in the original).

21. Freud, "Notes Upon a Case of Obsessional Neurosis," 105.

22. Herman Nunberg and Ernst Federn, eds., *Minutes of the Vienna Psychoanalytic Society*, vol. 1, *1906–1908* (New York: International Universities Press, 1962), 236; in the same volume, see also the Introduction, and chapter 28.

23. As quoted in Peter Gay, *Freud: A Life for Our Time* (New York: Norton, 1988), 244 (both quotations).

24. Freud's process notes for the "Rat Man" case are the only set of his case notes to survive; see Peter Gay, ed., *The Freud Reader* (New York: Norton, 1989), 309–50.

25. See Freud, "Notes Upon a Case of Obsessional Neurosis," 58, 60, and 80–100. Emphases are in the original for the first two quotes.

26. Freud, "Notes Upon a Case of Obsessional Neurosis," 40 (emphasis in the original).

27. Freud, "Notes Upon a Case of Obsessional Neurosis," 40.

28. Freud, "Notes Upon a Case of Obsessional Neurosis," 40.

29. Freud, "Notes Upon a Case of Obsessional Neurosis," 41.

30. Freud, "Notes Upon a Case of Obsessional Neurosis," 56 (all three quotations above).

31. Milgram, "Some Conditions of Obedience and Disobedience to Authority," 138.

32. Stanley Milgram, *The Individual in a Social World: Essays and Experiments*, ed. Thomas Blass (London: Pinter and Martin, 2010), 120–21.

33. Milgram, "Some Conditions of Obedience and Disobedience to Authority," reprinted in *The Individual in a Social World*, 128–50, at 132.

34. Milgram, "Some Conditions of Obedience and Disobedience to Authority," 147.

35. Milgram, "Some Conditions of Obedience and Disobedience to Authority," 146–47.
36. See www.roddickinson.net/pages/milgram/project-synopsis.php (accessed December 10, 2013).
37. Milgram, *Obedience to Authority*, 42.
38. Milgram, *Obedience to Authority*, 80.
39. Milgram, *Obedience to Authority*, 82.
40. Milgram, *Obedience to Authority*, 79–84.
41. See Arendt, *Eichmann in Jerusalem: A Report on the Banality of Evil*.
42. Burke, *A Grammar of Motives*, 60.
43. Burke, *A Grammar of Motives*, 61.
44. As well as the several case study-like vignettes reported in *Obedience to Authority*, see the brief discussion of "Tensions" in "Some Conditions of Obedience and Disobedience to Authority," 138–41. This section begins by stating that "the description of final scores does not fully convey the character of the subjects' performance, and it would be useful to interrupt our reporting of quantitative relationships to remark on the subjects' general reaction to the situation" (138). These remarks, however, remain captive to Milgram's inadequate "grammar of motives."
45. Burke, *A Grammar of Motives*, 324.
46. For a more detailed discussion of the obedience to authority experiments, see John Cash, "Obedience to Authority and Its Discontents," in *Responsibility*, ed. Ghassan Hage and Robyn Eckersley (Melbourne: Melbourne University Press, 2012), 5–28.

3 Influencing Public Knowledge
Erich Wulffen and the Criminal Case of Grete Beier

Birgit Lang

Wolf Hasso Erich Wulffen (1862–1936), state prosecutor in Dresden and later head of department in the Ministry of Justice in Saxony, was a prominent sexologist, criminologist, and legal expert in the late Wilhelminian era and the Weimar Republic. His mastery of the case study genre spanned a great variety of publications, ranging from judicial to literary cases, with a declared focus on the psychology of criminals. Amidst a climate of popular discontent, in which the justice system was widely criticized for class bias and alienation from social realities, Wulffen aimed to convey knowledge about the psychology of criminals to a wider audience. His explanations relied on a sexological framework, and he used case studies as his means of communication. While recent criticism on Wulffen has focused on the stereotyping effects of his academic works, this chapter investigates ways in which Wulffen used the case study genre to address his readers and to disseminate knowledge.[1] Detailed analysis of the case of Grete Beier, a convicted murderer who was executed in 1908, reveals how Wulffen simultaneously addressed and created a new educated public through his criminological case studies. He thus engaged in "poetic world-making"—Michael Warner's phrase for describing the attempt to imagine publics in advance.[2]

Wulffen envisaged a new audience that transcended dominant, class-biased notions of education (*Bildung*), and included the array of professionals working within the German criminal justice system. Writing about the Beier case, Wulffen carefully directed his presentation of select materials to his multiple perceived audiences, fostering active and purposeful learning on the part of readers. The Beier case also reveals how, under democratic rule in Weimar Germany, Wulffen was increasingly occupied with making the mainstream public conscious of its irrational behavior in relation to sensational trials. He did this by accommodating in his writing (albeit in a limited manner, and with limited success) what Todd Herzog calls the "criminalistic fantasies" of Weimar society.[3] The Beier case further allowed him to express cultural anxieties about the changing gender roles of young women in a postwar society. By the late 1920s, Wulffen's attempts to address an educated public had ceased to resonate with his anticipated readers. They were also stymied by the market forces of publishing as well as the changing literary status of the criminological case study. Hence this chapter demonstrates the increase and decrease in popularity of the criminological case study as a progressive educational genre during the late Wilhelminian and Weimar periods.

CASE STUDIES AND PUBLIC KNOWLEDGE

Wulffen's first verifiable encounter with the case study genre was through forensic medicine, a field that was central to nineteenth-century medical interest in sexuality and criminology.[4] The first medical case study compilation he referenced in his own writing was *Gerichtliche Psychiatrie. Ein Leitfaden für Mediziner und Juristen* (1897) written by the director of the psychiatric clinic in Göttingen, August Cramer (1860–1912). This volume was structured similarly to Richard von Krafft-Ebing's groundbreaking psychiatric sexological work *Psychopathia Sexualis*, and aimed to negotiate both legal and medical knowledge. Such case compilations comprised a distinctive mixture of analysis and casuistry. Tension between generalization and specificity made possible the formulation of new hypotheses, in the course of presenting noteworthy and remarkable cases.[5] Wulffen emulated this case-based model in many of his works in the field of criminal psychology.

Especially in the realm of psychiatry, the accessibility of case compilations beyond members of the profession caused a certain amount of unease amongst medical critics, such that, eventually, Krafft-Ebing used Latin for very explicit passages in the *Psychopathia Sexualis*. By contrast, Wulffen elevated the rich narrative appeal of case studies to draw in his nonprofessional as well as professional audiences. As a legal reformer, Wulffen was affiliated with the modern, sociological school of law of Franz von Liszt (1851–1919), and he sought to exploit the fact that case descriptions were easily understood in order to educate expert and lay readers.[6] His academic case studies were targeted at a professional, expert audience, often identified in the subtitle of the particular work, as in *Psychologie des Verbrechers; ein Handbuch für Juristen, Ärzte, Pädogogen und Gebildete aller Stände* (Psychology of the criminal: A handbook for lawyers, physicians, pedagogues and the educated of all classes, 1908). In such a handbook, Wulffen used the case materials presented for didactic purposes, drawing attention to practical matters and procedures, and preparing his readers for their roles in the court system. For instance, Wulffen explicated on unusual and lesser-known behavioral patterns of criminals; educated his readers about new casuistry; and, most importantly, elaborated on the tension between theory and practice, underlining that individual cases did not always fit criminological theories.

Wulffen's commitment to addressing both professional and lay audiences in his writing has to be seen in the overarching context of legal reform. His career spanned the late Wilhelminian era and the Weimar Republic, an era in which the German people's discontent with the court system focused on two key themes. The first of these was the court's apparent isolation from the broader public, conveyed by the alleged excessive punishment of convicted criminals. Directly connected with this concern was the charge of class bias, vehemently put forward by intellectuals of the political left, such as Kurt Tucholsky (1890–1935).[7] Those highly placed within the judicial system were aware of these issues, and attempts at reform accompanied the German penal code from the time of its first enforcement in 1872, with intensive periods of reformist activity in the late Wilhelminian and interwar periods. Nonetheless, the so-called Great Reform of the German Penal Code only came to fruition in 1969–70.[8]

When it came to the public realm, Wulffen went further than criticizing contemporary practices—he was a man of action. As discussed elsewhere, his 1907 study of con man Georges Manolescu represents the first expert legal commentary in Germany that aimed to address an educated audience outside the court system.[9] In line with Warner's description, Wulffen was highly alert to "the public" as a kind of social totality.[10] This was inevitable, due to his role as a member of the judiciary, and due to the court's institutional role: under German positive law, individual members of the public relinquish to the state—in the form of the court—their right to violence. From the beginning, in an extension of his engagement with legal reform per se, Wulffen showed an unusually strong commitment to communicating legal reform issues to the general public. In Wulffen's opinion, the daily press constituted the only effective way to inform the public of legal matters, and on numerous occasions he outlined and criticized the relationship between the press and the justice system. He deplored his legal colleagues' aversion to interacting with journalists, stating, for instance, that even though "attacks against the justice system may become over-exaggerated, seldom if ever are they addressed or clarified from the juristic side."[11]

Yet in a range of articles in legal journals, Wulffen also criticized the press on a number of fronts. He formulated his regrets that the press did not report on "the common touch" in the new penal reform code, which involved, for example, the inclusion of laypeople as assessors, and the widening of the right of appeal for those convicted of serious crimes.[12] Wulffen also criticized the fact that journalists were often misinformed, and maintained that certain journalistic practices were not in the interests of the people.[13] His 1906 article on "The detriments of press reports about criminal trials," published in a major German legal journal, discusses the impact of the divulgence of the full name, profession, and place of residence of the accused in all cases.[14] Due to their high workload and small salary, Wulffen argues, journalists sometimes confuse the public by reporting partial or incorrect statements. Meanwhile, the accused fear the crime reports in the media more than the public present at the trial, since the press "jeopardizes relatives, friendships, relations, social status, and economic interests." In doing so, he continues, "the press presumes a role that not even the judicial authorities enjoy."[15] In a further article published in 1908, Wulffen attributed the tense relationship between these institutions to a single cause: "they do not understand one another"—even though, as key "factors of culture," the judiciary and the press "share similar goals."[16]

SENSATIONALIZED CASES OF THE WILHELMINIAN ERA: WILHELM VOIGT (1849–1922), CARL HAU (1881–1926), AND GRETE BEIER (1885–1908)

To Wulffen, the analysis of sensational cases seemed especially pertinent, since these captured the imagination of the German public. They also caused anxiety within the courts, especially because they were capable of giving voice to a different sense of justice than that which the court engendered. To some extent such dissenting voices could be managed, whether by closing trials to the public or by bringing unduly provocative individuals before the law, but overall, any trial was considered capable of disturbing public order. In Wilhelminian society of the early twentieth century, three particular court cases became the focus of public and judicial contention.

In 1906, Wilhelm Voigt was sentenced to fifteen years imprisonment, having spectacularly robbed the city of Köpenick (today a suburb of Berlin). Voigt was a former prisoner who had been unable to find work. In October 1906 he donned the uniform of a Prussian military officer, and "arrested" the mayor of Köpenick; he was helped by army soldiers, who followed his orders on account of his disguise. Voigt then "confiscated" the fiscal funds of the city. After his arrest, Voigt became an international celebrity: at once a popular hero, and a hero for Wilhelminian and Weimar intellectuals. He was pardoned in 1908 by Wilhelm II.[17]

A year later, the lawyer Carl Hau was sentenced to death for the murder of his mother-in-law in Karlsruhe. Hau's trial was based on circumstantial evidence, a highly controversial issue in the public mind. A crowd of twenty thousand awaited the passing of judgment outside the court building, and public uproar about the verdict was considerable. The Hau case caused Wulffen to reflect on the "crisis" of penal law; in a public lecture of February 1908, given to a charitable association in Dresden (and published for circulation in the same year), he observed that never before had

> the defense lawyer challenged the state prosecutor to a duel in front of a jury court; [never before] had a member of the press who was called as a witness publically considered the state prosecutor's question "an unbelievable infamy"; [never before] had the police needed to read out the paragraph bringing the public to order during the state prosecutor's speech.[18]

These same complaints resurfaced in 1913 in Wulffen's *roman à clef* entitled *Frau Justitias Walpurgisnacht* (The Walpurgis night of justice), in which a state prosecutor named Löwe asks empathetically, "where is the famed people's sense of right and wrong, this alleged vibrant source of all legal development in the Hau trial?"[19]

While Hau, like Voigt, was eventually pardoned, Grete Beier, daughter of the mayor of Brand, became the last woman to be executed in the Kingdom of Saxony (later the Free State of Saxony), on July 23, 1908. For a variety of reasons her case held a special place for Wulffen, and was to become the most lastingly influential of these three high profile cases: the legal processes involving Beier took place within Wulffen's jurisdiction, at a relatively early time in his career, and he witnessed the consequences of the trial firsthand. The significance of this case for Wulffen is further underlined by the fact that the culprit was an intelligent young woman who had committed what were considered at the time a range of "sex crimes." Therefore, Beier was an obvious subject and source for Wulffen's areas of academic expertise in sexology, as well as the law.

As it became known over a matter of weeks in late 1907, the story of Grete Beier held the keen interest of the German populace. A middle-class woman living in the small Saxon city of Brand near Dresden, at twenty-two years old Beier committed a series of interrelated crimes: fraud; abortion of a child fathered by her clandestine fiancé Johannes Merker; and conspiracy to commit the murder of a witness, with the aim of concealing the actual murder of Heinrich Preßler, her formal fiancé. Beier poisoned Preßler with potassium cyanide, only to shoot him in order to fake his suicide. Immediately after the shooting she forged his will, naming herself as the main beneficiary. She also forged letters that pretended to explain Preßler's suicide. These missives, dubbed the "Feroni letters," were composed in the voice of Preßler's imaginary wife, who threatened to expose his supposed wrongdoing—that is, the murder of her sister. When Beier was incarcerated due to abortion charges, she sent a note to Merker, urging him to kill a female witness. Merker gave her up, and only then was Preßler's murder revealed.

Beier was brought to trial for murder, and sentenced to death on July 1, 1908. Her petition for pardon was put to the Saxon King Friedrich August III on July 15, who rejected it on July 21—Beier was guillotined two days later.[20] Throughout the month of July, members of the public wrote to the state court to express their opinions on the rejection, and to address Beier directly. The content of these letters revolved around two themes: an explanation of Beier's deeds, and criticism of the death penalty. Neither seems surprising considering the circumstances of the case. Beier had made known her motives and confessed in detail, more than likely to increase her prospects of a pardon by the king. The letters to the court offered a range of motives for the young woman's cruel and calculating behavior. They blamed her parents, especially her mother; one letter writer suspected that Beier had been hypnotized by Merker; other correspondents believed her to have been seduced by Satan, or evil spirits. With one exception, all the letters showed sympathy with the convicted murderer—a certain Heinrich Schneider from Karlsruhe even requested her autograph.[21] The vehemently moral opposition to her death penalty was based mainly on religious arguments, but could also include lese majesty. At least one writer expressed such opposition openly to the king, who was warned to refrain from taking his walks through Dresden "without shame." In academic journals, intellectual analysis of Beier's case circled around the same issues.[22]

Thanks to the efforts of the daily press, nationally and internationally the mainstream public soon became fascinated by Beier: by her youth; by her parents' adverse influence on her development; by Merker, her secret lover; and by Beier's cunning though calm and composed nature. Her execution by guillotine—attended by Wulffen—was a society affair. Two hundred witnesses were present, representing, according to writer and satirist Kurt Tucholsky, "ein kleines Volkfest," a small public fete.[23] The Beier case files include nineteen applications for admission to the event: six by members of the local press, and the rest by ordinary citizens, among them five medical doctors; a councilor; a surveyor; a teacher; three factory owners; a postal assistant; and a self-declared "man of the street."[24] According to one news article published in New York, 1,500 members of the public had applied to witness the execution in Freiberg.[25] Straight after the execution, the funeral carriage carrying Beier's body to her burial in Dresden was awaited by a crowd of about one thousand people.[26] Newspapers in Germany and abroad gave accounts of the execution, among them the *New York Herald* and London's *Daily Telegraph*.[27] As far away as South Australia a paragraph appeared in Adelaide's daily newspaper, the *Advertiser*.[28]

Following the execution, the press condemned this "anti-cultural retrograde step of Saxon justice," and noted with disdain that no one, not even the president of the Saxon court, had foreseen the possibility of an execution.[29] Indeed, for fifty years previously no woman had been executed in Saxony, and Beier's defense lawyer had not requested an appeal, since even the jury had recommended that the young woman be pardoned. In all, Beier's execution was felt to be deeply unfair. As a result, her grave in Dresden became a site of pilgrimage, to which members of the public brought great numbers of wreaths and flowers. The local newspaper *Dresdener Rundschau* commented on the aftermath of her sentence as follows: "Whoever might grace this grave with flowers may contribute to dispose of this superceded medieval cultural practice [the imposition of the death penalty]."[30] Wulffen openly regretted this widespread emotionalism that characterized the response to the guillotining. He also later bemoaned that Beier's grave had become an iconic site, and that near the grave, paraphernalia relating to Beier, such as photographs and brooches, continued to be sold.[31] The Beier case remained a reference point in the public mind for many years following the trial. Berlin court reporter Hugo Friedländer

(1854–1918) included Beier in his omnibus of sensational trials in Wilhel-minian Germany in 1910; in 1913 Tucholsky used the case to discuss the impenetrability of attitudes to sexuality.[32]

CRIMINOLOGICAL CASES FOR A NEW EDUCATED PUBLIC

In view of such intense fascination, concern, and sentimentalizing in the public domain, how did Wulffen himself recount the Beier case, and how did he address his respective audiences? Through and beyond his rise within the ranks of the Saxon court system, Wulffen wrote up the case for five different books published between 1913 and 1929. Three of these books targeted both academic and educated audiences; two were conceived more particularly for educated lay readers. In all five works, the Beier case was presented as one of a series of cases in a collection devoted to a specific topic, each topic identified in the publication title. The 1913 study *Das Kind: sein Wesen und seine Entartung* (The child: Its nature and degeneracy) focused on the nature and degeneration of children between the ages of five and eighteen. The various editions of *Der Sexualverbrecher: ein Handbuch für Juristen, Verwaltungsbeamte und Ärzte* (The sex offender: A handbook for jurists, civil servants and physicians) from 1915, 1920, and 1928, as well as the corresponding *Das Weib als Sexualverbrecherin: ein Handbuch für Juristen, Polizei- und Strafvollzugsbeamte, Ärzte und Laienrichter* (The female sex offender: A handbook for jurists, police and prison officers, phy-sicians and lay judges) from 1923 and 1925 focused on a broad range of crimes, including theft and forgery. These volumes were explicitly aimed at professionals in the criminal justice system, or, as the subtitles indicate, at physicians, jurists, lay judges, the police force, prison officials, and other public servants. The last two works in which Wulffen discussed the Beier case were directed not so much to a professional audience but to a more general readership. Specifically, the 1917 popular scientific treatise *Psy-chologie des Giftmordes*, and *Irrwege des Eros. Mit einer Einleitung für Mütter und Töchter* (Aberrations of Eros. With an introduction for mothers and daughters) of 1929, were envisaged for educated members of the work-ing and middle classes.

Close analysis of these texts reveals how Wulffen varied his approach to suit different publics. On all occasions the Beier case is made directly relevant to Wulffen's structuring theme. *Das Kind*, for instance, highlights Beier's normal childhood development, stressing her "modest and pleasant nature," her lack of "vanity, termagancy [violent temper] and any greed for sweets," and the change of behavior after becoming sexually active in puberty.[33] In this monograph, Wulffen also focuses on the poison murder of Preßler, which he sees in close relation to Beier's sexual excitability—for Wulffen a key factor in the development of criminality at puberty. Beier's shooting of Preßler is not mentioned, nor are other details of the case. Such carefully constructed interplay between overall narrative and individual case study is crucial to the book's rhetorical success, since, as a seasoned case writer, Wulffen knew that nonaligned examples divert readers, and can even contradict the very hypothesis that they mean to exemplify.[34]

Other publications written for a professional public focused on the presentation of evidence within the court, and debated possible classifications of Beier's crime. For example, in *Der Sexualverbrecher* Wulffen discusses at length Beier's haptic experience, or sense of touch. *Das Weib als Sexualverbrecherin* also quotes from original court materials, and reproduces photographs of Beier's different counterfeit handwritings. Such pieces of evidence were intended to help prepare Wulffen's target readership for court situations, in which they would encounter a comparable variety of information. In *Der Sexualverbrecher* Wulffen's treatment of the Beier case presents an otherwise inconspicuous female felon. It emphasizes that the court psychiatrist was unable to identify in Beier any physical signs of analgesia, physical insensibility, hypesthesia, paraesthesia, or hyperaesthesia: her sensitivity to physical pain was demonstrably normal. By asserting this in such detail, Wulffen is able to highlight factors that could usually assist the defense in pleading a defendant's insanity. He goes to great lengths to support the psychiatric assessment in the case, attempting to establish that the convicted criminal was "morally degraded"—in Wulffen's view, Beier exhibited limited feelings of shame and felt little remorse.[35] This conclusion seems especially pertinent as information for prison officials and those who supervised prisoners; in 1905 Wulffen had bemoaned the fact that leading prison staff often lacked any background or training in criminology. Case writings could allow them intricate insight into criminals' unexpected and contradictory behavior.[36]

The case compilations written for an educated, wider public do not differ greatly from those presented to professional audiences. In these, Wulffen's summary of Beier's case remains largely the same, with no obvious factual omissions. If anything, more relevance is given to the social factors in Beier's demise, and to her avid passion for reading novels, which in Wulffen's eyes inspired the "Feroni letters."[37] At times Wulffen adopts a more informal register to communicate his account, and avoids specialized terminology. However, in *Psychologie des Giftmordes* he includes up-to-date academic references concerning the case, including his own works, enabling interested readers to further explore relevant issues of criminality.[38] This presents clear testimony to Wulffen's attempt to educate a wider audience and to disseminate criminological knowledge through case studies.

WEIMAR PERSPECTIVES: SENSATIONALISM AND GENDER

The most poignant differences in Wulffen's descriptions of the Beier case are not based on class bias. Rather, they are closely connected to the changing

German political landscape between the turn of the century and the Weimar era. For intellectuals such as Wulffen, the new democratic Germany was a complicated place. In his seminal study *The German Mandarins* (1969), Fritz Ringer was the first to point out the ambiguous role played by the old intellectual elite—the mandarins—in Weimar Germany. Many members of this group harbored an ambivalent if not negative view of the republic.[39] Whereas for many German mandarins education (*Bildung*) remained an elitist concept and a key to their identity, Wulffen consistently took a more egalitarian approach, as seen in the inclusive address of his writings. With his seat in the Saxon parliament for the DDP (the young, liberal German Democratic Party), Wulffen actively participated in democratic politics. What troubled him about the republic, however, was the increased violence in a destabilized and brutalized postwar society. This becomes particularly obvious in his comments on the Beier case during the 1920s.

In both *Das Weib als Sexualverbrecherin* (1923) and *Irrwege des Eros* (1929), Wulffen's reflections on the Beier case shift towards the public's reaction. Now writing some twenty years after the time when the young woman's trial and execution were most topical, Wulffen is attuned to the case's changing political meanings over time. In *Das Weib als Sexualverbrecherin* he details the martyr status Beier initially held for the general populace, both because she was betrayed by Merker (who revealed her attempt to incite him to the murder of a witness), and because she was the first woman in fifty years to be decapitated in Saxony.[40] Wulffen outlines the dissatisfaction caused by the case within the court system, and public discontent with the response of King Friedrich August III; reporting on the rumors that surrounded the king's decision to sentence Beier to death, he observes that the sentence had supposedly been a result of the queen's unfaithfulness, and the king's consequent negative relationship to the female sex.[41] Following the German revolution of 1918–19, the case was interpreted in an even more sensationalist manner: Wulffen cites an unnamed German writer who launched an article (republished several times) claiming that, on realizing she was sentenced to death, Beier had been so distraught that her prison ward told her she would be pardoned by the king just before ascending the scaffold. Wulffen criticizes this report on the grounds that its author was far removed from the actual incident. Having been present at the execution, Wulffen can vouch personally for Beier's composure. For him, such responses illustrate how intensely "the revolution wanted to revive the martyr."[42] Wulffen also reproduces a recent exchange with a university professor, who assumed that the king had pardoned Beier, and asked Wulffen if she was subsequently executed on behalf of the judiciary. Wulffen takes this inquiry as a further example of the "fantasy of the people" and here, as elsewhere, he includes the German mandarins—represented by the writer and the professor—in his address to the general populace.[43]

The Weimar Republic's "love relationship" with crime and criminality has been widely noted in secondary literature.[44] In his work on crime fiction,

Herzog analyzes the criminalistic fantasies in key Weimar literary texts.[45] When Walter Benjamin famously asks his readers, "But isn't every square inch of our cities a crime scene? Every passer-by a culprit?" criminality offers him, like other intellectuals of the left, "a point of access into modernity, an investigation not just of modern society but of modernity itself."[46] As a criminologist, this broad fascination and its generalizations worried Wulffen. He saw the underlying romanticization of criminality as the flipside of a brutalized postwar society, and became increasingly outspoken about changes in the German understanding of criminality and the law. Accordingly, in *Das Weib als Sexualverbrecherin* he compares the sentencing of Grete Beier with that of Elisabeth Hemberger. The latter was acquitted of the manslaughter and murder of her husband in 1920; her accomplice was sentenced to five years in prison.[47] The comparison of the two cases allows Wulffen to underline the dramatic decrease in the severity of sentencing between the prewar and postwar eras.

Like *Das Weib als Sexualverbrecherin*, *Irrwege des Eros* (1929) offers an exhaustive account of the public response to the Beier case, including the rumors mentioned above. And like *Psychologie des Giftmordes*, this book was targeted at a wide readership, and discussed Beier's execution in detail. At the time of its publication, Wulffen had recently retired from his leading position in the Saxon Ministry of Justice, and here for the first time he relates his personal experience of events surrounding Beier's case. The jurists and the townspeople were deeply affected by Beier's impending death, Wulffen asserts. He writes of himself and the other Dresden jurists going to bed with a heavy heart the night before her execution—not because they doubted their sentence, but due to compassion for the accused.[48] Significantly, in these lines Wulffen's register clearly denotes that he sees himself as a man among equals with the German people: he uses the possessive adjective "our" to describe the people's reaction to the haunting case of Beier.[49]

In writing *Irrwege des Eros*, Wulffen also aimed to engage specifically with "mothers and daughters," as stated in the subtitle of the book. More than a decade earlier, *Psychologie des Giftmordes* had informed its audience through carefully considered and accessible information, offering interested readers a way to deepen their understanding of the matter via bibliographic references. In contrast, although Wulffen is consistent in underlining the factual nature of his case descriptions, *Irrwege des Eros* does not present further references to specialist literature.[50] A key innovation in this book is Wulffen's direct address to the mothers of the new generation of middle-class women: he contends that a lack of mothering played a role in all the criminal cases included in *Irrwege des Eros*.[51] He perceptively comments that young women's increasing independence, due both to emancipation and, after the war, the lack of suitable marriage partners, has produced a new relationship to the opposite sex.[52] Yet, he continues, very rarely are young women given advice, especially in sexual matters, by their mothers. Such detailed observations on shifting social relations represent Wulffen's strength, as Jason Crouthamel has pointed out—but Wulffen's explanatory framework also departed from contemporary, otherwise like-minded explanations based on gender and socioeconomic factors.[53]

Wulffen's insistence on sexual activity as the key factor behind the emergence of criminal behavior in women differed from his views on male criminality—he considered the latter a combined result of nature, nurture, and fate, and consequently included more extensive sociological explanations of crimes committed by men. As discourses on prostitution in Weimar society proliferated, Wulffen felt affirmed in his assumptions concerning female criminality, although he was directly challenged by fellow sexologists.[54] Amongst them was psychiatrist Otto Juliusburger (1867–1952), a close affiliate of Magnus Hirschfeld's *Institut für Sexualwissenschaft* (Institute for Sexual Science) in Berlin; in an otherwise very positive review of Wulffen's *Das Weib als Sexualverbrecherin*, Juliusburger pointed out that he could not follow the author when it came to the proclaimed gender difference in the causes of criminality.[55]

For Wulffen, Beier perfectly exemplifies the downfall of a middle-class daughter. Wulffen underscores Beier's fraught relationship with her mother, and the fact that she was raised for several years by her grandmother. Her early seduction by a dancing partner, and the strongly sexual relationship to her fiancé Merker are prominent in Wulffen's account.[56] It can be assumed that his vivid description of Beier's execution—the preparation of the guillotine, the strapping of the young woman to the bascule, and the mention of Beier's low-cut dress (which left her neck free)—were all intended to accommodate the criminalistic fantasies of Wulffen's readers. At the same time, they served as an alarm, warning readers about the potentially dire consequences of a mother's neglect.[57]

This warning was positively received by those who reviewed the book for the newspapers. In the well-known liberal German paper *Vossische Zeitung*, one reviewer commented favorably on Wulffen's portraits of female criminals who had been at the center of sensational trials, declaring that these presented "gripping images in vibrant colors and with details of which any newspaper article was deprived as a result of the hearing in camera."[58] The *Hamburger Neueste Nachrichten* similarly attested that the volume was "written vividly," and that Wulffen avoided generalization and dogmatic one-sidedness.[59] The *Berliner Tageblatt*, another stronghold of German liberalism, stressed the importance of the author's critical presentation of the case files and authentic sources, all of which had been at least partly at Wulffen's disposal.[60]

In the liberal circles represented by such newspapers, Wulffen was an established and highly esteemed author. Yet what garnered praise in that particular milieu no longer translated into sales numbers: throughout the wider public realm, Wulffen's appeal in *Irrwege des Eros* fell largely on deaf ears. In a letter to the author of July 1930, publisher Julius Brüll complained that sales were "catastrophic," hence plans for a volume that had been discussed earlier were dropped.[61] Brüll saw the grim economic circumstances after Black Friday as the reason for disinterest in Wulffen's latest book, and commented dryly, "only crime novels sell."[62] Even so, the marked interest expressed in the same letter about a new edition of one of Wulffen's crime novels did not eventuate in a publication. Around the same time, and in a similar vein, Ullstein publishers also wrote to Wulffen. A vast, highly respected publishing house based in Berlin, Ullstein was the long-standing publisher of Wulffen's crime fiction. This letter declined the third reissue of Wulffen's *Michael Argobast* (first published in 1917) in the popular "yellow series" of contemporary novels. *Michael Argobast* centers on the eponymous hero's struggle to hide and transcend a previous criminal conviction, illustrating the terrible consequences of his criminal record being read aloud in an open court. Ullstein argued that, while the depiction of the main theme seemed convincing enough, the yellow series required less tendentious works, since it was premised on allowing readers to take their minds off problems "in such times of hard life."[63]

Although Wulffen's publishers explained the decline in sales with reference to external circumstances—mainly the economic collapse and readers' consequent longing for escapist fiction—an additional factor was at play. For nearly thirty years, case writings had held a genuine fascination for the public, but in the concrete world in which discourse circulates and relies on specific vernaculars, the novelty value of the case study had waned, and its authority had declined. In Wilhelminian Germany, authentic case files had been published only rarely, and were often edited or commented upon by legal or psychiatric experts. In the Weimar Republic, the topical "edge" and intellectual cachet of Wulffen's compilations and expert analyses dwindled, not least because case writing had become a more common form in which convicted felons could present their voice. As early as 1908 Grete Beier herself had produced a twenty-four-page autobiographical account of her life and deeds as part of her court case; however, this file was never made public. After her execution her lawyer insisted that, in accordance with Beier's wish, even the defense statement should be entirely withheld in her court file, so as not to create prejudice against her mother.[64] By contrast, early in 1924 Carl Hau was released on parole from prison in Bruchsal, and a year later he was the published author of two books with Ullstein: one outlining the history of his trial, the other giving an account of his imprisonment.[65] The availability of Hau's writing produced disastrous results: in the eyes of the legal authorities it constituted a violation of his parole, and a renewed warrant of arrest was issued. Hau fled to Italy, where he committed suicide, presumably to escape impending imprisonment. This denouement contributed to a shift concerning the case study genre that was already underway. In Wilhelminian Germany case writings had carried with them the respectability of the legal and psychiatric professions, a respectability that Wulffen skillfully exploited to pedagogical ends. At this period convicted criminals such as Hau popularized the genre and such texts both imitated and subverted their original context. They also fueled Weimar's "criminalistic fantasies" and presented an attempt to communicate the viewpoint of convicted criminals.

* * *

Beginning at the turn of the century, Wulffen imagined in advance the educated and professional publics he wrote for. He engaged in poetic world-making, and successfully positioned his writing beyond prevailing notions of the German judiciary's class bias and isolation from the German people. To use Warner's terms, Wulffen thus made legal discourse accessible to the "indefinite strangers" of the public. For better and for worse, Wulffen's emancipatory project was bound to the case study genre as the key means of engaging his readers. By the late 1920s this emerged as an obstacle to the appeal of his publications, for as a writer he faced a crisis of uptake. Whereas Wulffen had freed the case study genre from its specialist academic setting in order to educate the public in Wilhelminian Germany, the dynamic circular relationship between his texts and his presumed readers now ruptured. Confronted with the Weimar Republic's romanticization of crime and case writings, he chose a more direct and moralizing tone in his case writings. Such a register resonated with liberal readers invested in legal reform, yet in broad terms this was a diminishing readership, given the political developments in 1920s Germany. The limited uptake of his works in the wider public domain at this period makes plain that Wulffen no longer wrote for the public at large. To invoke Warner's useful distinction, late in his career, Wulffen was obliged to accept that his case studies no longer conveyed knowledge to "the" public, but to "a public."

NOTES

1. In German cultural history and the history of criminology in particular, Wulffen's work is generally considered to have perpetuated Italian criminal anthropologist Cesare Lombroso's biological theories, and to have disseminated stereotypes about criminals, furthering the dreaded "Biologisierung des Sozialen" (biologization of the social sphere) that culminated in discriminatory and calamitous National Socialist policies (see for example Monika Frommel, "Internationale Reformbewegung zwischen 1880 und 1920," in *Erzählte Kriminalität. Zur Typologie und Funktion von narrativen Darstellungen in Strafrechtspflege, Publizistik und Literatur zwischen 1770 und 1920*, ed. Jörg Schönert (Tübingen: Niemeyer, 1991), 447–96, at 489). Historian Silviana Galassi has argued that from the 1880s onwards, such political appropriations of criminology were facilitated by two factors: the close alignment between criminology and politics in Wilhelminian Germany, and the insufficient academic professionalization of criminology as a field of study (Silviana Galassi, *Kriminologie im Deutschen Kaiserreich. Geschichte einer gebrochenen Verwissenschaftlichung* (Stuttgart: Franz Steiner, 2004), 424ff.). Indeed, the prevalent cultural pessimism that went hand in hand with the biologization of

crime engulfed many German criminologists in the early twentieth century (Galassi, *Kriminologie im Deutschen Kaiserreich*, 424–28; Richard F. Wetzell: *Inventing the Criminal: A History of German Criminology, 1880–1945* (Chapel Hill: University of North Carolina Press, 2000), 125–78). Wulffen, however, always assumed criminality to be the result of three key factors: nature, nurture, and fate. By contrast, in the English-speaking world, Wulffen is commonly viewed as a modern intellectual, and one of the early twentieth century's most discerning observers of the psychological effects of war, who was also able to present "a multifaceted picture of members of the criminal class." (Jason Crouthamel, "Male Sexuality and Psychological Trauma: Soldiers and Sexual 'Disorder' in World War I and Weimar Germany," *Journal of the History of Sexuality* 17, no. 1 (2008): 60–84, at 75.)

2. Michael Warner, "Publics and Counterpublics," *Public Cultures* 14, no. 1 (2002): 49–90, at 82.

3. See Todd Herzog, *Crime Stories: Criminalistic Fantasy and the Culture of Crisis in Weimar Germany* (New York: Berghahn Books, 2009).

4. Wulffen quotes Cramer's monograph in a short study on the representation of justice in the works of Gerhart Hauptmann: Erich Wulffen, "Gerhart Hauptmann's 'Rose Bernd' vom kriminalistischen Standpunkte," *Juristisch-psychiatrische Grenzfragen. Zwanglose Abhandlungen* 4, no. 3 (1906), 20; for the role of forensics see: Harry Oosterhuis, "Sexual Modernity in the Works of Richard von Krafft-Ebing and Albert Moll," *Medical History* 56, no. 2 (2012): 133f.

5. John Forrester, "If *p*, then what? Thinking in cases," *History of the Human Sciences* 9 (1996), 1–25, at 18.

6. The following works discuss the history of the International Criminological Association in more detail: Elisabeth Bellmann, *Die Internationale Kriminal-istische Vereinigung, 1889–1933* (Frankfurt: Lang, 1994); Frommel, "Internationale Reformbewegung," 447–96; Sylvia Kesper-Biermann, "Wissenschaftlicher Ideenaustausch und 'kriminalpolitische Propaganda'. Die Internationale Kriminalistische Vereinigung (1889–1937) und der Strafvollzug," in *Verbrecher im Visier der Experten: Kriminalpolitik zwischen Wissenschaft und Praxis im 19. und frühen 20. Jahrhundert*, ed. Desiree Schauz and Sabine Freitag (Stuttgart: Steiner, 2007), 79–97.

7. Benjamin Carter Hett, *Death in the Tiergarten: Murder and Criminal Justice in the Kaiser's Berlin* (Cambridge MA: Harvard University Press, 2004), 3f.

8. For a valuable summary of the ongoing changes to the Penal Code from 1877 onwards, see Gabriele Zwiehoff, *Änderungsgesetze und Neubekanntmachungen der Strafprozessordnung und strafverfahrensrechtlicher Bestimmungen des Gerichtsverfassungsgesetzes*, vol 1: *1877–1949* (Münster: MV Wissenschaft, 2013).

9. Birgit Lang, "Verbrecher im Fokus. Zur Zirkulation verbrecherischer und kriminalpsychologischer Fallgeschichten um 1900," *Stimulus. Mitteilungen der Österreichischen Gesellschaft für Germanistik* 19 (2014): 301–13; Birgit Lang, "The Case of the Con Man: Criminal Writers, Legal Experts, and the Question of Culture," in *Intercultural Encounters in German Studies*, ed. Alan Corkhill and Alison Lewis (St Ingbert: Röhrig, 2014), 359–75.

10. Warner, "Publics and Counterpublics," 49.

11. "Die Angriffe gegen die Justiz mögen bei uns sich ins Maßlose steigern, eine Abfertigung oder Aufklärung in der Tagespresse von juristischer Seite erfolgt so gut wie nie." Erich Wulffen, "Die Protokolle der Kommission für die Reform des Strafprozesses," *Archiv für Kriminalanthropologie und Kriminalistik* 23 (1906): 347–64, at 349.

12. Wulffen, "Protokolle," 350–51, 360–61.

13. Wulffen, "Protokolle," 349.

14. Erich Wulffen, "Die Schäden in der Berichterstattung der Presse über Gerichtsverhandlungen," *Deutsche Juristen-Zeitung* 11, no. 22 (1906): 1231–35.
15. "Er gefährdet Verwandtschaft, Freundschaft, gesellschaftlichen Verkehr, soziale Stellung und wirtschaftliche Interessen. Damit maßt sich die Presse eine Kompetenz an, die den rechtsprechenden Behörden selbst nicht zusteht." Wulffen, "Schäden in der Berichterstattung," 1233.
16. Erich Wulffen, "Justiz und Presse," *Deutsche Juristen-Zeitung* 13, no. 12 (1908): 676–80, at 676.
17. Benjamin Carter Hett has written extensively about the Voigt case: see his monograph *Death in the Tiergarten*, 182–94, and also Hett, "The 'Captain of Köpenick' and the Transformation of German Criminal Justice, 1891–1914," *Central European History* 36, no. 1 (2003): 1–43.
18. "Was im Karlsruher Mordprozeß gegen den Rechtsanwalt Hau geschah, das war noch niemals da, weder vereinzelt noch gleichzeitig, daß der Verteidiger im Schwurgerichtssaale dem Staatsanwalt eine Herausforderung zum Zweikampfe ankündigte, daß ein als Zeuge vernommener Vertreter der Presse die Frage des Staatsanwaltes als unerhörte Infamie bezeichnete, daß während des Plaidoyers [!] des Staatsanwaltes der vor dem Gerichtsgebäude tobenden Volksmenge von den Polizeibeamten die Aufruhrparagraphen verlesen wurde." Erich Wulffen, *Der Strafprozeß: ein Kunstwerk der Zukunft. Ein Vortrag gehalten im gemeinnützigen Verein zu Dresden am 5. Februar 1908* (Stuttgart: Deutsche Verlagsanstalt, 1908), 3.
19. Erich Wulffen, *Frau Justitias Walpurgisnacht. Roman* (Berlin: Duncker, 1913), 223f.
20. Case File 11121/5, Hinrichtung Marie Margarete Beier wegen Ermordung ihres Verlobten Heinrich Moritz Ernst Preßler und Urkundenfälschung, Staatsanwaltschaft beim LG Freiberg, Saxon State Archives, Dresden.
21. Case File 11121/5, Hinrichtung Marie Margarete Beier wegen Ermordung ihres Verlobten Heinrich Moritz Ernst Preßler und Urkundenfälschung, Staatsanwaltschaft beim LG Freiberg, Saxon State Archives, Dresden.
22. Glaser highlights the contradictory nature of Beier's statements and her mental health, while Paul Lindau focuses on the role of Beier's clandestine fiancé Merkel. See Dr. Glaser, "Grete Beier," in *Der Pitaval der Gegenwart. Almanach interessanter Straffälle*, vol. 5, ed. Reinhard Frank, G. Roscher, and H. Schmidt (Tübingen: Mohr [Siebeck], [1909?]), 209–81; Paul Lindau, *Ausflüge ins Kriminalistische* (Munich: Langen, 1909).
23. Kurt Tucholsky, "Hinrichtung," *Gesammelte Werke 1, 1907–1924*, ed. Mary Gerold-Tucholsky and Fritz J. Raddatz (Frankfurt: Zweitausendundeins, 2005), 19.
24. Case File 11121/5 Hinrichtung Marie Margarete Beier wegen Ermordung ihres Verlobten Heinrich Moritz Ernst Preßler und Urkundenfälschung, Staatsanwaltschaft beim LG Freiberg, Saxon State Archives, Dresden.
25. *New Yorker Morgen*, August 8, 1907. Case File 11121/5, Hinrichtung Marie Margarete Beier wegen Ermordung ihres Verlobten Heinrich Moritz Ernst Preßler und Urkundenfälschung, Staatsanwaltschaft beim LG Freiberg, Saxon State Archives, Dresden.
26. Unknown newspaper, n.d., Mannl Family Archive; see www.ysio.de/beier/seite18.html (accessed June 18, 2013). Dr. Mannl was the responsible state prosecutor in the Beier case.
27. Case File 11121/5, Hinrichtung Marie Margarete Beier wegen Ermordung ihres Verlobten Heinrich Moritz Ernst Preßler und Urkundenfälschung, Staatsanwaltschaft beim LG Freiberg, Saxon State Archives, Dresden.
28. The brief report in Adelaide's *Advertiser* of July 27, 1908, was titled "The Saxon Murder."

29. "Kulturfeindliche Rückschrittsbewegung der sächsischen Justiz," *Dresdener Rundschau*, August 1, 1908.
30. "Wer dieses Grab mit einem Blümchen schmücken mag, der trage auch mit dazu bei, die überlebten Kulturgepflogenheiten des Mittelalters zu beseitigen," *Dresdener Rundschau*, August 1, 1908.
31. Erich Wulffen, *Das Weib als Sexualverbrecherin. Ein Handbuch für Juristen, Verwaltungsbeamte und Ärzte* (Berlin: Paul Langenscheidt, 1923), 210.
32. Hugo Friedländer, "Grete Beier, Tochter des Bürgermeisters Beier zu Brand, wegen Ermordung ihres Bräutigams vor dem Schwurgericht zu Freiberg i. Sa.," in *Interessante Kriminalprozesse von kulturhistorischer Bedeutung. Darstellung merkwürdiger Strafrechtsfälle aus Gegenwart und Jüngstvergangenheit* (Berlin: Barsdorf, 1910), 204–40; Kurt Tucholsky, "Laster und Liebe," *Gesammelte Werke 1, 1907–1924*, ed. Mary Gerold-Tucholsky and Fritz J. Raddatz (Frankfurt: Zweitausendundeins, 2005), 109–12, especially 110.
33. Erich Wulffen, *Das Kind: sein Wesen und seine Entartung* (Berlin: Langenscheidt, 1913), 272.
34. Gert Ueding and Bernd Steinbrink, *Grundriß der Rhetorik. Geschichte—Technik—Methode*, 2nd ed. (Stuttgart: Metzler, 1986), 268.
35. Erich Wulffen, *Der Sexualverbrecher. Ein Handbuch für Juristen, Verwaltungsbeamte und Ärzte* (Berlin: Langenscheidt, 1915–28), 365.
36. Erich Wulffen, *Reformbestrebungen auf dem Gebiete des Strafvollzugs. Bearbeitet für das Jahrbuch der Gehe-Stiftung zu Dresden* (Dresden: von Zahn & Jaensch, 1905), 12.
37. Erich Wulffen, *Psychologie des Giftmordes* (Vienna: Urania, 1917), 73.
38. Wulffen, *Psychologie des Giftmordes*, 73.
39. Fritz Ringer, *The Decline of the German Mandarins: The German Academic Community, 1890–1933* (Hanover: University Press of New England, 1990), 241–252.
40. For criminologist Franz Exner (1881–1947), Saxony itself would become a case study for the limited preventative use of the death penalty. In his influential 1929 study titled *Mord und Todesstrafe in Sachsen (1885–1921)*, Exner demonstrated that in Saxony—where there were two lengthy periods without the death penalty—no correlation could be shown to exist between death penalty and the frequency of crime.
41. Wulffen, *Weib*, 210.
42. Wulffen, *Weib*, 211.
43. Wulffen, *Weib*, 211.
44. Compare Udi E. Greenberg, "Criminalization: Carl Schmitt and Walter Benjamin's Concept of Criminal Politics," *Journal of European Studies* 39, no. 3 (2009): 305–19; Daniel Siemens, "Explaining Crime: Berlin Newspapers and the Construction of the Criminal in Weimar Germany," *Journal of European Studies* 39, no. 3 (2009): 336–52; Maria Tatar, *Lustmord: Sexual Murder in Weimar Germany* (Princeton: Princeton University Press, 1995).
45. Herzog, *Crime Stories*, 14.
46. Walter Benjamin, "Little History of Photography," in *Selected Writings*, vol. 2, *1927–1934*, trans. Rodney Livingstone and others (Cambridge MA: The Belknap Press of Harvard University Press, 1999), 507–30, at 527.
47. Wulffen explains that Hemberger's husband, a teacher, had had various affairs with his pupils, and that after his death she accused him of domestic violence. Yet Wulffen also points out that Hemberger's considerable efforts to conceal the crime undermine her credibility. She had wrongly identified a suicide victim as her husband, and she had slipped keys into the pocket of the deceased; she was also present when her husband's body was dismembered,

her co-accused indicating that she herself had cut up the body—see Wulffen, *Weib*, 229; Sace Elder argues that the Hemberger case became a means to reinscribe traditional gender roles for the cultural elite of which Wulffen was a part. See Sace Elder, *Murder Scenes: Normality, Deviance, and Criminal Violence in Weimar Berlin* (Ann Arbor: University of Michigan Press, 2010), 164–69.

48. Erich Wulffen, *Irrwege des Eros. Mit einer Einleitung Mütter und Töchter* (Hellerau bei Dresden: Avalun, 1929), 221.

49. Wulffen, *Irrwege des Eros*, 231f.

50. Wulffen, *Irrwege des Eros*, 5.

51. Wulffen, *Irrwege des Eros*, 10f.

52. Wulffen, *Irrwege des Eros*, 10.

53. Crouthamel, "Male Sexuality," 74.

54. On Wulffen and his view on prostitution see Peter Becker, "Weak Bodies? Prostitutes and the Role of Gender in the Criminological Writings of 19th-Century German Detectives and Magistrates," *Crime, History & Societies* 3, no. 1 (1999): 45–70.

55. Otto Juliusburger, "Das Weib als Sexualverbrecherin," *Vorwärts*, February 15, 1923. File 1477, Papers Erich Wulffen, Saxon State and University Library, Dresden.

56. Wulffen, *Irrwege des Eros*, 222f; 231.

57. Wulffen, *Irrwege des Eros*, 230.

58. "Irrwege des Eros," *Vossische Zeitung*, October 19, 1930. File 1478, Papers Erich Wulffen, Saxon State and University Library, Dresden.

59. "Irrwege des Eros," *Hamburger Neueste Nachrichten*, June 20, 1930. File 1478, Papers Erich Wulffen, Saxon State and University Library, Dresden.

60. [*Berliner*] *Tageblatt*, undated. File 1478, Papers Erich Wulffen, Saxon State and University Library, Dresden.

61. Letters Julius Brüll to Erich Wulffen, January 1, 1927, and May 11, 1928. Files 456 and 460, Papers Erich Wulffen, Saxon State and University Library, Dresden.

62. Letter Julius Brüll to Erich Wulffen, July 30, 1930. File 479, Papers Erich Wulffen, Saxon State and University Library, Dresden.

63. Letter of Ullstein Verlag to Erich Wulffen, November 26, 1931. File 731, Papers Erich Wulffen, Saxon State and University Library, Dresden.

64. Case File 11121/1b, Strafsache gegen Marie Margarete Beier wegen Ermordung ihres Verlobten Heinrich Moritz Ernst Preßler und Urkundenfälschung, Staatsanwaltschaft beim LG Freiberg, Saxon State Archives, Dresden.

65. Carl Hau, *Das Todesurteil: Die Geschichte meines Prozesses* (Berlin: Ullstein, 1925); Carl Hau, *Lebenslänglich: Erlebtes und Erlittenes* (Berlin: Ullstein, 1925).

4 A Case for Female Individuality
Käthe Schirmacher—Self-Invention and Biography

Johanna Gehmacher

Feminist challenges to the heteronormative gender system and controversies around essentialism and performativity are not specific to the late twentieth century, but in their various terminologies they can be traced back over more than one hundred years. Denouncing idealized images of femininity, women have been claiming their right to define their own identities since at least the middle of the nineteenth century.[1] Rhetorics of a female essence that needed to be developed, and strategies of deliberate self-invention, fueled these struggles. The idea of self-definition that they shared, however, rested on what has been shown to be a powerful myth—the modern concept of identity.[2] This concept informed political discourses of the twentieth century in unprecedented ways, and continues to entail the reorganization of all relationships between individuals and collectives. In many respects, the fight for female individuality by the women's movement at the end of the nineteenth century can be analyzed as an early example of the struggles with, and the political use of, the concept of identity.[3] Formulating their protests against being made into an "Other"—a woman, a nonwhite, a colonized, or a nonheterosexual individual—the protagonists of the women's movement and other social and political movements were, at the same time, inextricably embroiled in processes of othering.[4]

In this chapter I discuss processes of self-definition, as well as the complications encompassed by this endeavor. Taking the example of Käthe Schirmacher (1865–1930), a well-known writer and journalist, women's rights activist, and German nationalist politician, I wish to make a case for analyzing biographies of political activists as case studies in the context of a specific political agenda. Such an approach must take into account the possibility that the political activists themselves (or, in some instances, their fellows) already presented their careers as "cases." I argue that biographical research must deconstruct these "preconstructions" if it is to produce case studies of lasting historical relevance. Therefore, I aim to discuss correspondences as well as differences between the concepts of "biography" and "case." I show how Schirmacher invented herself as a "modern woman" for changing publics—a strategy that was of major importance for her political and her professional careers. As I will argue, this strategy is fruitfully discussed with reference to the transformation of concepts of individual-ization and scientification, both of which have produced highly gendered strategies and narratives.

The fact that Schirmacher already aroused controversy and ambivalent reactions during her own lifetime makes her an excellent case through which to discuss these questions. Widely traveled, highly educated, and economi-cally independent, Schirmacher was seen as an encouraging example of a "modern woman" by many of her contemporaries. Her ambitious endeav-ors, however, also aroused the intense hostility of the more conservative fac-tions of society; her outspoken views often divided audiences. Moreover, her radical change of political camps—from international radical women's activ-ism to German and *völkisch* nationalism—appalled many of her former political allies. Today Schirmacher is known only to specialists of German gender history and German nationalism. Her contradictory, even warring political engagements have rendered her a peripheral figure in the histo-ries of the movements in which she participated. It is, however, exactly this ambivalence that precludes an attitude of identification on the part of the historian, and allows for differentiated insights into the development and performance of a public figure.

BIOGRAPHIES AS CASES

To work in the field of biography always involves negotiating the ideologi-cal dimension of the very concept of biography. In modernity the biographi-cal narrative has become a key site in which the subject is produced and promulgated as a historically specific figure: gendered and pervaded by cat-egories such as race and class.[5] As a result, through powerful discourses, the individual is singled out from a dense web of social relations.[6] Thus while some critics describe the modern subject as a mere effect of discourse, others contend that the modern subject must be analyzed above all in terms of the site in which those discourses are being produced and reproduced.[7]

The place occupied by biographical research within historical stud-ies was rather unstable for a long period, at least in the German-speaking countries.[8] Not accepted as a science proper by many historians, ironically biography often was and is mistaken by a wider public as history's main concern. The refusal with which biographical research has been met in the academy can be at least partly ascribed to the ideology of wholeness that the biographical narrative all too readily suggests.[9] As a powerful cultural form, biography tends to transform contingencies into destiny and to construct fictions of individual unity and uniqueness. All too often, biography sup-ports the assumption that a life course can be narrated as a consistent and complete story, safely anchoring the protagonist in time and space.[10] The issue at stake, therefore, is whether biographical research is able to decon-struct these "preconstructions." There have been different ways to answer this question. Some, rejecting the idea of a coherent story altogether, have shattered the biographical narrative into fragments.[11] Others have relied on anonymous data, focusing on the "story" they hoped to detect through the connection and comparison of many biographies.[12] The first approach is relevant when it comes to deconstructing the idealizing concept of the singularity of the biographical "hero." The second approach strives to make visible and relevant—as part of a collective—the many who have hitherto remained nameless.[13] I argue that it would be most fruitful to understand both types of biographies as cases that are at once unique, and examples of a general structure or rule.[14] Such an argument takes up the issues of singularity and generalization in a productive way, thus allowing a clear distinction to be made between the often problematically converging interests of researcher and autobiographer.

The shift of focus in historiography to marginalized groups and movements, which also informs theoretical conceptions of biographical research and representation, has often been construed in the sense that the "old biography" represents heroic individuals, while the new approaches reveal anonymous examples of lives structured through political, economic, and cultural patterns. Even so, I hold that the antagonism between singularity and exemplarity is part of both forms of biography: to show how a protagonist is at once equal to all others (of a group, a nation, or a gender) and different from those others is surely the central task of all biographical constructions.

Like the biographical narrative, the case negotiates the relation between singularity and generalization.[15] It has aptly been described as a narrative form referring to a (practical or theoretical) norm, which it questions at the same time. A case, therefore, is neither merely an example of something already sufficiently known, nor a singular and incomparable event. Carlo Ginzburg, among others, has argued that a case is an argument for normative or theoretical transformation.[16] As such, the case never stands for itself; it always formulates a question within a larger context, and is therefore a means to an end.[17] Hence to narrate a biography as a case means to deliberately reduce its complexity and heterogeneity. At the same time, this explicit focus allows for the disruption of the ideology of wholeness that biography entails. Unlike biography, a case formulates a question and calls for a decision. Rife with tensions and contradictions, it strives for theoretical transformation. Biography, on the other hand, can have multiple meanings, including admonition, idealization, and edification, as well as the construction of commonalities and continuities within social networks.[18] To present a biography as a case, therefore, means to reduce its communicative functions and to focus the narrative in order to address a more specific public.

Both biographical narratives and case narratives are always addressed to a public or to publics. Michael Warner's differentiation between "the public" and "publics" is extremely useful in social movement theory, but can pose problems in a German-writing context, since the particular German word cannot be made plural: the German equivalent to "public"—"Öffentlichkeit"—is used only in the singular.[19] Nonetheless the difference is pertinent within my field of research, that of the women's movements before World War I. For the women engaged in these movements were fighting to become members of *the* public, and not just *a* public that could be qualified by a diminishing characterization such as "the women's movement."[20] And yet, it was women's fight for participation that provided evidence of the fact that *the* public was simply *a* public, because it excluded half of the population. In a way, these women destroyed the image of that which they wanted to join: *the* public lost its purported universality through having been criticized by the women's movements.

THE CASE OF KÄTHE SCHIRMACHER

Born in 1865 in Danzig, Germany, Käthe Schirmacher was a prolific journalist, a writer of fiction and nonfiction, and a well-known radical political activist. She was involved in the most different, even warring political movements: having been previously an important figure in the radical women's movement in Germany, and a protagonist of the international women's movement, she became an activist on behalf of a racist version of German Nationalism before World War I. Schirmacher came from a once well-to-do family that had lost its fortune during the economic crisis of the 1870s; she was obliged to provide for herself until the end of her life. She did so as a popular writer and speaker in the context of her political activism. Publishing in a wide range of journals, and regularly undertaking extended lecture tours, in a sense she made political activism her profession, in an epoch and a context that refused women formal political participation.[21]

Existing biographies of Schirmacher exemplify the challenges inherent to biographical studies, and have deepened my questions concerning the benefits and shortcomings of reading a biography as a case. Schirmacher could be depicted—indeed has been depicted—as a rather singular personality. She was a woman who earned her money in the male field of professional journalism.[22] She was a disputatious political speaker who often divided audiences, a feminist-turned-racist nationalist who thereby combined seemingly contradictory political views.[23] She was unmarried, and shared a household with a lifelong female partner.[24] In all, she did not really comply with any generalizations about Wilhelminian society. By the same token, it is also possible to interpret Schirmacher's biography as a telling example of specific circumstances in European societies during this period. That is, her biography allows for discussion of developments such as the economic decline of the middle classes; this decline forced a large proportion of young middle-class women into a labor market that was ill-prepared to offer them jobs other than those of governess or school mistress.[25] Schirmacher's biography can equally illustrate the growing political awareness of middle-class women who were confronted with distressing economic developments, and with their own lack of political or social rights.[26] If nothing else, Schirmacher's contradictory political path might stand for growing nationalistic identification among huge factions of European societies before World War I, which also affected liberal movements such as the women's movements.[27]

The different forms of narrating Schirmacher's biography are mainly found within histories of the women's movement, which in turn form part of the wider field of historical and theoretical analysis of social movements.[28] There are also some references to Schirmacher in right-wing and extreme right political contexts. An apologetic biography was published during the National Socialist period, and even today she is occasionally hailed in right-wing newspapers as an exemplary nationalist.[29] All of these accounts struggle in their own way with the contradictions that Schirmacher's life course apparently presents. They either elide aspects that fail to fit into the chosen narrative, or split their protagonist into two persons, "the younger" and "the elder" Schirmacher—as did fellow feminist activist Lida-Gustava Heymann, in her obituary, when she wrote, "the keen, happy, fresh and eager fighter for women's liberation became a chauvinistic, embittered, hard-hearted woman, fraught with Prussian militarism."[30] French historian Liliane Crips subordinated every other biographical aspect to the question of how to explain Schirmacher's transformation from a liberal feminist to a *völkisch* nationalist.[31] While I do appreciate Crips's conception of Schirmacher's biography as an "exemplary case," I challenge the way she focuses on political orientations that strongly echo Schirmacher's own autobiographical account in her 1921 memoirs.[32]

Instead, I propose to focus more generally on the apparently awkward process of identity construction that can be observed in Schirmacher's life history, and to search for contexts that might explain it. Andrea Bührmann's lucid analysis of discourses of first wave women's movements in Germany provides an extremely useful context for considering these questions. In her 2004 study, Bührmann develops her concept of gender as a form of subjectification; she argues that feminist discourses are to be read as the struggle with the hegemonic form of female subjectification that activists of the women's movement were seeking to transform. Women's radical discourses disputed the hegemonic gender apparatus (*Dispositiv*) that conceded individuality only to men, while women were merely seen as a "sexualized species" ("sexualisiertes Gattungswesen").[33] Schirmacher's biography, as well as her oeuvre, can be analyzed as a specific intervention in this struggle against hierarchical gender relations, and in support of a concept of "female individuality." Her position within these discourses was simultaneously central and marginal. Her egalitarian model of gender identities was far more radical than the concept of "spiritual motherhood" ("geistige Mütterlichkeit") proposed by the liberal women's movement, but Schirmacher also constituted an elitist link between academic education and the concession of political rights. I suggest that the research program proposed by Bührmann can be gainfully developed and differentiated by testing her theses on select biographical cases. Schirmacher proves to be a rewarding example in this respect, for she explicitly interfered in the debate; she also vehemently reacted to hegemonic gender structures performatively, through her personal life plan.

Schirmacher's biography does not conform to the dominant conceptions of femininity of her time, and is too ambivalent to serve the purposes of idealization (positive or negative), without cutting out vital elements of her life. For this reason, narrating her biography as a case helps to highlight contradictions that were central to the society in which she lived. As a matter of course it should be stated that the case of Käthe Schirmacher will never be more than a specific perspective on her biography. Likewise it must be noted that more than one case can be made from one biography.

THE "MODERN WOMAN": SELF-INVENTIONS AND LITERARY IMAGINATION

A pivotal concept in Schirmacher's writings is that of the "modern woman." In coining this concept she took up a rather ambivalent contemporary term that she sought to transform in two ways. On the one hand, she tried to strip the term of its connotations of immorality, by reformulating it as a sociological category comprising all women affected in a certain way by processes of (economic, cultural, or political) modernization. On the other hand, she recast the term in a political sense, developing the "modern woman" as an idealized model. She saw herself as a "modern woman" in both senses. She worked with this concept in different textual genres, and on different biographical levels. I argue that, in a way, Schirmacher presented the narrative of her life as "a case" for the benefit of her political demands.

In 1893 Schirmacher delivered in English a lecture at the International Women's Congress in Chicago, to which she gave the fairly misleading title "The marriage prospects of the modern woman." This political text exemplifies her use of the concept of the modern woman as a descriptive category and as a political ideal. Before a huge audience, she outlined the economic and demographic bases of the strong quest among middle-class women to study, and to be admitted to professions through which they could earn a living. In this first sense, "modern woman" referred generically to those growing numbers of middle-class women who, in the context of industrialization and social change, were no longer guaranteed maintenance through marriage and their families. At the same time, Schirmacher propagated a model that must have appeared utopian to many of her contemporaries: that of "the modern woman" who had gained knowledge, competence, and independence; who had found her place and income in society through a regular occupation—this was the other way to use the term. Schirmacher's analysis of women's marriage prospects was structured by a doubling of meanings as well. As one—sociological—aspect, she pointed out that women made up well over 50 percent of the German population, a fact that by itself would make it impossible for all women to marry.

> The marriage prospects of every woman depend . . . upon the number of eligible men living in the country. In this respect the German women are not particularly favored for their number exceeds that of the men by around one million and a half, so that it is impossible for every German woman to marry, unless we institute polygamy, put a tax on bachelors, or forbid young men to emigrate.

Yet in her opinion the well-trained, self-supporting "modern woman"—the idealized model she promulgated—had the worst marriage prospects of all, since the average German man preferred an ignorant and subordinate wife.

> Unless the modern woman find[s] a man to appreciate her strength of will and tenacity of purpose, . . . unless he admit[s] her on a footing of perfect equality, . . . I think she will not marry. She supports herself, and so does not want to marry in order that she may be provided for. She is fond of her work, absorbed by it, makes friends by it, is respected for it, and so need not marry in order to obtain the regard due to a useful member of society.[34]

Against the background of this grave situation, Schirmacher demanded the right of women to refuse marriage without being pitied or scolded. Even so, she also developed the utopian model of an ideal marriage grounded on equality and mutual respect. Both models of gender relations were based on the prerequisite of equal opportunities for education. Obviously in her lecture Schirmacher used the factual report as a framework that allowed her to formulate political demands. I argue that she developed the concept of the woman without marriage prospects as a case that called for a revision of a political situation in which women were excluded from universities and professions. But because her concept remained rather ambiguous (were all women potentially to be seen as "modern women," or just those who matched the ideal model?), the range of her demands could remain open as well, and thus adaptable to quite different publics.

Schirmacher's own prospects in 1893 were quite dark. Although apparently she had no intention of marrying, her expectations regarding her plans to earn money on the basis of an academic education were bleak. In her own country she could neither find employment nor could she continue her studies—Prussian universities did not admit women at that time. Besides, she lacked the resources necessary to study abroad. Her letters and diary from around 1893 show a young woman who looks much like a case illustrating her own analysis, and indeed she made her own circumstances part of her public discourse.

Hence Schirmacher promulgated the concept of the "modern woman" in political speeches and articles, but also worked on representing that type in a way that would be most rewarding. This can be illustrated by an incident of some years after 1893. In the meantime Schirmacher had graduated from university, and become a professional speaker on behalf of the women's movement. (She had financed her studies in Paris and Zurich by giving lessons, and with the help of her prosperous brother-in-law.) Having been asked to give a speech in a rather conservative German town, she agreed with the organizer that her university education should not be mentioned in the biographical note attached to the public announcement of her lecture; she did so in order to win a larger audience for her lecture. That she had earned an academic title would be revealed only after the audience had been given the opportunity to appreciate her female charm. The expectation was that once the audience had come to perceive her as an endearing young lady *and* as an educated speaker, this revelation (along with causing astonishment) would allow her elaborate self-presentation as a "modern woman" to serve as proof that university training did not necessarily ruin women's femininity. This deliberate staging was even more clearly mirrored in later newspaper reports on Schirmacher's frequent public appearances.[35]

"If there is any lady at all who embodies the auspicious development of the women's movement it is Miss Dr. Schirmacher."[36] When Schirmacher was greeted with these words at the International Women's Conference in Berlin 1904, she was already considered a kind of celebrity. One of the first German women to obtain a doctorate, she would enchant her audiences with her charming, feminine appearance. Her case was, in fact, presented as evidence that higher education did not masculinize a woman, or worse, "make her a disoriented cross between male and female."[37] This was an important prerequisite for calls to open the universities to all women—and not just in cases of exceptional aptitude. It also meant that Schirmacher had to stand for her own exceptional path, and simultaneously for all women; therefore she was obliged to prove that she was a "real woman." Once again, the singularity of a specific case and a general claim merged into a powerful political argument.

It is interesting to note that Schirmacher's enactment of the "modern woman" worked vis-à-vis quite different publics. Along with conservative bourgeois audiences in German provincial towns, it also appears to have convinced liberal or even progressive participants of an international women's congress. This might indicate that the concept was open to adaptation, while also able to win broader acceptance precisely because of the ambiguity between general description and singular case.

Schirmacher's literary texts prove to be another context in which she developed the concept of the "modern woman." In different ways these works all circle around the question of the appearance, or characteristics, of a new life plan for women—especially for educated, intellectual, university-trained women. One of Schirmacher's characters, Victoria Stein (who later reappears as Victoria Barr, Fräulein Barr, and Dr. Victoria Barr) is a never-tiring student and ardent political fighter, who remains unaffected by any temptation of luxury, love, or rest. Featuring in several texts, Victoria Stein/Barr makes her first appearance in a play written by a twenty-four-year-old Schirmacher shortly after her "Aggrégation" at the University of Paris. In the play "Sturm" ("Storm"), Stein is likewise about to pass her final exams at the University of Paris. Discussing her future plans, colleagues and friends try to dissuade her from returning to her conservative and antimodern native country of Germany. Stein, determined to lead the fight for women's rights, obviously represents the ideal type of the "modern woman."[38]

Written during the 1890s, the novella "Libertad," and especially the novel "Halb" ("Half"), both contain more ambiguous characters.[39] In each book the main characters are a group of young women studying, or who had previously studied together with Fräulein Barr/Victoria Barr in Paris. Their life circumstances, decisions, and careers are featured as para-digmatic: the French teacher Judith Delorme, safely installed as a civil ser-vant after her "Aggrégation," who takes life rather lightly; the gifted jurist Charlotte Weiler, married to an American lawyer with whom she runs a successful law firm and lives in a marriage full of sympathy but without real love; the promising artist Ann-Marie Althauser, who, too proud to ask for support when she runs out of funds, finally succumbs to a heart disease.

While the earlier novella "Libertad" depicts ideal personalities who are confronted with insurmountable antagonisms, the novel "Halb" addresses the tensions and inner contradictions haunting the protagonist Ethel Rodd, a young American engaged to a Prussian officer. She begins studying during her long engagement, gaining knowledge, opinions, and independence by which she becomes increasingly unacceptable to her conservative groom. After severe emotional conflict, she breaks off the engagement, and then finds herself unable to complete her studies. Therefore she becomes "stuck in-between," having failed to become either a successful wife or a woman with a formal qualification, and hence a new identity. At the end of this gloomy novel Rodd comes to recognize herself as a desperate "transitional type" ("Übergangstypus"), unable to conform to traditional norms; unable to match up to the new ideal of the "modern woman."[40] This is the point at which Schirmacher is most explicit about her central issue: the devel-opment of a new gender concept. Undoubtedly it would be interesting to discuss similarities between the protagonists of these texts and Schirm-acher's biography, as well as the problematic effects inherent in reading women's novels as autobiographically informed and motivated.[41] For the purpose of this chapter, however, it seems more rewarding to emphasize a more general commonality between Schirmacher's autobiographical and fictional texts. Although written in different contexts and addressing different publics, both kinds of text nonetheless use the narration of a life as an argument within a specific political agenda—they make a case for female individuality.

SCHIRMACHER'S TRANSITIONS AND TRANSFORMATIONS

In the course of her own life, Käthe Schirmacher adapted the concepts of "modernity" and "femininity" in very particular ways. During the 1890s her plan was to earn money by writing popular literary texts such as "Libertad" and "Halb" while continuing her studies in Paris and Zurich. It was the best hope for this polyglot young woman to gain a professorship in modern languages in the United States.[42] For manifold reasons she was never able to reach her ambitious goal, which was, in fact, nearly unattainable for a woman at that time. In a way, she became "stuck in transition" herself. Instead of being successful in academia, she became a successful campaigner for the right of women to study, embodying the best example of the cause.

This leads, finally, to the question of how to explain Schirmacher's break with the international women's movement, and her later commitment to German nationalism, especially in relation to the concept of the "modern woman." There is certainly more than one answer to this question, including economic reasons, and transformations in personal relationships. Yet among the possible interpretations, I find compelling the fact that Schirmacher's change to nationalist politics allowed her to move to a new and larger political arena. In my view, the decision to enter "real politics"—that is, to address *the* public and not just *a* public centered on the women's movement—can probably be understood as a means of escaping another "in-between" status. Having campaigned for women's political rights for years, shortly before World War I Schirmacher began to act as if these rights were already granted. This is not to say that nationalist identification was a logical consequence of the fierce conflicts surrounding the transformation of gender concepts. It is noteworthy that Schirmacher was not the only woman among former feminist campaigners who strove for new publics. There were others, such as Anita Augspurg and Lida-Gustava Heymann, once Schirmacher's political companions, and later her fierce opponents within the women's movement, who became courageous pacifists during World War I. However, it can be stated that, at some point in their lives, quite a number of campaigners within the women's movement decided to act as if the political arena was already open to them.

Clearly Schirmacher's biography cannot be reduced to the political case she made out of her personal destiny. Nor can it be reduced to the context created by a historian in order to set the stage for Schirmacher's life story. During the past decades of feminist research, Schirmacher has been met with interest and with hesitation. The fascination as well as the ambivalent feelings aroused by her case probably reflect the difficulty of placing the radical feminist and ardent nationalist, the suffragist and elitist activist, the accurate journalist and the writer of polemical pamphlets, the academic and the literary author, into a single context. Yet it is exactly the challenging heterogeneity of Schirmacher's personality that makes her case so interesting.

In this chapter I have tried to show how Schirmacher connected biographical and autobiographical narratives with strategies of the case narrative to transform them into a political argument. Both forms of narrative refer to central transformations in European discourses of the nineteenth century: the scientification of social life, and the increase in self-reflexivity and individualization—at least amongst the middle classes. And both of these processes were gendered, if in different ways. Developed as a male concept since the Renaissance, individuality had begun to be connected with the idea of equal and individual political representation since the French Revolution. As Joan Scott has convincingly shown, the antagonism between uniqueness and equality that characterized the abstract concept of the individual as a subject of equal rights was stabilized by the exclusion of women from nineteenth-century political discourses.[43] Striving for political rights, feminists were faced with the need to point out the inconsistencies of this concept, but they were also obliged to accept the "ambiguities of the republican notion of the individual."[44] The fight for "female individuality" was therefore doomed to failure, due to the antagonisms it encountered in a male-dominated society, and to the paradox of equality and difference it inevitably entailed.[45] The political use of the biographical genre by activists within the women's movement such as Käthe Schirmacher can only be understood in this context. The literary figures they invented, like their own autobiographical narratives, were constructed as strong arguments for political change. At the same time, they exposed the paradoxical nature of "female individuality" in an exemplary manner. The stirring narratives they presented emphasized women's commonalities as a group excluded from rights, and the extraordinary capacities and goals of individual women.

The case study narrative, on the other hand, became a distinct form for scientific description of the social world. It would be worth researching in greater detail the ways in which the case study was structured by the gender order established through the sciences during the eighteenth and nineteenth centuries. "Gender" became a major signifier within systematic descriptions of nature, whereas the human sciences split into many disciplines. These disciplines discussed both the male nature of the modern subject, and the comprehensive discipline of gynaecology that constituted "women" as a species.[46] I suggest that gender can be understood as the blind spot as well as the symptomatic feature of case studies *and* biographical narratives. To understand how a specific narrative functions, we must analyze how it constructs gender.

Autobiographical and biographical writings—and specifically, texts penned by the protagonists of women's movements of the late nineteenth and early twentieth centuries—appear to be an extremely rich body of material for understanding the specific rhetorics of the case developed within the political discourse of those years. Assuming that Käthe Schirmacher was not the only woman to construct her own biography as a political case, I would call upon historians of social movements to integrate biographical perspectives into their studies more often. I would add that, in my experience, the most rewarding biographical subjects are those "uncategorizable," ambivalent figures who did not meet the expectations of their contemporaries, and who continue to disrupt the expectations of today's historians.

NOTES

1. This is demonstrated, for instance, by Kali Israel, *Names and Stories: Emilia Dilke and Victorian Culture* (Oxford: Oxford University Press, 2002).
2. Rogers Brubaker and Frederick Cooper, "Beyond 'Identity,'" in *Ethnicity without Groups* (Cambridge MA: Harvard University Press, 2004), 28–63.
3. Andrea Bührmann, *Der Kampf um weibliche Individualität. Zur Transformation moderner Subjektivierungsweisen in Deutschland um 1900* (Münster: Westfälisches Dampfboot, 2004).
4. A foundational text for any theory about hierarchical processes of othering is, of course, Edward Said's *Orientalism*, repr. with a new preface (London: Penguin, 2003). The term, however, was introduced in an early article by Gayatri Chakravorty Spivak, "The Rani of Sirmur," *History and Theory* 24, no. 3 (1985): 247–72. The involvement of women's movements in the production of colonial others is, for instance, discussed in Sara Mills, *Discourses of Difference: An Analysis of Women's Travel Writing and Colonialism* (London: Routledge, 1991); also Anne McClintock, *Imperial Leather: Race, Gender and Sexuality in the Colonial Contest* (New York: Routledge, 1995).
5. See Bernhard Fetz, "Die vielen Leben der Biographie. Interdisziplinäre Aspekte einer Theorie der Biographie," in *Die Biographie—Zur Grundlegung ihrer Theorie*, ed. Bernhard Fetz and Hannes Schweiger (Berlin: Walter de Gruyter, 2009), 3–66; Bettina Dausien, *Sozialisation—Geschlecht—Biografie. Theoretische und methodologische Untersuchungen eines Zusammenhangs* (Wiesbaden: Verlag für Sozialwissenschaften, 2009); Teresa Iles, ed., *All Sides of the Subject: Women and Biography* (New York: Teachers College Press, 1992); Anne-Kathrin Reulecke, "'Die Nase der Lady Hester.' Überlegungen zum Verhältnis von Biographie und Geschlechterdifferenz," in *Biographie als Geschichte*, ed. Hedwig Röckelein (Tübingen: Edition Diskord, 1993), 117–42; Angelika Schaser, "Bedeutende Männer und wahre Frauen. Biographien in der Geschichtswissenschaft," in *Biographisches Erzählen*, ed. Irmela von der Lühe and Anita Runge (Stuttgart: Metzler, 2001), 137–52.

6. Monika Bernold, "Anfänge. Zur Selbstverortung in der popularen Autobiographik," *Historische Anthropologie. Kultur—Gesellschaft—Alltag* 1 (1993): 5–24.

7. Thomas Schäfer and Bettina Völter, "Subjekt-Positionen. Michel Foucault und die Biographieforschung," in *Biographieforschung im Diskurs*, ed. Bettina Völter et al. (Wiesbaden: Verlag für Sozialwissenschaften, 2009), 161–88.

8. Ulrich Raulff, "Das Leben—buchstäblich. Über neuere Biographik und Geschichtswissenschaft," in *Grundlagen der Biographik. Theorie und Praxis des biographischen Schreibens*, ed. Christian Klein (Stuttgart: Metzler, 2002), 55–68, at 55–56.

9. Reulecke, "Die Nase der Lady Hester," 326.

10. Pierre Bourdieu, "Die biographische Illusion (1986)," *Bios: Zeitschrift für Biographieforschung und Oral History* 1 (1990): 75–89. An early critique of this ideological use of the biographical form was formulated by Siegfried Kracauer, "Die Biographie als neubürgerliche Kunstform (1930)," in *Theorie der Biographie. Grundlagentexte und Kommentar*, ed. Bernhard Fetz and Wilhelm Hemecker (Berlin: Walter de Gruyter, 2011), 119–23.

11. See Liz Stanley, "Process in Feminist Biography and Feminist Epistemology," in *All Sides of the Subject: Women and Biography*, ed. Teresa Iles (New York: Teachers College Press, 1992), 109–25; also, by the same author, *The Auto/biographical I: The Theory and Practice of Feminist Auto/biography* (Manchester: Manchester University Press, 1995).

12. Detlev Garz distinguishes three aspects of biographical analysis, which, in his opinion, must discern what is universal for all human beings from features typical for a specific group, and from individual characteristics. See Detlev Garz, "'Das Leben stört natürlich ständig.' Qualitativ—biographische Verfahren als Methoden der Bildungsforschung," in *Die Fallrekonstruktion. Sinnverstehen in der sozialwissenschaftlichen Forschung*, ed. Klaus Kraimer (Frankfurt: Suhrkamp, 2000), 157–78, at 165–66. The search for specific characteristics of a group is the rationale behind many projects of biographical interviews in sociology as well as in the field of oral history. This is most explicitly the case in the collective biography method. Compare, for instance, Christian Fleck, "Probleme beim Schreiben einer Kollektivbiografie deutschsprachiger Soziologen," *Österreichische Zeitschrift für Soziologie*, Sonderheft 31, no. 8 (2006): 22–53.

13. See, for instance, Sherna Berger Gluck and Daphne Patai, eds., *Women's Words: The Feminist Practice of Oral History* (New York: Routledge, 1991).

14. On the concept of the case see Lauren Berlant, "On the Case," *Critical Inquiry* 33, no. 4 (2007): 663–72; John Gerring, "What Is a Case Study and What Is It Good For?," *American Political Science Review* 98, no. 2 (2004): 341–54; Klaus Kraimer, "Die Fallrekonstruktion—Bezüge, Konzepte, Perspektiven," in *Die Fallrekonstruktion. Sinnverstehen in der sozialwissenschaftlichen Forschung*, ed. Klaus Kraimer (Frankfurt: Suhrkamp, 2000), 23–57; Johannes Süßmann, "Einleitung: Perspektiven der Fallstudienforschung," in *Fallstudien: Theorie—Geschichte—Methode*, ed. Johannes Süßmann, Susanne Scholz, and Gisela Engel (Berlin: Trafo, 2007), 7–27. On the concept of the exemplary see *Das Beispiel. Epistemologie des Exemplarischen*, ed. Jens Ruchatz, Stefan Willer, and Nicolas Pethes (Berlin: Kadmos 2013).

15. Berlant, "On the Case," 664; Süßmann, "Einleitung: Perspektiven der Fallstudienforschung," 12.

16. Carlo Ginzburg, "Ein Plädoyer für den Kasus," in *Fallstudien: Theorie—Geschichte—Methode*, ed. Johannes Süßmann, Susanne Scholz, and Gisela Engel (Berlin: Trafo, 2007), 29–48, at 30.

17. Berlant, "On the Case," 666: "[A case] can bear the weight of an explanation worthy of attending to and taking a lesson from."
18. On different uses of biography see Hans Erich Boedeker, ed., *Biographie schreiben* (Göttingen: Wallstein, 2003); Peter France and William St. Clair, eds., *Mapping Lives: The Uses of Biography* (Oxford: Oxford University Press for the British Academy, 2002); Hedwig Röckelein, ed., *Biographie als Geschichte* (Tübingen: Edition Diskord, 1993).
19. Michael Warner, "Publics and Counterpublics," *Public Culture* 14, no. 1 (2002): 49–90, at 50.
20. Ulla Wischermann, *Frauenbewegung und Öffentlichkeiten um 1900. Netzwerke, Gegenöffentlichkeiten, Protestinszenierungen* (Königstein: Helmer, 2003).
21. On Schirmacher's biography see Liliane Crips, "Comment passer du libéralisme au nationalisme völkisch, tout en restant féministe? Le cas exemplaire de Käthe Schirmacher (1865–1930)," in *Femmes—Nations—Europe*, ed. Marie-Claire Hoock-Demarle (Paris: Université de Paris VII Denis Diderot 1995), 62–77; Johanna Gehmacher, "Der andere Ort der Welt. Käthe Schirmachers Auto/Biographie der Nation," in *Geschlecht und Nationalismus in Mittel- und Osteuropa 1848–1918*, ed. Sophia Kemlein (Osnabrück: Fibre, 2000), 99–124; Johanna Gehmacher, "De/Platzierungen. Zwei Nationalistinnen in der Hauptstadt des 19. Jahrhunderts. Überlegungen zu Nationalität, Geschlecht und Auto/Biographie," *Werkstatt Geschichte* 32 (2002): 6–30; Johanna Gehmacher, "Moderne Frauen, die Neue Welt und der alte Kontinent. Käthe Schirmacher reist im Netzwerk der Frauenbewegung," *Österreichische Zeitschrift für Geschichtswissenschaft* 22 no. 1 (2011): 16–40; Johanna Gehmacher, "Reisende in Sachen Frauenbewegung. Käthe Schirmacher zwischen Internationalismus und nationaler Identifikation," in *Ariadne. Forum für Frauen- und Geschlechtergeschichte* 60 (2011): 58–65; Wolfgang Gippert, "'Ein kerndeutsches nationalbewußtes starkes Frauengeschlecht.' Käthe Schirmachers Entwurf einer völkisch-nationalen Mädchen- und Frauenbildung," in *Ariadne. Forum für Frauen- und Geschlechtergeschichte* 53–54 (2008): 52–59; Ulla Siebert, "'Von Anderen, von mir und vom Reisen.' Selbst- und Fremdkonstruktionen reisender Frauen um 1900 am Beispiel von Käthe Schirmacher und Emma Vely," in *Nahe Fremde—Fremde Nähe. Frauen forschen zu Ethnos, Kultur, Geschlecht*, ed. Wissenschaftlerinnen in der europäischen Ethnologie (Vienna: Wiener Frauenverlag, 1993), 177–216; Anke Walzer, *Käthe Schirmacher. Eine deutsche Frauenrechtlerin auf dem Wege vom Liberalismus zum konservativen Nationalismus* (Pfaffenweiler: Centaurus-Verlagsgesellschaft, 1991).
22. Wischermann, *Frauenbewegung und Öffentlichkeiten um 1900*, 150–53; Gehmacher, "Reisende in Sachen Frauenbewegung."
23. This is the focus in Crips, "Comment passer du libéralisme au nationalisme völkisch," and Gehmacher, "Der andere Ort der Welt."
24. Leila J. Rupp, *Worlds of Women: The Making of an International Women's Movement* (Princeton: Princeton University Press, 1998), 96; Gehmacher, "Moderne Frauen, die Neue Welt und der alte Kontinent," 27. On the concept of the female couple in women's movements of the late nineteenth and early twentieth centuries, see Margit Göttert, *Macht und Eros. Frauenbeziehungen und weibliche Kultur um 1900—eine neue Perspektive auf Helene Lange und Gertrud Bäumer* (Königstein: Helmer, 2000); Angelika Schaser, *Helene Lange und Gertrud Bäumer. Eine politische Lebensgemeinschaft* (Cologne: Böhlau, 2000). On female homosexuality at that time, see Hanna Hacker, *Frauen und Freundinnen. Studien zur "weiblichen Homosexualität" am Beispiel Österreich 1870–1938* (Weinheim: Beltz, 1987); Marti M. Lybeck, "Gender,

Sexuality, and Belonging: Female Homosexuality in Germany, 1890–1933," PhD dissertation, University of Michigan, 2007; Katie Sutton, *The Masculine Woman in Weimar Germany* (New York: Berghahn Books, 2011).

25. Gisela Bock, *Frauen in der europäischen Geschichte. Vom Mittelalter bis zur Gegenwart* (Munich: C.H. Beck, 2000), 142–76.

26. Karen Offen, *European Feminisms, 1700–1950: A Political History* (Stanford: Stanford University Press, 2000).

27. Ute Planert, ed., *Nation, Politik und Geschlecht. Frauenbewegungen und Nationalismus in der Moderne* (Frankfurt: Campus, 2000).

28. For a theoretical approach to the integration of women's movement history into theories of social movements: Myra Marx-Ferree and Carol McClurg Mueller, "Gendering Social Movement Theory: Opportunities, Organisations and Discourses in Women's Movements Worldwide," in *Das Jahrhundert des Feminismus. Streifzüge durch nationale und internationale Bewegungen und Theorien*, ed. Anja Weckwert and Ulla Wischermann (Königstein: Helmer, 2006), 39–60.

29. Hanna Krüger, *Die unbequeme Frau. Käthe Schirmacher im Kampf für die Freiheit der Frau und die Freiheit der Nation 1865–1930* (Berlin: Bott, 1936); Rüdiger Ruhnau, "Eine unbeugsame Dame. Die Danzigerin Käthe Schirmacher setzte sich energisch für den deutschen Osten ein," *Preußische Allgemeine Zeitung*, June 18, 2005.

30. Lida-Gustava Heymann, "Käthe Schirmacher," *Die Frau im Staat*, no. 12 (1930): "Aus der begeisterten, frohen, frischen, arbeitsfreudigen Kämpferin für die Befreiung der Frau war eine chauvinistische, von preußischem Militärgeist erfüllte, verbitterte, ungütige Frau geworden."

31. Crips, "Comment passer du libéralisme au nationalisme völkisch."

32. Käthe Schirmacher, *Flammen. Erinnerungen aus meinem Leben* (Leipzig: Dürr & Weber, 1921).

33. Bührmann, *Der Kampf um weibliche Individualität*, 20, 240.

34. Käthe Schirmacher, "The marriage prospects of the modern woman. Speech held at the International Women's Congress, Chicago 1893," Schirmacher Papers 174/001, University of Rostock Library, Rostock. The printed version of the lecture in the original English is included in Käthe Schirmacher, *Aus aller Herren Länder. Gesammelte Studien und Aufsätze* (Paris: Welter, 1897), 285–90.

35. For biographical data, and a more in-depth analysis of this argument, see Gehmacher, "Moderne Frauen, die Neue Welt und der alte Kontinent."

36. M. Rapsilber, "Vom internationalen Frauenkongreß," *Kleines Journal*, September 23, 1896; my translation.

37. Mathilde von Mevissen to Käthe Schirmacher, January 24, 1896, Schirmacher Papers 567/027, University of Rostock Library, Rostock; my translation.

38. Käthe Schirmacher: Sturm (MS 1889), Schirmacher Papers 369/001, University of Rostock Library, Rostock.

39. Käthe Schirmacher, *Die Libertad. Novelle* (Zurich: Verlags-Magazin, 1891); Käthe Schirmacher, *Halb. Roman* (Leipzig: Wilhelm Friedrich, 1893).

40. Schirmacher, *Halb. Roman*, 252.

41. Anita Runge, "'Leben'—'Werk'—'Profession.' Zum Umgang mit biographischen Dokumenten bei Schriftstellerinnen," in *Biographisches Erzählen*, ed. Irmela von der Lühe and Anita Runge (Stuttgart: Metzler, 2001), 70–84.

42. Schirmacher, *Flammen*.

43. Joan W. Scott, *Only Paradoxes to Offer: French Feminists and the Rights of Man* (Cambridge MA: Harvard University Press, 1996), 7–10.

44. Scott, *Only Paradoxes to Offer*, 11.
45. Bührmann, *Der Kampf um weibliche Individualität.*
46. See Londa Schiebinger, *Am Busen der Natur. Erkenntnis und Geschlecht in den Anfängen der Wissenschaft* (Stuttgart: Klett-Cotta, 1995); Claudia Honegger, *Die Ordnung der Geschlechter. Die Wissenschaften vom Menschen und das Weib, 1750–1850* (Frankfurt: Campus, 1992).

Part II
Historical Cases

5 Sexological Cases and the Prehistory of Transgender Identity Politics in Interwar Germany

Katie Sutton

"A general need has been met now that we finally have the opportunity to have our say," declared self-identified male-to-female transvestite Toni Fricke in 1924, responding to the appearance of a new magazine column called "Der Transvestit" (The transvestite) in a Berlin-based homosexual women's magazine.[1] Coined in 1910 by German doctor, sex researcher, and homosexual rights activist Magnus Hirschfeld (1868–1935), the term *Transvestit/in*, "transvestite," was used in the early decades of the twentieth century to refer not just to cross-dressing but to a broad spectrum of what would now be described as "transgender" experiences and identifications; from self-defined heterosexual male transvestites with wives and children who cross-dressed only at home, to biological females and males living permanently as a member of the "opposite" sex.[2] Fricke's relief at having found the forum of "Der Transvestit" was echoed by fellow reader Dolly S., who warmly welcomed the opportunity "to talk about our sensibility and our condition."[3] Together with a number of similar magazine columns, supplements, and entire publications produced during the interwar period in Germany, this was one of the first examples of print media worldwide to specifically address "transvestite" issues, targeting individuals who were starting to identify with this still-new sexological category.

In the following I examine how this new branch of subcultural media negotiated questions of transvestite identity, and in doing so adapted the narrative model of the sexological case history. Drawing on Michael Warner and Lauren Berlant's formulations of "sexual publics," I explore how these mediated cases developed into a new subgenre of confessional transvestite autobiography, helping to create a distinct transvestite reading public and subcultural identity during the Weimar Republic.[4] The circulations, adaptations, and applications of the sexological "transvestite" classification at this period provide, I submit, an important instance of the "looping effects" described by Ian Hacking. The classification of human "kinds," according to Hacking, can change how people designated as "of that kind" see themselves: "that is, new knowledge about 'the criminal' or 'the homosexual' becomes known to the people classified, changes the way these individuals behave, and loops back to force changes in the classifications and

knowledge about them."[5] The "looping" of transvestite cases and classifications between sexology and an emerging subculture suggests sexological literacy beyond the immediate sphere of the medical profession in this
period. At the same time, this "looping" was a process of critical negotiation, with subcultural authors appropriating sexological models for their
own purposes.

A crucial feature of this adaptation from medical case to autobiographical
narrative was, I will argue, the recurring trope of "sich bekennen," which
can be approximately translated as "to confess" or "to openly acknowledge"
something. This trope bears strong links to the traditions of religious confession, identified by Michel Foucault as a crucial "technology of the self"
in the creation of modern understandings of subjectivity.[6] Reading Weimar
transvestite confessional literature through the lens of late twentieth-century
scholarship on "coming out" as gay, lesbian, or transgender demonstrates
how such narratives do much more than simply "loop back" or mediate sexological definitions and narrative structures to a broader subcultural public.
Rather, they function as strategic "performances" of identities that served
to simultaneously constitute and naturalize the transvestite subjectivities in
question.

At a broader level, the present chapter explores how an analysis of transvestite "cases," both medical and autobiographical, might contribute to a
more critical historiography of transgender identity politics. Articulating a
need to "disturb" common approaches to the history of sexuality, Laura
Doan identifies two key branches of scholarly endeavor. The first is the
more established form of "ancestral genealogy"—a mode of history writing
aimed at "recovering" nonheteronormative subjectivities in the past whose
characteristics resemble, and thus reaffirm, sex-gender identities in the present. Alternatively, historians of sexuality pursue "queer genealogy"—a
mode inspired by Foucauldian critiques to "unsettle and destabilize" identity categories. Yet each of these modes, insists Doan, "remains tethered . . .
to the logic of lineage," and to the negotiation of ideas about identity (even
if this tethering is more "precarious" in the latter mode).[7] In order to open
up sexual historiography to other, less genealogically oriented approaches,
she postulates a "queer critical history" that "turns to the past not to 'look
for' evidence of queerness-as-being in texts and objects, but to deploy
queerness-as-method to 'look through' the archive to see what is unknown
at the present moment."[8]

Doan's approach provides a productive basis for analyzing 1920s transvestite narratives in ways that go beyond the affirmation of non-gender-normative
identities in the present. In particular, this chapter challenges conventional
queer temporalities that situate the birth of LGBTQ activism in the second
half of the twentieth century—marked symbolically by the 1969 Stonewall riots—by exploring what might be called the "prehistory" of contemporary sexual identity politics. From this perspective, it is important to
read the "identity work" of Weimar transvestite autobiography not only

as a technology of the individual self, but also as a process of discursively constituting—and simultaneously delimiting—a politicized transvestite public oriented towards rights and recognition.[9] While such an analysis does not escape the "logic of lineage," it does attempt to produce a more "undetermined history" (Joan Scott's phrase) than a straightforward narrative of emergence would allow.[10]

PERFORMATIVE TECHNOLOGIES OF THE TRANSVESTITE SELF: MEDICAL CASES AND AUTOBIOGRAPHY

The historical context in which the transvestite media of 1920s Germany emerged was one of rapid social change and an increasingly active homosexual rights movement. Historians have shown that interwar sexual identity politics were in many respects a response to the ongoing criminalization of male homosexuality under Paragraph 175 of the Criminal Code. Homosexual rights activism was spearheaded by Hirschfeld and the Wissenschaftlich-humanitäres Komitee (Scientific Humanitarian Committee) from as early as 1897, and was spurred along by homosexual "scandals" among the Kaiser's inner ranks in the decade before World War I.[11] Ongoing urbanization, the end of the war, the advent of Weimar parliamentary democracy, and a corresponding liberalization of the public sphere all contributed to new forms of social and subcultural organization, including the consolidation of a mass movement based on notions of sexual and gender identity.[12] For transvestites, this liberalization encompassed more relaxed police attitudes (although harassment remained a problem), making it possible to apply for official certificates allowing the bearer to wear gender-atypical clothing in public, or to assume a gender-neutral name.[13] Meanwhile, the two largest homosexual rights organizations in interwar Germany encouraged the formation of affiliated transvestite groups: the Bund für Menschenrechte, or BfM (League of Human Rights) established a short-lived "Sondergruppe Transvestiten" ("Special Transvestite Group") in 1929, and in 1930 the Deutscher Freundschafts-Verband, or DFV (German Friendship Association) oversaw the foundation of the "Vereinigung D'Eon" ("D'Eon Organization").[14]

Although the transvestite magazine columns of the Weimar era were associated with these Berlin-based organizations, letters to the editor indicate that they attracted many more readers—both within Germany and beyond—than were ever members of the metropolitan associations. The longest running column was "Die Welt der Transvestiten" (Transvestites' world), published in conjunction with homosexual women's magazine *Die Freundin* (Girlfriend, affiliated with the BfM) from 1924–33. At various points this column bore the alternative titles "Der Transvestit" (The transvestite), or "Meinungsaustausch der Transvestiten" (Transvestite forum). A shorter column, also called "Der Transvestit" (The transvestite) appeared from 1926–32 in the magazine *Frauenliebe* (Womanly love, later renamed *Garçonne*, both affiliated with the DFV).[15] This period also witnessed at least one exclusively transvestite magazine, *Das 3. Geschlecht* (The third sex), published by the Berlin-based Radszuweit Verlag for a brief interlude from ca. 1930–32.[16] While the content of these columns and publications was diverse, ranging from historical and scientific articles to self-help sections on dress and relationships, autobiographical confessional narratives regularly dominated the available column space.

Through these autobiographical narratives, cross-identifying individuals negotiated what it might mean to call oneself a transvestite, developing a number of recurrent tropes, or "sexual scripts."[17] Emphasizing certain aspects of their life stories and brushing over others, these narratives began to assume the contours of a recognizable genre of transvestite life writing. The preference of many columnists to sign their contributions in semi-anonymous fashion, using either initials or a pseudonym (often only a first name) served a number of purposes. At one level, a pseudonym protected the author's privacy and reputation, allowing even individuals whose personal transvestite history was unknown to friends, family, or colleagues to narrate that history in a public forum. At the same time, appropriately (cross-)gendered pseudonyms served the important function of affirming the author's "true" gender identification.

That there soon developed a shared understanding of a "typical" transvestite autobiography is evident from Gertrud Kollmann's reflections in the "Welt der Transvestiten" column in 1932:

> It is probably not necessary to reiterate in too much detail to the thoughtful, sensitive, experienced individual the intricacies of our lonely process of coming into being. Every sincere transvestite knows what they are: the first "misunderstood" childhood inclination, the failed "first" "true" love, the first doubt, the horrible awakening and—the struggles, the hot, bitter, secret, lonely struggles, and if all goes well and does not result in exhausted resignation, the final secret, conscious confession to oneself! [*das letzte heimliche, bewußte Sich-Dazu-Bekennen!*][18]

The familiar content of transvestite life writing that Kollmann outlines had some subcultural precedents, including two 1907 book publications. *Aus eines Mannes Mädchenjahren* (Memoirs of a man's maiden years), which told of a "pseudo-hermaphrodite" who had been assigned a female gender identity at birth but later chose to live as a man, was published posthumously under the pseudonym N. O. Body (Karl M. [Martha] Baer); the fictionalized *Tagebuch einer männlichen Braut. Aufzeichnungen eines Homosexuellen* (Diary of a male bride: Notes of a homosexual) by Walter Homann charted the experiences of a female imitator (*Damen-Imitator*), who lived as a woman both on and off stage.[19] In key respects, however, the autobiographical narratives in the Weimar transvestite media pointed to their discursive origins in the medical case history, or *vita sexualis*, developed in the context of late nineteenth- and early twentieth-century sexology.

Prominent fin-de-siècle sex researchers including Richard von Krafft-Ebing, Havelock Ellis, and Magnus Hirschfeld had each incorporated patient histories of what they variously termed "inversion," "transvestism," "sexoaesthetic inversion," or "Eonism" into their case-based studies of sexual pathologies.[20] The compilation of anonymized patient cases was essential to the professionalization of a discipline still struggling to differentiate itself from its origins in psychiatry, and to establish itself, in Foucault's terms, as "legitimate knowledge"; Harry Oosterhuis describes how early sexologists relied almost entirely on the "voices of perverts" in their attempts to delineate new sexual categorizations.[21] Taking Ellis's study of "Eonism," Ivan Crozier identifies a series of key elements in the cases of transvestism published by sexologists, including cross-dressing during childhood, a growing awareness of one's difference during puberty, and the first experiences of successfully "passing" as a member of the opposite sex. In most cases, the patient's narrative ends with a report on their current situation, including the impact of their cross-dressing on their intimate relationships. In some there is also an attempt at self-classification, revealing the narrator's awareness of sexological theories of inversion.[22] By the 1910s and 1920s, such sexological studies were joined by psychoanalytic investigations of transvestism, which likewise used patient histories as their central form of evidence.[23]

Like the transvestite cases of sexology, the transvestite autobiographies published in Weimar subcultural magazines reveal a predictable structure and confessional tone, and both consist of a retrospective narrative told in the hope of receiving enlightenment or affirmation. These parallels suggest familiarity with medical discourses among at least some cross-identifying individuals in this period, particularly among more educated, urban transvestites with the means to access sexological publications, present as sexological patients, and write for subcultural publications. The first recurring element of these autobiographical narratives is an account of transgendered experiences in childhood. Male-to-female transvestites recount their memories of being little boys who wanted to be girls, who played with dolls and had girls as playmates, and who dressed up in their sister's, female cousins', or governess's clothes, while female-to-male transvestites describe their childhood refusal to wear frilly dresses, their envy of boys' trousers, and their preference for toys such as air rifles. The happiness resulting from such cross-gendered childhood dress and play, as author Lu L. recounted, "cannot be understood and certainly cannot be described by anyone who doesn't share my predisposition [*Veranlagung*]."[24] By focusing on a life stage when, as another contributor insisted, the subjects were far too young for "perversity" to play a role, accounts of transvestite childhoods functioned as discursive "proof" of transvestism as a natural, inborn condition.[25] This was not unlike their role in the sexological case studies, which were generally selected by the physician author for their capacity to illustrate theories of transvestism as a "congenital" or "intermediary" sexual form.[26]

Autobiography scholarship describes the importance of establishing "coherence systems" in life writing: sets of assumptions that provide "a means for understanding, evaluating, and constructing accounts of experience."[27] Just as Foucault has famously argued that in the nineteenth century the "homosexual" cohered into "a personage, a past, a case history, and a childhood," Weimar subcultural authors retrospectively fashioned their childhood memories to fit what was quickly becoming a coherent narrative of transvestite causality.[28] Underlining discursive constructions of the "naturalness" of the transvestite condition is the identification, in several narratives, of an accidental initial catalyst for cross-dressing. Scenarios such as becoming drenched in a thunderstorm and being "forced" to change into the only dry clothes available emphasize the innocence of the young transvestite protagonist, but also the admiration of onlookers for how convincingly the child is able to "pass" as the "other" sex.[29]

Seeking new, more scientific ways of describing and understanding their experiences and desires, subcultural authors thus drew on sexological narrative models and medical theories of congenital transvestism as productive resources in the process of identity construction. Examples of such writing support the recent move among historians of sexuality to revisit Foucault's *History of Sexuality* in ways that highlight the more emancipatory aspects of the doctor-patient relationship, challenging earlier critiques of sexologists' hierarchical and pathologizing authority. The "looping effect" between sexology and an emerging transvestite public was not a matter of straightforward uptake: more differentiated historical accounts are required to account for the transfers of knowledge that took place between sexologists, patients, and the wider society, and for the agency of transvestite authors in that process.[30]

A crucial affirmation of such authorial agency took the form of the confessional trope of *sich bekennen*. From the perspective of a queer genealogy interested in "dialogic temporalities," this trope can be roughly—if anachronistically—aligned with late twentieth-century discourses of "coming out" as gay, lesbian, or transgender. As Doan observes, such comparisons remain tied to an identity-based project that risks brushing over the experiences of individuals who did not formulate their sense of self in these terms.[31] Yet they also enable a closer analysis of the performative identity work being undertaken by authors of 1920s transvestite autobiographies and post-Stonewall coming out narratives alike. Scholars of the latter demonstrate that tales of homosexual identity formation since the late 1960s have tended to follow a conventional narrative paradigm that begins with feelings of otherness in childhood, and culminates in a sense of gay identity and community belonging. Kenneth Plummer describes these narratives as "'modernist tales' in that they use some kind of causal language, sense a linear progression, talk with unproblematic language and feel they are 'discovering a truth'." Biddy Martin similarly remarks on the tautological aspect of coming out stories, which "describe a process of coming to know something that has always been true, a truth to which the author has returned."[32] Taking a broader view of the "reflexive project of the self" in late modernity, philosopher Anthony Giddens examines how the notion that one can discover the "truth" of one's sexual self has become central to the way in which the individual conceives of his or her very identity.[33] Such linking of sexuality and modern subjectivity also underwrites transgender life writing; here, however, it is the author's "true" gender identity rather than sexual orientation that is affirmed.

Autobiography's function as a "technology of the self" in late modernity has its roots, as Foucault points out, in the traditions of religious confessional literature: "the confession was, and still remains, the general standard governing the production of the true discourse on sex."[34] Reflecting these discursive origins, many of the autobiographical contributions to the Weimar transvestite columns use the religiously infused terminology of the "Beichte," or "confession," in addition to the verb *sich bekennen*. Introduced by the Catholic Church "as a technique of power that works by exposure and individuation," confessions, as Wendy Brown observes, are "construed as liberation from repression or secrecy"—even as the narrator's belief in this emancipation encourages a forgetting of the disciplinary framework within which the truth telling occurs.[35] Despite such limitations, scholars emphasize the ways in which the autobiographical tradition, with its Enlightenment focus on the sovereignty of the narrating subject, has historically provided an emancipatory alternative to medical discourses of sexual subjectivity.[36] This promise of emancipation is implicit in many of the Weimar transvestite narratives, where the confessional motif structures the author's life story from childhood through to the moment of writing.

The first stage of this confessional process charts the narrator's self-acknowledgement of the "inner truth" of his or her transgendered desires during childhood or puberty; as commentator Fred Ursula remarks, "my female soul showed itself from an early age." Authors recount the pain of being forced to keep their gender identity a secret, but also the satisfaction accompanying their first purchase of non-gender-normative clothing—as Ursula declares, "I was utterly satisfied, even though only half of my wishes had so far been fulfilled."[37] Although less common than male-to-female narratives, female-to-male transvestites often include a further critical moment centered on chopping off their long hair, with author E.K. describing how "all at once things got better with this drive to cross-dress [*Umkleidung-strieb*]. It was like a big letting out of breath."[38] The next stage of the confessional narrative recounts the authors' first public outing during which they successfully "passed" in public as a member of their nonbiological sex, a moment that Lilly from Hamburg describes as "the most beautiful, happy, pure moment of my life to date."[39] This is generally followed by accounts of the narrator's initial, often hesitant contacts with other transvestites, a step that might be termed a "subcultural coming out."

Some stories end at this point, and can therefore be interpreted as examples of coming out only in a limited sense. This is particularly the case with narratives that were published either anonymously, under the author's initials, or using a pseudonym—an anonymity that further aligns the stories with both the religious confession and the sexological case. But other accounts go further, describing a more public declaration of a transvestite identity to family, friends, or colleagues, which may or may not have been warmly received. In almost all instances, the confessional narrative concludes with an account of the author's current situation, which could range from financial destitution and rejection by friends and family, to happy marriage to an understanding spouse. In the latter vein, male-to-female transvestite E. B. describes the immense happiness she has achieved by finding a girlfriend "who understands me, and with whom I can be exactly who I am."[40] Although columnists frequently articulated concern that their confession could end in disaster and rejection, many also stressed its cathartic or emancipatory potential, viewing the act of public declaration as a kind of symbolic rebirth. Wally M., for example, recounts the immense relief that followed his own revelation: "some time ago now I confessed my condition to my wife and since then I have become a thoroughly different person."[41]

In his study of contemporary homosexual literature, Volker Woltersdorff draws on the work of Foucault and Judith Butler to characterize the coming out narrative as a "performative technology of the gay self"; a process, in other words, though which gay identity is both anchored and publicly declared. The act of coming out, scholars insist, not only references a particular identity and associated political and cultural agenda, but also actively *produces* that identity, making it legible and visible through a lifelong series of differentiated repetitions.[42] Similarly, Weimar-era narratives of "confessing" to one's transvestism can be seen as a project of strategic and creative self-transformation, through which individuals sought to establish and reaffirm emancipatory possibilities of identification. These autobiographical narratives, I suggest, can be productively characterized as performative technologies of the transvestite self, creating a coherent sense of transvestite subjectivity based on the narrative model of *sich bekennen*. The sense of predictability and generic familiarity surrounding these narratives is further enhanced by the conditions of relative anonymity under which they often appeared. Through the repeated publication of life stories that differed only in details, but not in fundamental form, the 1920s transvestite media established a distinct subcultural genre that actively produced transvestite subjects through discourse.

CREATING A TRANSVESTITE PUBLIC: "LOOPING EFFECTS" AND IDENTITY POLITICS

The strength of contributors' identification with this still-new sexological category—or, to follow Hacking, the "looping" of sexological classifications into new subcultural contexts—is evident from such self-reflexive titles as "Transvestitenglück" (Transvestite happiness), or "Leben und Sehnsucht eines Transvestiten" (The life and longing of a transvestite).[43] Many commentators also explicitly approved of sexologists' congenital explanations of transvestism: Fred Ursula declared that "transvestism . . . is a predisposition [Veranlagung], just like homosexuality, although these are not identical"; Friedel Werner insisted that, far from being a an acquired "aberration" (Verirrung), science had shown transvestism to be an "inborn predisposition"; and Toni Fricke described undergoing blood tests with the famous researcher Professor Abderhalden in Halle to prove "that I am, so to say, internally a hermaphrodite."[44] Yet columnists also used the magazine forum to explore more complete, nonscientific identifications as members of their preferred sex, appealing to a broader transvestite public in ways that differed from both the sexological case study and the religious confession. Male-to-female transvestites, for example, referred to one another as "fellow sisters," and to themselves as "women" or "ladies," often signing off, as noted above, with an acquired female name, rather than the male name given to them at birth. As Maria declared, "I want to be judged and recognized as a woman"; another contributor described how "from the moment when I could feel myself to be truly a woman, I became happy."[45]

Hacking observes that, just as the imposition of classifications can loop back to affect individual behavior and identity, the individuals "sorted" by this effect can become rebellious, rearranging classifications imposed from above. Late twentieth-century gay liberation, he adds, represents "only the most successful example of this type of interaction."[46] The appropriation of sexological classifications by the 1920s transvestite media, I suggest, constitutes precisely such a "rebellious" intervention into the looping effect between sexologists and the "human kinds" they sought to categorize. A key effect of the autobiographical narratives examined above was to establish a transvestite identity that could form a basis for a sense of community and solidarity—a transvestite "public." Anna Maria H. thus declares that she is sharing her story in order to "show that it is also possible for us transvestites to structure our lives and achieve happiness in a way that is in line with our nature."[47] Other contributors told of how reading others' life stories had opened their eyes to their own transvestite "tendencies" (Neigung) or "predisposition" (Veranlagung), about which they had not previously dared to speak for fear of ridicule.[48] Such solidarity offered many readers a crucial psychological crutch in the face of ongoing social and legal discrimination. As Mimi lamented, "if people knew what we transvestites suffer, they would certainly be milder in their judgments." Another (anonymous) contributor declared it "bitterly difficult" for transvestites, "hermaphrodites," and "homoeroticists" (Homoeroten) to live lawfully in the face of widespread bigotry.[49] By linking their individual situation to the broader plight of sex-gender minorities, such authors called on their transvestite peers to become politically active in the defense of a shared identity.

Thus sexological classification of the "transvestite" did more than loop back to shape the identity of the individuals it described; the classification was also strategically redirected by those individuals towards the formulation of a broader identity politics based around notions of "rights" and "recognition." The urgent need for such a political agenda was underlined by numerous reports of mental health problems, social rejection, and suicides affecting transvestite-identifying individuals. Toni Fricke delineated the "persistent, nerve-murdering [*nervenmordenden*] psychological pressure" constantly threatening to undermine the health of transvestite individuals, while Loni Rex reported that it was only thanks to the "Welt der Transvestiten" column that "I now dare to walk out onto the street as a woman, and it is not going too far when I say that the enlightenment [*Aufklärung*] you have given me [through your magazine] saved my life."[50] At the same time, a number of columnists point to the sacrifices involved in publicly identifying as a transvestite, with at least one commentator suggesting that it was the privilege of a wealthy few: "the only people who can openly confess to being a transvestite are those who are completely financially independent and who can go abroad if necessary."[51] Nor was it unusual for authors to observe that, because of the expected fallout, their spouses, partners, or families remained ignorant of their tendencies.

Friedel Werner was among those to insist, in "Welt der Transvestiten," that despite the difficulties involved in openly acknowledging one's transvestism, only by organizing collectively and being recognized as transvestites would it be possible to improve things to a stage where individuals could live and move according to their innermost disposition. Similarly, Werner Kn. argued elsewhere in *Die Freundin* that transvestites had "had enough of hiding away like burglars," demanding that fellow transvestites "come out of your own four walls" and "make suggestions as to how we can achieve victory and happiness."[52] Others urged fellow readers to distribute their copies of the magazines widely, and even to leave them in the train or on the bus, so that people moving in so-called normal circles could be enlightened about the transvestite condition.[53] In such ways, the narrative strategy of *sich bekennen* characteristic of the autobiographical writings became crucial to the demand for recognition formulated by this emerging transvestite public.

The Weimar transvestite media thus worked to establish an "imagined community" of transvestite-identifying individuals, complementing the grassroots political activities of the Berlin-based organizations, which included hosting meetings and organizing public lectures.[54] This discursively created public aligns with Michael Warner's definition of a "counterpublic": an entity that comes into being through "an address to indefinite strangers," but where the "strangers" addressed are "not just anybody"; rather they are "socially marked by their participation in this kind of discourse." Warner's formulation is particularly interesting here both because it shows how participation in a counterpublic impacts upon individual identity formation, and for the way it expresses a relationship of conflict and subordination within a broader public sphere: "the subordinate status of a counterpublic does not simply reflect identities formed elsewhere; participation in such a public is one of the ways its members' identities are formed and transformed."[55] Contributors to the Weimar transvestite magazines addressed fellow readers *as* transvestites, assuming a shared identification within the space of the publication. On this basis, they provided advice on personal matters, such as where to find sympathetic retailers, or how to apply for a legal name change.[56] At the same time, this imagined transvestite community had a broader, political dimension, with authors beginning to formulate claims for social and legal recognition in relation to a larger, national German public.

AUTOBIOGRAPHICAL FILTERING AND THE LIMITS OF TRANSVESTITE POLITICS

There were, however, distinct limits to what I have characterized here as critical interventions into the "looping effect" in the service of a transvestite identity politics. At one level, this delimitation resulted from a policing on behalf of a "respectable" transvestite public—a policing internal to the transvestite community. As I have argued elsewhere, the mostly middle-class contributors to the transvestite magazines accepted respectability as the price of legal and political recognition. Consequently, individuals who did not conform to self-imposed standards of bourgeois decency, including prostitutes, criminals, those perceived as "excessively" flamboyant, and sometimes even homosexual and female-to-male transvestites, were largely marginalized within the terms of Weimar transvestite politics.[57]

Yet equally important from the perspective of a critical genealogy of transgender identity politics was the policing of identity that took place at the level of genre. Just as I have argued above that the autobiographical narratives used repeated tropes and familiar structures to discursively produce transvestite subjectivities, they also served an important filtering function. Only certain life experiences were accepted by authors, editors, and readers as pivotal to the process of "confessing" to one's transvestism, while others were brushed over as irrelevant, or were even seen to discount the author's claim to an authentic transvestite identity.

As autobiography scholars observe, narrative filtering is essential in order to impose on a life history a formal structure that life itself does not have. For the narratives in question here, filtering is that which allows the stories to become intelligible as transvestite narratives. Yet such intelligibility comes at a cost, for in the process, other stories are made unintelligible, and the number of legitimate tales is censored. In one such account, author Fräulein Gerda describes how she had been forced as a child to wear girls' clothing, and subsequently resisted cross-dressing for an extended period before returning to it later in life. This account was denied legitimacy as a transvestite narrative by fellow readers of "Die Welt der Transvestiten," one of whom declared, "if you have managed to remain without disguise [*ohne Verkleidung*] for fifteen years, then it is out of the question that you are a genuine transvestite, in my opinion you are a bisexual [*ein Bisexueller*]."[58] In another example, the editors of the "Welt der Transvestiten" column distanced themselves from a contribution by male-to-female transvestite Irene D., who had reported how her cross-dressing began during childhood, when she was forced to wear her female cousin's clothing due to financial necessity, and how she only gradually developed a real taste for this practice as an adult. The editors explain that this piece was published only in order to show Irene D. how wrong she is:

> Miss Irene D. really does not deserve to have her opinion communicated to the general public [*Öffentlichkeit*], but we are doing so in order to convince her of the complete falseness of her point of view. We do not agree with the thoughts outlined here, on the contrary, we cannot, on the basis of our years of experience, identify with them at all. . . . The transvestites have the floor, and points of view such as those of the reader Irene may not be permitted to go unchallenged.[59]

As these examples show, by the late Weimar period the sexological "transvestite" label had, for some readers at least, acquired the status of an essential identity, which could be proven or disproven based on the evidence provided by one's life story.

The stakes of narrative intelligibility are particularly high in the case of transgender life writing. In his study of contemporary transsexual autobiographies, Jay Prosser gives the example of the modern transsexual who must tell a coherent narrative of him/herself *as* a transsexual, carefully following an established pattern of generic expectations, before his/her diagnosis is approved by psychologists, and access is granted to the medical and surgical means of physical transition.[60] For Weimar-era transvestites the stakes were of a somewhat different order—by the early 1930s, surgical transformation was possible only in a limited sense, and only for a select few; in this context, the judging of "intelligible" narratives was predominantly undertaken by fellow readers rather than physicians or psychologists. Nonetheless, accounts such as Fräulein Gerda's or Irene D.'s were refused the status of genuine transvestite narratives for failing to adhere to certain generic conventions. These conventions had their roots, in turn, in congenital sexological understandings of the transvestite condition. In both contexts, medical and subcultural, transvestite narratives were subject to processes of selection and filtering for the sake of coherence, but at the expense of diversity.

Whereas scholars of contemporary transsexual autobiography tend to consider the case histories of sexology as the genre's main historical precedent, the predominance of life writing in the Weimar transvestite magazines suggests a need to revise this view.[61] Enabling a degree of transgender consciousness and activism that would not be achieved again for several decades, the interwar German transvestite media comprise sources for a "prehistory" of transgender identity politics. From the perspective of critical historiography, the writers' negotiations around what constituted an acceptable transvestite identity, community, and politics in Weimar Germany offer an opportunity to challenge more progress-oriented, genealogical modes of LGBTQ history writing. Scholarly efforts to trace a post-Stonewall narrative of emancipation based on notions of "identity," "pride," and "recognition," as Doan emphasizes, often brush over the "topsy-turvydom" of gendered and sexual identities in the past.[62] In contrast, a critical perspective on how a transvestite public and identity politics emerged in the 1920s can encourage us to take a closer look at the structures and ongoing dominance of identity-based activism for queer politics in the present.

Critiquing the lack of futurity inherent in current models of identity politics, Wendy Brown argues that "the language of recognition becomes . . . a vehicle of subordination through individualization, normalization, and regulation, even as it strives to produce visibility and acceptance." The focus on achieving recognition of a "marginalized" identity, she argues,

> reiterates the existence of an identity whose present past is one of insistently unredeemable injury. . . . Politicized identity thus enunciates itself, makes claims for itself, only by entrenching, restating, dramatizing, and inscribing its pain in politics; it can hold out no future—for itself or others—that triumphs over this pain.[63]

Such articulation of the limits of sexual identity politics in the present and into the future points to the further need to look more critically at the historical "birth" or "emergence" of this political model in the context of twentieth-century modernity. Rather than simply affirming and celebrating the beginning of a progress narrative that continues to the present, critical genealogies of queer identity politics will benefit from being as attentive to the limits of historical sexual publics as to their formation. By observing how certain narratives and identities were rendered unintelligible in the process of creating an interwar transvestite public, I have attempted to suggest a somewhat different history of early LGBTQ activism.

CONCLUSION

The new genre of transvestite life writing established in the subcultural periodicals of the Weimar era exhibited strong links to, but also significant differences from, the medicalized framework of the sexological case history from which it emerged. At one level, sexological theories of congenital transvestism productively "looped back" into subcultural contexts, contributing to the active discursive construction of a transvestite public. By adapting medical narrative models—and thus critically intervening in the "looping" process of classifying human "kinds"—transvestite autobiographers developed a discursive basis from which to expound the wider interests and political goals of an emerging "transvestite public." By sharing their life stories, and particularly by emphasizing those aspects of their experience that aligned with solidifying subcultural understandings of what it meant to call oneself a "transvestite" at this historical moment, they offered a critical support to fellow readers in the face of social discrimination.

This strategic use of narrative, including the confessional trope of *sich bekennen*, bears comparison, I have argued, to late twentieth-century coming out discourses, functioning as a "performative technology of the transvestite self." In an instance of queer dialogic temporality, both of these narrative forms functioned in their respective historical contexts as a basis for establishing an identity politics based on notions of "recognition" and "rights." Consequently, I have characterized the 1920s transvestite narratives in terms of a "prehistory" of post–World War II sexual identity politics. At the same time, however, a critical approach toward progress-oriented genealogies of sexual identity politics has enabled this analysis to point toward some of the identities and experiences at whose cost this political identity was formed. Further consideration of such exclusions might require the analysis of quite different source materials—novels, perhaps, or criminal records on prostitution and "gross mischief" arrests, where the perceived boundaries of transvestite identity or respectability may be less clear-cut. Although such work remains to be done, by deploying "queerness-as-method," rather than simply searching the sources for self-affirming narratives of "queerness-as-being," this chapter has sought to contribute to a more critical historiography of transgender experience and sexual identity politics in the early twentieth century.

NOTES

1. Toni Fricke, "Aus dem Empfindungsleben eines 'Transvestiten'!," in "Der Transvestit," *Die Freundin* 1, no. 2, September 12, 1924, 1–2. Unless otherwise stated, all translations from the German are my own. The research for this chapter was supported by the Australian Research Council and the German Academic Exchange Service. I am indebted to Laura Doan for the "prehistory" angle and further suggestions, including the reference to Ian Hacking's work; thanks also to Birgit Lang and Cynthia Troup for helpful comments.
2. Magnus Hirschfeld, *Die Transvestiten. Eine Untersuchung über den erotischen Verkleidungstreib* (Berlin: Alfred Pulvermacher, 1910).
3. Dolly S., "Transvestitenfragen," *Die Freundin* 4, no. 9, April 30, 1928, 6–7.
4. These scholars emphasize that, while many studies of historical gay communities have tended to imagine "community" in terms of "whole-person, face-to-face relations," "queer" forms of social organization do not always take

such traditional forms: Lauren Berlant and Michael Warner, "Sex in Public," *Critical Inquiry* 24, no. 2 (1998): 547–66, at 54 n15; see also Michael Warner, "Publics and Counterpublics," *Public Culture* 14, no. 1 (2002): 49–90.

5. Ian Hacking, *The Social Construction of What?* (Cambridge MA: Havard University Press, 1999), 105.

6. Michel Foucault, *The History of Sexuality*, trans. Robert Hurley, vol. 1, *The Will to Knowledge* (London: Penguin, 1998), 63.

7. Laura Doan, *Disturbing Practices: History, Sexuality, and Women's Experience of Modern War* (Chicago: University of Chicago Press, 2013), 58–59. Doan argues for the need to "examine how queer genealogy's steadfast interest in sustaining a dialogical interest between present and the past complicates its claims to be a critical history practice": 61.

8. Doan, *Disturbing Practices*, 90.

9. Sociologists use "identity work" to describe the "processes and procedures engaged in by groups designed to effect change in the meanings of particular identities": Barbara Ponse, *Identities in the Lesbian World: The Social Construction of Self* (Westport CT: Greenwood, 1978), 208.

10. Doan, *Disturbing Practices*, 141, citing Joan Scott (n21).

11. The Wissenschaftlich-humanitäres Komitee focused primarily on petitioning the Reichstag for reform of Paragraph 175, and from 1899 to 1923 oversaw publication of the *Jahrbuch für sexuelle Zwischenstufen*. See Manfred Baumgardt, "Die Homosexuellen-Bewegung bis zum Ende des Ersten Weltkrieges," in *Eldorado: Homosexuelle Frauen und Männer in Berlin 1850–1950. Geschichte, Alltag und Kultur*, ed. Michael Bollé (Berlin: Rosa Winkel, 1984), 17–27; Robert Beachy, "The German Invention of Homosexuality," *The Journal of Modern History* 82, no. 4 (2010): 801–38.

12. On the significance of urban spaces, and the expansion of capital and wage labor for the development of sexual subcultures and politicized identities, see e.g. George Chauncey, *Gay New York: Gender, Urban Culture, and the Makings of the Gay Male World, 1890–1940* (New York: Basic Books, 1994); John D'Emilio, "Capitalism and Gay Identity," in *Powers of Desire: The Politics of Sexuality*, ed. Ann Snitow, Christine Stansell, and Sharon Thompson (New York: Monthly Review Press, 1983), 100–13; Jeffrey Weeks, *Sexuality and Its Discontents: Meanings, Myths and Modern Sexualities* (London: Routledge, 1985), 191–93.

13. Rainer Herrn, *Schnittmuster des Geschlechts: Transvestitismus und Transsexualität in der frühen Sexualwissenschaft* (Gießen: Psychosozial-Verlag, 2005), 134–42.

14. The Vereinigung D'Eon was named after the same eighteenth-century crossdressing French diplomat who had inspired Havelock Ellis's coinage of "Eonism," see n20. The subtlety of this name, as leader Marie Weis observed, was intended to protect the privacy of club members: Marie Weis, "Die Aufgaben der Vereinigung D'Eon," in "Der Transvestit," *Garçonne*, no. 4, December 1, 1930, 10. On the links between *Vereinigung D'Eon* and Hirschfeld's Institute for Sexual Science see Herrn, *Schnittmuster*, 111ff.

15. While the column in *Die Freundin* attracted a wide range of contributors, the *Frauenliebe* column was dominated by contributions from chief editor Marie Weis. On these sources see Herrn, *Schnittmuster*, 142ff.

16. Advertisements in BfM magazines *Die Freundin* and *Der Insel* indicate that at least five issues of *Das 3. Geschlecht* were published between May 1930 and June 1932. The library of the Kinsey Institute for Research in Sex, Gender, and Reproduction at Indiana University in Bloomington holds an undated copy of issue 5, featuring photographs, scientific articles, as well as fiction and nonfiction.

17. On "sexual scripts" and "sexual stories" see Michael Kimmel, ed., *The Sexual Self: The Construction of Sexual Scripts* (Nashville: Vanderbilt University Press, 2007); Kenneth Plummer, *Telling Sexual Stories: Power, Change and Social Worlds* (New York: Routledge, 1995).

18. Gertrud Kollmann, "Die Liebes-Maske," in "Die Welt der Transvestiten," *Die Freundin*, 8, no. 20, May 18, 1932, 6–7.

19. N. O. Body, *Aus eines Mannes Mädchenjahren*, ed. Hermann Simon (Berlin: Hentrich, 1993); first published 1907 in Berlin by Riecke. An English translation was published in 2005 as *Memoirs of a Man's Maiden Years*, with a foreword by Sander Gilman (Philadelphia: University of Pennsylvania Press). Geertje Mak examines this text as an example of "hermaphrodite" life writing in *Doubting Sex: Inscriptions, Bodies and Selves in Nineteenth-Century Hermaphrodite Case Histories* (Manchester: Manchester University Press, 2012), 205–24. Walter Homann, ed., *Tagebuch einer männlichen Braut* (Hamburg: Männerschwarm Verlag, 2010); first published 1907 in Berlin by Dreyer.

20. Richard von Krafft-Ebing, *Psychopathia Sexualis: Mit besonderer Berücksichtigung der konträren Sexualempfindung: Eine medizinisch-gerichtliche Studie für Ärzte und Juristen*, 15th ed. (Stuttgart: F. Enke, 1918); Havelock Ellis, *Eonism and Other Supplementary Studies*, vol. 7, *Studies in the Psychology of Sex* (Philadelphia: F. A. Davis, 1919); Hirschfeld, *Die Transvestiten*.

21. Harry Oosterhuis, "Sexual Modernity in the Works of Richard von Krafft-Ebing and Albert Moll," *Medical History* 56, no. 2 (2012): 133–55; Harry Oosterhuis, *Stepchildren of Nature: Krafft-Ebing, Psychiatry, and the Making of Sexual Identity* (Chicago: University of Chicago Press, 2000); Foucault, *History of Sexuality*, 72. On the role of patient histories in the professional institutionalization of medicine see Julia Epstein, "Historiography, Diagnosis, and Poetics," *Literature and Medicine* 11, no. 1 (1992): 23–44, at 26.

22. Ivan Crozier, "Havelock Ellis, Eonism and the Patient's Discourse; or, Writing a Book About Sex," *History of Psychiatry* 11 (2000): 125–54, at 138–46. On the early sexological treatment of transvestism see also: Darryl Hill, "Sexuality and Gender in Hirschfeld's *Die Transvestiten*: A Case of the 'Elusive Evidence of the Ordinary'," *Journal of the History of Sexuality* 14, no. 3 (2005): 316–32; Geertje Mak, "'Passing Women' im Sprechzimmer von Magnus Hirschfeld. Warum der Begriff 'Transvestit' nicht für Frauen in Männerkleidern eingeführt wurde (transl. Mirjam Hausmann)," *Österreichische Zeitschrift für Geschichtswissenschaften* 9, no. 3 (1998): 384–99; Jay Prosser, "Transsexuals and the Transsexologists: Inversion and the Emergence of Transsexual Subjectivity," in *Sexology in Culture: Labelling Bodies and Desires*, ed. Lucy Bland and Laura Doan (Cambridge: Polity, 1998), 116–31.

23. For example, Wilhelm Stekel, "Fragmentary Analysis of a Transvestite," in *Frigidity in Woman, Disorders of the Instincts and the Emotions. The Parapathia Disorders* (New York: Liveright, 1926), 237–72; Karl Abraham, "Über hysterische Traumzustände," *Jahrbuch für psychoanalytische Forschung* 2 (1910): 1–32.

24. Lu L., "Briefe, die man der 'Freundin' schreibt," *Die Freundin* 3, no. 20, October 17, 1927, 6.

25. Mimi, "Was wir Transvestiten leiden," *Die Freundin* 4, no. 10, May 14, 1928, 2–3.

26. As Crozier observes, Ellis considered any sexual behavior to have a certain congenital component, and thus his cases all contain descriptions of early childhood development: "Havelock Ellis, Eonism," 138f.

27. Charlotte Linde, *Life Stories* (New York: Oxford University Press, 1993), 164; on autobiography and coherence see also A. C. Liang, "The Creation of Coherence in Coming-out Stories," in *Queerly Phrased: Language, Gender, and Sexuality*, ed. Anna Livia and Kira Hall (New York: Oxford University Press, 1997), 287–309, at 302f; Jay Prosser, *Second Skins: The Body Narratives of Transsexuality* (New York: Columbia University Press, 1998), 103, 107f.

28. Foucault, *History of Sexuality*, 43. For discussion of the "ensemble of [often overlapping] sub-childhoods" that developed during the twentieth century to describe various aspects of "sexual inversion" see Annette Runte, *Biographische Operationen. Diskurse der Transsexualität* (Munich: Wilhelm Fink, 1996), 210. See also discussion of the "authentische schwule Kindheitserinnerung" in Volker Woltersdorff, *Coming Out: Die Inszenierung schwuler Identitäten zwischen Auflehnung und Anpassung* (Frankfurt: Campus, 2005), 224.

29. See e.g. Gerd Gerda El., "Transvestitenglück," *Die Freundin* 3, no. 20, October 17, 1927, 4–5; Ilse v. R., "Aus der Jugendzeit," in "Die Welt der Transvestiten," *Die Freundin* 9, no. 7, February 15, 1933, 6–7; Ingeborg Wilhelm, "Wie Fritz Weidlich die schönste Braut von Wiesenthal wurde (Fortsetzung)," *Die Freundin* 4, no. 1, January 9, 1928, 6.

30. As Foucault insists, we are dealing "not nearly so much with a negative mechanism of exclusion as with the operation of a subtle network of discourses, special knowledges, pleasures, and powers": *History of Sexuality*, 72. See for example essays in Scott Spector, Helmut Puff, and Dagmar Herzog, ed., *After The History of Sexuality: German Genealogies with and beyond Foucault* (New York: Berghahn Books, 2012).

31. As Doan explains, citing Valerie Traub, "queer genealogy operates as a site where it not only possible but desirable to 'stage a dialogue between one queer past and another'": *Disturbing Practices*, 77.

32. Plummer, *Telling Sexual Stories*, 83; Biddy Martin, "Lesbian Identity and Autobiographical Difference(s)," in *The Lesbian and Gay Studies Reader*, ed. Henry Abelove, Michèle Aina Barale, and David M. Halperin (New York: Routledge, 1993), 274–94, at 281; see also Judith Roof, *Come As You Are: Narrative and Sexuality* (New York: Columbia University Press, 1996); Liang, "The Creation of Coherence," 291; Woltersdorff, *Coming Out*, 173, 218.

33. Anthony Giddens, *Modernity and Self-Identity: Self and Society in the Late Modern Age* (Stanford: Stanford University Press, 1991), 9, 32f.; see also Stevi Jackson, "The Sexual Self in Late Modernity," in Kimmel, ed. *The Sexual Self*, 3–15, at 8.

34. Foucault, *History of Sexuality*, 63. An expanded genealogical analysis of "technologies of the self" in the context of Christian spirituality can be found in Luther H. Martin, Huck Gutman, and Patrick H. Hutton, ed., *Technologies of the Self. A Seminar with Michel Foucault* (Amherst: University of Massachusetts Press, 1988), 4. On autobiography as a secularized form of confessional ritual see Alois Hahn, "Zur Soziologie der Beichte und anderer Formen institutionalisierter Bekenntnisse: Selbstthematisierung und Zivilisationsprozeß," *Kölner Zeitschrift für Soziologie und Sozialpsychologie* 34, no. 3 (1982): 407–34, at 407.

35. Wendy Brown, *States of Injury: Power and Freedom in Late Modernity* (Princeton: Princeton University Press, 1995), 41–42.

36. Woltersdorff, *Coming Out*, 31. See also Sidonie Smith and Julia Watson, *Reading Autobiography: A Guide for Interpreting Life Narratives* (Minnesota: University of Minneapolis Press, 2001), 2, 91ff.

37. Fred Ursula, "Wär' ich doch eine Frau…," *Die Freundin* 3, no. 3, February 21, 1927, n.p.
38. E. K., untitled contribution, *Die Freundin* 3, no. 13, July 11, 1927, n.p.
39. Lilly aus Hamburg, "Mein erster Ausgang als Dame," *Die Freundin* 6, no. 11, March 12, 1930, 4.
40. E. B., "Meinungsaustausch der 'Transvestiten'," *Die Freundin* 3, no. 9, May 16, 1927, n.p.
41. Wally M., "Zwei Zuschriften" [one of two letters], in "Die Welt der Transvestiten," *Die Freundin* 8, no. 34, August 24, 1932, 6–7. Woltersdorff compares tropes of symbolic rebirth and religious conversion in *Coming Out*, 106, 116–17.
42. Woltersdorff, *Coming Out*, 27f., 266. On coming out as a performative speech act in the context of the US military see Judith Butler, *Excitable Speech: A Politics of the Performative* (New York: Routledge, 1997), 76ff., and 107ff.
43. Gerd Gerda El., "Transvestitenglück," *Die Freundin* 3, no. 20, October 17, 1927, 4–5; [no author given] "Meinungsaustausch der Transvestiten: Leben und Sehnsucht eines Transvestiten," *Die Freundin* 3, no. 12, June 27, 1927, n.p. Some contributors, however, used the term more cautiously, referring to themselves as "so-called transvestites": Toni Fricke, "Ein Transvestit ist vogelfrei," *Die Freundin* 3, no. 18, September 19, 1927, 5–6.
44. Fred Ursula, "Wär' ich doch eine Frau . . . ," *Die Freundin* 3, no. 3, February 21, 1927, n.p.; Friedel Werner, "Das transvestitische Empfinden," in "Die Welt der Transvestiten," *Die Freundin* 5, no. 10, September 4, 1929, 5–6; Toni Fricke, "Ein Transvestit ist vogelfrei," *Die Freundin* 3, no. 18, September 19, 1927, 5–6. Some contributors also explored the newer psychoanalytic language of the "drives," e.g., Gerda, "Die Welt der Transvestiten," *Die Freundin* 6, no. 38, September 17, 1930, 5–6.
45. Maria, "Brief eines Transvestiten," in "Die Welt der Transvestiten," *Die Freundin* 7, no. 52, December 28, 1932, 6–7; [no author given] "Meinungsaustausch der Transvestiten: Leben und Sehnsucht eines Transvestiten," *Die Freundin* 3, no. 12, June 27, 1927, n.p.
46. Hacking, *The Social Construction of What?*, 131.
47. Anna Maria H., "Warum verzagen?" in "Die Welt der Transvestiten," *Die Freundin* 7, no. 33, August 19, 1931, 6.
48. R. C., "Meinungsaustausch der 'Transvestiten': Der alternde Transvestit," *Die Freundin* 3, no. 11, June 13, 1927, n.p.
49. Mimi, "Was wir Transvestiten leiden," *Die Freundin* 4, no. 10, May 14, 1928, 2–3; [no author given] "Verzweiflungskampf eines weiblichen Transvestiten," *Die Freundin* 4, no. 13, June 25, 1928, 3 [possible error in printed date, which should perhaps read July].
50. Toni Fricke, "Aus dem Empfindungsleben eines 'Transvestiten'!" in "Der Transvestit," *Die Freundin* 1, no. 2, September 12, 1924, 1; Loni Rex, "Die Welt der Transvestiten. Briefe die uns erreichen," *Die Freundin* 6, no. 43, October 22, 1930, 5.
51. Letter to the editor, *Die Freundin* 6, no. 5, January 29, 1930, 6.
52. Friedel Werner, "Das transvestitische Empfinden," in "Die Welt der Transvestiten," *Die Freundin* 5, no. 10, September 4, 1929, 5–6; Werner Kn., "Der Kampf der Transvestiten," *Die Freundin* 4, no. 7, April 2, 1928, 4.
53. Mimi, "Was wir Transvestiten leiden," *Die Freundin*, 4, no. 10, May 14, 1928, 2–3.
54. Benedict Anderson, *Imagined Communities: Reflections on the Origin and Spread of Nationalism* (London: Verso, 1983).
55. Warner, "Publics and Counterpublics," 86–87.

56. See e.g. "Aus dem Empfindungsleben eines 'Transvestiten'!" in "Der Transvestit," *Die Freundin* 1, no. 2, September 12, 1924, 1–2; D. Gr. T., "Meinungsaustausch der Transvestiten," *Die Freundin* 3, no. 13, July 11, 1927, n.p.

57. Katie Sutton, "'We Too Deserve a Place in the Sun': The Politics of Transvestite Identity in Weimar Germany," *German Studies Review* 35, no. 2 (2012): 335–54.

58. Reply to Fräulein Gerda by Emma, "Die Welt der Transvestiten," in *Die Freundin* [cover missing, probably volume 6, no. 41, October 8, 1930].

59. Editorial commentary on article by Irene D., "Kann Transvestitismus anerzogen sein?" in "Die Welt der Transvestiten," *Die Freundin* 7, no. 48, December 2, 1931, 6.

60. Prosser, *Second Skins*, 10, 101ff., 107, 115f.

61. Like the sources examined above, the contemporary transsexual autobiographies typically chart a shift from a childhood characterized by confusion and non-gender-normative activities, through to self-discovery and finally transformation. In addition to Prosser see Runte, *Biographische Operationen*, 208, 631; Joanne Meyerowitz, *How Sex Changed: A History of Transsexuality in the United States* (Cambridge MA: Harvard University Press, 2002), 365f.

62. Doan, *Disturbing Practices*, 97–133.

63. Brown, *States*, 66, 73–74. See also the critique of "identity knowledges" in Robyn Wiegman, *Object Lessons* (Durham NC: Duke University Press, 2012).

6 The Sad Tale of Sister Barbara Ubryk
A Case Study in Convent Captivity

Timothy Verhoeven

In July 1869, the international press was filled with accounts of a terrible case of convent captivity. According to the reports, a magistrate in Cracow (at that time part of the Austrian province of Galicia) had discovered a hidden cell within the city's Carmelite convent. The sight that greeted the magistrate when he opened the cell door was horrifying. Inside was a naked and emaciated figure, its body smeared with mud and excrement, and cowering in fear as light streamed into the rat-filled cell. This "creature," as the press termed the figure, was a nun named Barbara Ubryk (1817–91), and it was soon established that she had spent no less than twenty-one years in her terrible prison.

Narratives of convent abuse flourished in the nineteenth century across a range of nations.[1] Some offered graphic descriptions of physical and sexual abuse, while others focused on the emotional torment endured by the cloistered nun. Some were written in the form of testimony from escaped nuns; others were more openly works of imagination. But whatever their form or focus, these narratives of convent abuse shared a central message: that the convent was a physical and spiritual prison in which young women were stripped not only of their freedom, but of their feminine identity.

As an attack on the convent, the case of Barbara Ubryk was not, therefore, unique. Nevertheless, several features of her sad story and its reception make it deserving of specific attention. The first aspect that set the Ubryk case apart from other stories of convent atrocity was its transnational scope. Previous studies of the Ubryk scandal have limited their reach to the borders of the nation-state.[2] However, the case immediately crossed national borders—one of its most striking features. Newspaper accounts of the discovery of Ubryk appeared across Europe, North America, and Australia. The second intriguing aspect of the case was the manner in which it was understood as simultaneously extreme and typical. Jean-Claude Passeron and Jacques Revel argue that this ability to reconcile two seemingly opposed concepts, the singular and the general, is crucial to the case study's explanatory power. A case study is by definition singular, but to be more than a mere example it must illuminate larger, intelligible patterns.[3] One person's story becomes an exemplary narrative on which generalized claims can be grounded. In Lauren Berlant's terms, this is the "canny negotiation" that marks the case study. Freud could take the singular narrative of Dora and, as Berlant writes, "claim to be able to discern in her life exemplary patterns that warranted fundamental changes in how we understand people generally."[4] This exemplary ambition is a central and defining feature of the case study.

The Ubryk case worked in this manner. The ambitious claim at the heart of the case was not linked to a broader understanding of human nature, but rather to a specific institution, the convent. The suffering of Barbara Ubryk was understood as both singular and typical. On the one hand, certain details of the Ubryk case were shocking. In particular, the pitiful physical state in which Ubryk was discovered, as well as the incredible length of her confinement, made the case particularly notorious. Yet far from an aberration, the cruel regime of punishment and incarceration that reigned in the Cracow convent was seen to be representative of all convents. It was widely believed that, even if spared the same level of torture and brutality, all nuns were held against their will and left at the mercy of cruel convent authorities.

The extent to which this shocking narrative was understood to be exemplary became clear in the loud calls for state supervision of convents that followed Ubryk's discovery. The *Journal des Débats* used the case to insist that convents "be submitted to common law, and that supervision on the part of the authorities be exercised at any time in these mysterious retreats."[5] For the *Albion* newspaper (New York), the significance of the Ubryk story was equally clear: "The moral we draw from this horrible story is that monasteries and nunneries must be thrown open to the free inspection of the civil power."[6] The London *Times* suggested that the Ubryk case proved how cruel men and women could be when their actions were screened from public view. "Where such communities are secluded from public inspection," the paper commented, "such things as this Cracow history are not unlikely to happen."[7] Such views won widespread public support. In England, petitions requesting government inspection of convents attracted thousands of signatures. In 1869, some ninety-five petitions bearing a total of sixteen thousand signatures reached parliament; in 1870, the number of petitions was 134, with a total of over thirty-three thousand signatures. Finally, in 1870 the member of Parliament Charles Newdegate (1816–87) managed to win a majority for the establishment of a House of Commons Select Committee to investigate convents.[8]

The Ubryk case, then, worked to bridge the specific and the general. It also combined the voyeuristic and the didactic, a feature it shared with the medical case study. The erotic confessions contained in texts such as Richard von Krafft-Ebing's *Psychopathia Sexualis* introduced an educated public to the origins of perversions and disorders, and thus worked to deepen sexual knowledge. Their aim was, on one level at least, didactic, but such accounts of perversion also titillated—a factor that helped to drive their sales.[9] Vernon A. Rosario argues that, by the late nineteenth century, the public was increasingly turning to medical texts to be entertained by stories of erotic perversity. Erotic medical confessions, he argues, were "liminal narratives" that lay in the "shady boundary between scientific documents and licentious popular literature."[10] The sales of such medical texts owed as much to public curiosity as to scientific endeavor.

The Ubryk case worked in exactly this manner. As we shall see, one of the reasons for its appeal was the opportunity it provided for graphic depictions of sexual abuse and torture. Stories of concealed torture chambers and sadomasochistic violence began to circulate almost immediately after the discovery of Ubryk in Cracow. Yet newspapers and publishers escaped any accusation of lewdness, for there was a reassuringly didactic element to the story. What was the lesson of the Ubryk case? On one level, the answer is clear. The captive nun's suffering provided shocking proof of the cruelty at the heart of the Catholic Church. There were other lessons as well. In its description of sexual aberration, the Ubryk narrative threw into relief the contours of accepted sexual and gender norms. The key issue here was Catholic celibacy. Nuns such as Ubryk were understood to be suffering the effects of sexual abstinence. Indeed, doctors soon intervened in the scandal by debating the extent to which Ubryk was a victim of the two disorders most associated with celibate nuns, namely hysteria and nymphomania. Ubryk was also a victim of her decision to renounce the true feminine path of marriage and motherhood. Very few women would be punished to the same degree, but there was nevertheless a clear moral to her story. Women who strayed from the protective sphere of the home were vulnerable to the darkest forms of abuse. The Ubryk narrative thereby worked to reinforce sexual and gendered norms.

THE CREATION OF A RECEPTIVE PUBLIC

The public for the case of Barbara Ubryk was initially the international readership of newspapers. News of the discovery of the captive nun spread very quickly. The initial reports appeared in the Austrian and German press, but the story was soon front-page news in France and Britain as well. By late August American newspapers were carrying reports, and in early October the *Sydney Morning Herald* had the story.[11] The Ubryk case exemplified the manner in which communication networks, notably the news agencies Havas and Reuters, were creating an international public. Many of the articles appeared in identical form from nation to nation. The *Sydney Morning Herald*, for example, reprinted an article from the *Presse* in Vienna; American papers took articles from the *Siècle* in France. In many cases, editorialists added their own reflection on the story's significance, but these too were essentially similar in tone and content. The *New York Times* denounced the "horrible cruelties practiced upon the unfortunate Carmelite nun at Cracow"; the *Journal des Débats* condemned what it described as "the odious imprisonment of the Cracow nun."[12]

Importantly, the initial discovery of Ubryk was followed by a steady drip of further revelations, thereby sustaining this public that had been created. Michael Warner argues that the "punctual" temporality of circulation is essential in the emergence of modern publics. For Warner, the pace and timing with which discourse is put into circulation is as important in the creation of a public or counterpublic as what is actually said.[13] The discovery of Ubryk raised a series of further questions. How had she entered the convent? Why had she been locked up? Who was responsible for tipping off the authorities about her plight? Over the succeeding weeks, answers to these questions gradually emerged. The identity of the informant was revealed as a fellow nun. The details of Ubryk's entry into the convent soon followed, with most accounts pointing to a failed love affair as the decisive reason. Embittered by her cruel treatment at the hands of a callous suitor, and rejected by her own family, the young Ubryk had, in this account, joined the convent in a desperate act of protest. Dramatic developments in the story contributed to the maintenance of its public, such as the news that one of the suspects in the case, the convent confessor, had died in mysterious circumstances. Throughout this series of revelations, national differences remained of little importance; the newspaper accounts that appeared were not reshaped to fit particular national publics.

In addition to its transnational scope, one of the features of this public was its willingness to believe. The story was, after all, incredible—a woman imprisoned and abused for no less than twenty-one years in one of Europe's most sophisticated cities. A skeptical reader might have noticed significant inconsistencies in the press accounts. These included the location of the cell, the number of people present at Ubryk's liberation, and even the spelling of her name. There was also a plausible counternarrative. The Catholic press soon published the defense of the convent's mother superior. In the account of the head nun, Ubryk had been dumped in the convent by her family, who could no longer cope with her mental instability. The family had concealed this illness from the convent authorities, and once Ubryk had begun to show signs of her derangement—tearing off her clothes, biting other nuns—there had been very little choice but to isolate her from the rest of the community. The mother superior even claimed medical approval for this course of action; the doctor who attended the convent, she stated, had confirmed this decision.[14]

But these defenses had little effect in quieting public outrage. Even the revelations, some months after the scandal first erupted, that the charges against the convent authorities had been dropped, and that Ubryk was hopelessly insane, failed to shake conviction in the secular press that a horrible crime had been committed. The mother superior's account was dismissed by a series of commentators. The doctor who had allegedly approved the confinement of Ubryk seemed to have disappeared; the current physician, as the *Philadelphia Public Ledger* noted, "stated that he had never even seen Barbara once."[15] In France, the *Moniteur Universel* ridiculed the head nun's account as well.[16] And what about Ubryk's insanity that, several papers reported, had been confirmed by the examining doctors after her liberation? Here the explanation was simply that her derangement had followed rather than preceded her captivity. Furthermore, according to some accounts, her mental state seemed to be improving. As the *Moniteur Universel* reported, once she had been clothed in secular and appropriately feminine attire, Ubryk had almost immediately "come out of her mindlessness and [out] of the savage state into which isolation and solitude had plunged her."[17]

How had such a receptive public been created? Here another of Warner's propositions concerning the creation of publics, the role of a "concatenation of texts," provides a persuasive answer. As Warner argues, one text alone is unlikely to create a public; rather, a series of related stories combine to create the reflexivity, or cross-circulation, essential to the formations of a public.[18] This sense of connectedness to other related narratives is clear in the Ubryk case. Narratives describing the abuse and incarceration of nuns were wildly popular from the era of the Enlightenment to the late nineteenth century. Some reached an international audience. The most notorious American narrative, *The Awful Disclosures of Maria Monk*, contained graphic scenes of torture and sexual abuse. Young nuns are whipped, their naked flesh is branded with hot irons, and their cheeks are pierced with pins. The book was a best seller at home, and was soon published in the United Kingdom and in Australia. Yet even if not reaching an international audience, these narratives showed that each nation had its own Barbara Ubryk. In France, court cases and popular novels had long presented the convent as a site of incarceration. Leading anticlericals took great interest in accounts of convent captivity. Among the private papers of the republican historian Jules Michelet, there is a folder with handwritten copies of press extracts concerning one such case, that of Soeur Sainte-Marie de Colombes in the town of Bayeux in 1845. Like Ubryk, Soeur Sainte-Marie was forced into a *cachot*, or cell, by a tyrannical mother superior; after eight days she was transferred to the Bon-Sauveur religious house in Caens, where she was locked up for a further ten months in a cell filled with "folles furieuses." In another parallel with the Ubryk case, Sainte-Marie's mother superior defended this action on the grounds of her charge's mental derangement.[19]

Even cases that diverged from the standard narrative of confinement could be read as indictments of the convent. In Britain, just months before the revelations concerning Ubryk, the public had been fascinated by a court case, *Saurin v. Star*, which appeared to expose the pettiness as well as the cruelty of convent life. In *Saurin v. Star*, the complainant, Sister Saurin, was in fact suing to be allowed to return to a convent from which she had been excluded. What fascinated the British public, however, was the picture of harassment and cruelty at the hands of an authoritarian mother superior that emerged from her testimony. Sister Saurin claimed that the mother superior had inflicted upon her a series of demeaning punishments, including cutting off all communication with her family, before unjustly excluding her from the community.[20]

The concatenation of texts that produced a public primed to believe the worst about convents was not limited to judicial cases. Much of the public would have recognized Ubryk's story from the plotlines of best-selling novels. In Isaac Kelso's sensational novel *Danger in the Dark*, published in the United States in 1854, the heroine Isadora is locked up in a tiny cell in a convent; she has been imprisoned on the pretext that she is insane.[21] Fictional depictions of the convent invariably emphasize its fortress-like qualities. To cite one example, Alfred Villeneuve's *Les mystères du cloître*, the high walls and reinforced gates of the Abbaye-aux-Dames conceal a regime of punishment. The heroine Blanche soon finds herself locked up in a tiny cell by a cruel and vindictive superior.[22]

Commentators on the Ubryk case sometimes made clear such links with best-selling novels. In France, for example, the Ubryk tale was read in the context of perhaps the most famous narrative of convent abuse, Denis Diderot's *La religieuse*. In Diderot's text, the heroine, Suzanne, undergoes a series of trials and punishments at the hands of her fellow nuns as well as superiors. In one episode, she is locked up in a subterranean cell and becomes near-insane as a result. A highly controversial work, Diderot's account was periodically banned throughout the nineteenth century, but it nonetheless served as a framing device for many of the public reactions to the Ubryk tale. "This poor woman," wrote F. X. Trébois in the *Tribune*, "reminds us of Diderot's nun. Like Diderot's heroine, Barbara suffers from hunger, thirst, and the most unspeakable humiliations."[23]

This kind of genre-mixing accounts for another curious aspect of the public reception of the Ubryk case, namely the manner in which readers seemed implicitly to understand what had happened to Ubryk. The initial newspaper reports were coy on the question of her imprisonment and treatment. Very few details were given as to the reasons for her incarceration, or the nature of her suffering. This was partly a question of censorship and of public standards. Arguably, however, the newspapers did not need to spell out what had happened to Ubryk; for a public primed by a series of similar revelations, and steeped in a popular literature of convent atrocity, the facts were only too clear. This was a narrative of sexual vice. As all of the press accounts indicate, Ubryk had almost immediately confessed to her liberators that she had broken the vow of chastity. Her crime was mitigated to some degree by the atmosphere of sexual corruption that apparently reigned in the convent. Again, few details were given in the initial reports. Yet at the point of her liberation, the weak and miserable Ubryk had found the strength to launch the following accusation at the nuns around her: "But these, too, are not angels."[24]

The ease with which the Ubryk case escaped the boundaries of genre is further evident in the largely fictionalized accounts of her life that were rushed into print. These works, which appeared with astonishing speed in Germany, France, Britain, and the United States, were advertised as "true narratives," thereby creating an expectation of authenticity among the reading public.[25] They also employed many of the devices of sentimental fiction of the era. As in such fiction, the reader is incited to feel sympathy for the plight of the suffering heroine, cruelly betrayed by her family and her lover, and forced to rely on her own fortitude and courage to survive her ordeal.[26] In grafting fictional conventions onto a contemporary controversy, these "true narratives" fit what Barbara Foley has defined as the "documentary novel." This novel, as Foley argues, claims to represent reality through "agreed-upon conventions of fictionality," while at the same time making "some kind of additional claim to empirical validation."[27] The authors of Ubryk's "life story" included long passages of "testimony," made, allegedly in the first person, by key individuals involved in the case, including Ubryk herself; they also included judicial reports and press clippings. Alongside these are imaginative reconstructions of key scenes in Ubryk's life.

Many of the imagined scenes concern affairs of the heart. The American account begins with Ubryk arguing with her father over her choice of suitor. She is determined to marry the young man she loves; her father, however, insists that she take a nobleman. The narrative suggests that the torment and misery experienced by the young woman will drive her to the mad act of joining the convent. Furthermore, the fictionalized accounts included a level of sexual explicitness that was unavailable to newspaper editors. While the press reports had hinted at sexual crime within the convent, the authors of these works left little doubt on the question. According to these narratives, Ubryk had been raped by the nuns' confessor soon after entering the convent. Upon discovering this crime, the mother superior, far from responding with pity, had flown into a jealous rage, as she had once been the confessor's sexual favorite. Then, so these stories claim, in collusion with the confessor, the mother superior had locked Ubryk in her subterranean cell.

FUSING THE SENSATIONAL AND THE DIDACTIC

One of the reasons for the public interest in the narrative of Barbara Ubryk was no doubt its blending of sexually graphic detail with moralistic intent. In his analysis of sensational literature in antebellum America, David S. Reynolds has classified the convent atrocity story as part of the "immoral reform" genre. This genre, he suggests, had a dual purpose: demonstrating a high-minded commitment to social reform, while allowing a largely male readership to indulge in sexual fantasy. These works are filled with scenes of innocent women subjected to cruel and sadistic punishment, whether at the hands of drunk husbands, heartless brothel owners, or cruel Catholics.[28] The appeal of such works, he speculates, lay as much their pornographic dimension as in their serious message of moral reform.

Sadomasochism appears with startling intensity in many of the accounts of Ubryk's ordeal. Several newspapers noted that a group of investigators sent to search the convent in the wake of Ubryk's liberation had stumbled upon a hidden torture chamber containing heavy crosses, girdles with inward pointing nails, and a crown of thorns with long sharp spikes.[29] Fictionalized accounts provided more graphic details. In one scene in the French version, *Les amoureuses cloîtrées*, a nun is tied to an iron ring, stripped to the waist, and whipped mercilessly by the other nuns. In a frenzy of cruelty and sadism, the torturers then begin inflicting such punishments on one another. Following an attempt to escape, Ubryk, too, is whipped; such is the ferocity of her torturers that drops of blood splatter their faces.[30]

The sensational element of the Ubryk case seems clear. But what of the didactic aspects? For opponents of the Church, the most immediate lesson was the backwardness of Catholicism. The status of women was considered a marker of civilization in the nineteenth century. Only societies that sheltered women within the domestic sphere could lay a claim to civilization. European and American travelers pointed to the degrading treatment of women in Asia and the Middle East as proof of the primitive nature of those societies. Women in such "lesser" societies, they argued, were forced into manual work, subjected to violence and intimidation, and denied the protection of the one institution—the home—which was the appropriate framework for their peculiar virtues. At the same time, as Louise Michele Newman has argued, white women's activists claimed to be agents of civilization, particularly as reformers of "savage peoples."[31] Protestant missionaries, for example, sought to uplift "heathen" women by rescuing them from manual drudgery and showing them, instead, the benefits of companionate marriage and childrearing.[32]

In its cruel treatment of the women under its command, and particularly in its determination to prevent them enjoying the benefits of marriage and childrearing, the Catholic Church loomed as a backward, even uncivilized institution, and one alien to the spirit of the nineteenth century. The captive nun was a ghost from Europe's dark, medieval past. Much of the press commentary expressed this sense of being transported back to the era of the Medieval Inquisition. "You would think yourself," as one paper declared in the days after Ubryk's liberation, "taken back to the dark centuries of the Middle Ages."[33] The physical location of the Carmelite convent itself reinforced this contrast with the enlightened modern age. Nearby in the city of Cracow were the Botanical Gardens and the Observatory, two exemplary institutions of science and inquiry. Next to these the convent was a dark and forbidding space that seemed impervious to modern progress. As many of the reports in the press concluded, "And is this the nineteenth century?"[34]

The cruelty and backwardness of Catholicism did not exhaust the ideological potential of the Ubryk narrative. Like the medical case study, the Ubryk narrative provided a lesson in sexual aberration. If rape and sexual violence were at the heart of the story, Ubryk's sexual behavior was also called into question by members of the medical fraternity. One of the fictionalized accounts of her captivity and liberation included documents from the trial of convent authorities. At that trial, several doctors testified that Ubryk was suffering from hysteria and nymphomania. During their examination, they reported, she had stripped off her clothing, and "winked quite unambiguously at them."[35] Another medical journal reported that she "used the most vulgar and lascivious expressions, which even completely degraded women only seldom use."[36]

The doctors' diagnosis of Ubryk built on a long-standing association between Catholic celibacy and hysteria, an association that medical doctors had played a large role in validating. Classical authorities had explained the link between sexual abstinence and hysteria through the accumulation of female sperm in the uterus. Nineteenth-century doctors abandoned this notion, but many continued to adhere to the association between hysteria and prolonged abstinence. A leading French authority, Dr. Hector Landouzy, argued that whenever an organ was deprived of its normal function, the equilibrium of the body was disturbed. The nun, by not employing her reproductive organs, was thus inherently vulnerable to the disease of hysteria.[37] Medical writers with a more popular audience referred at length to the hysterical nun. For example, Auguste Debay's *Hygiène et physiologie du mariage*, which had reached 172 editions by 1883, included just such a case study. Debay reported knowing a young woman who had been forced into a convent by her father—a story that echoed the fictionalized accounts of Ubryk's clash with paternal authority. The result for Debay's subject was predictable. First she "slipped into a deep state of exhaustion, then passed through all the stages of hysteria, erotomania, and nymphomania."[38] In this instance, however, the woman's sickness prompted her family to take her back into the home, where her recovery was astonishing. Soon the young woman married, and became "remarkable for her sweetness of character."[39]

The association between sexual abstinence and hysteria did not go unchallenged. Another leading French authority, Paul Briquet, vigorously refuted the link, and instead argued that sexual excess was most often the cause. For the rest of the century, doctors argued about whether the nun or the prostitute was more vulnerable to hysteria.[40] Psychiatrists, however, found another means to link Catholic celibacy with aberrant behavior in women. The intense emotional devotion that characterized female religiosity stemmed, these psychologists argued, from repressed eroticism. In Britain, Henry Maudsley argued that many young women confused deep religious feeling with what was really "a morbid self-feeling, arising out of an unsatisfied sexual instinct." Such unsatisfied instincts, he argued, often led to "hysterical excitement."[41] Richard von Krafft-Ebing went further, suggesting that the relationship between religious and sexual excitement was easy to establish. An unfulfilled sexual desire, he argued, was often channeled into religious fervor.[42] The linkage between religious fervor in young women and hysteria was put most forcefully by the alienists of the renowned Salpêtrière asylum in Paris. As Jan Goldstein has argued, the psychiatric profession used the hysteria diagnosis to debunk traditional Catholic interpretations of aberrant behavior in women, and at the same time to impose itself as the only reliable authority in cases of female illness. The exalted mysticism of female saints was diagnosed by the psychiatrists of the Salpêtrière as episodes of hysterical delirium. In 1891, Henri Legrand du Saulle, who had trained at the Salpêtrière in the 1850s, declared that many Catholic female saints were, in his words, "nothing more than simple hysterics."[43]

The concern on the part of doctors and psychiatrists to label Catholic female piety as pathological points to a broader imperative related to gender and sexual norms. Such norms could be established by prescriptive ideals. But more often, this goal was achieved through the presence of the deviant Other. By throwing into relief the contours of the normal, the presentation of deviancy helped to shore up conventional gender and sexual norms. This explains the medical preoccupation with the abnormal rather than the normal. The "norm," as Peter Cryle and Lisa Downing observe in their study of female sexual pathologies, was very rarely presented to readers of medical texts; instead, the pages of these texts were replete with cases of perversion. The reason was simple: this was the most efficient means of giving an otherwise elusive clarity to models of proper sexual behavior.[44] Convent captivity narratives employed a similar strategy. The convent that was the scene of Ubryk's sufferings was presented as a deviant space in which perverse sexual practices were free to flourish—a closed-off institution filled with women whose unnatural state of sexual abstinence left them vulnerable to the most serious sexual pathologies. Fascination with such imagined spaces was no doubt a product of voyeurism, but there was an earnest message as well. The fate of the captive nun highlighted the virtues of "normal" sexual behavior. These vivid accounts of the captive nun's suffering announced that women's natural destiny was not celibacy and the grim life of the convent, but rather the natural and benign states of marriage and maternity.

This message was made explicit in medical reflections on the Ubryk case. A long account of the scandal published in the medical weekly *Wiener medizinische Wochenschrift* ended with a stirring defense of marriage against all forms of the celibate state. A young woman who chooses to embrace chastity, the authors declared, "rejects the noble gifts of nature, being destined for childbearing and family. Her old age will be dreadful and sad as she is bereft of the sympathy of her husband and the love of her children." Other women who might be tempted by the life of the nun should take note. Marriage, the authors affirmed, is "the means by which the physical as well as mental and moral welfare of man and wife are best assured."[45] The urgency of this message was increased by evidence that more and more young women were choosing the convent over the home. In many nations, Catholic female religious orders experienced a boom in recruitment during the nineteenth century. In France, the number of nuns and novices increased from 13,900 in 1808 to 66,000 in 1850, and in 1878 stood at 127,000.[46] Even Protestant nations witnessed a growth in numbers. In 1840, there were fewer than twenty convents in England; by 1900, there were 113 congregations running 596 convents.[47] The number of nuns in the United States increased from 1,344 in 1850 to 40,340 in 1900.[48]

Many factors were driving this growth, but from the perspective of secular commentators, the fact that more and more women were renouncing marriage and childrearing was deeply troubling. Not only was their individual health at risk, but the future prosperity of the nation would be imperiled by the loss of so many women of childrearing age. In this context, the sufferings of Barbara Ubryk assumed a heightened importance. Here was the life of the convent laid bare. Rather than a refuge from worldly disappointment, these young women would find in the convent only torture and misery. When set against this miserable fate, marriage and childrearing could take on the air of welcome havens.

* * *

Long after the outrage surrounding the discovery of Barbara Ubryk had subsided, her fate continued to interest the international public. On October 9, 1869, *Harper's Weekly* ran a portrait of Ubryk recuperating in her asylum. In February 1870, the same journal published the observations of a visitor to Ubryk's asylum. The ex-nun, the journal reported, "looks extremely well," and "conversed freely, though rather incoherently."[49] In May 1891, Ubryk's death afforded many newspapers the opportunity to repeat her story, and new editions of her story were published in Canada and Australia.[50]

For scholars of case studies and their publics, the Ubryk case points to the importance of transnational networks. While of most immediate concern to German-speaking liberals, the narrative of this Cracow nun soon reached an international audience. The broad reception of this narrative was due to its capacity, as a case study, to encapsulate the shocking and the familiar. The Ubryk case won such a wide public not simply because of its graphic detail, but because its outline was familiar to a reading public steeped in the literature of convent atrocity. Like the medical case study, the Ubryk case afforded this public the opportunity to indulge in sexual fantasy while deflecting the charge of lewdness. Readers of the lurid details of her confinement, rape, and torture could react with public outrage and secret pleasure.

The voyeuristic element should not eclipse, however, the power of such cases to reinforce sexual norms. As Michel Foucault has argued, discourses on perverse sexuality attained such disciplinary power because they simultaneously incited pleasure; "pleasure and power do not cancel or turn back against each other: they seek out, overlap, and reinforce one another."[51] The norm-creating function of the convent atrocity case becomes even more evident if we consider its mass public. The works of sexologists, for example, often had a small readership, but anti-Catholic narratives such as those concerning Ubryk captured an enormous audience, and, as such, they were crucial in establishing and reinforcing an ideology of gender and sexuality. Ubryk, after all, was both victim and villain. As the subject of rape and torture, she was clearly a figure of sympathy. Nevertheless, within conventional views of women's social destiny, Ubryk had erred in renouncing marriage and reproduction, and in embracing the alternative life of the nun. In so graphically describing the price to be paid for such a choice, cases such as that of Barbara Ubryk were a powerful means of establishing and maintaining gender and sexual norms.

NOTES

1. The convent captivity narrative has been most studied in the United States—see Jenny Franchot, *Roads to Rome: The Antebellum Protestant Encounter with Catholicism* (Berkeley: University of California Press, 1994); Barbara Welter, "From Maria Monk to Paul Blanchard," in *Uncivil Religion: Interreligious Hostility in America*, ed. Robert N. Bellah and Frederick E. Greenspahn (New York: Crossroad, 1987), 43–71, at 44; Daniel A. Cohen, "Miss Reed and the Superiors: The Contradictions of Convent Life in Antebellum America," *Journal of Social History* 30, no. 1 (1996): 149–84; Susan M. Griffin, "Awful Disclosures: Women's Evidence in the Escaped Nun's Tale," *PMLA* 111, no. 1 (1996): 93–107; Tracey Fessenden, "The Convent, the Brothel, and the Protestant Woman's Sphere," *Signs* 25, no. 2 (2000): 451–78; Marie Anne Pagliarini, "The Pure American Woman and the Wicked Catholic Priest: An Analysis of Anti-Catholic Literature in Antebellum America," *Religion and American Culture* 9, no. 1 (1999): 97–128. In France, see Caroline Ford, *Divided Houses: Religion and Gender in Modern France* (Ithaca NY: Cornell University Press, 2005). In Britain, see Rene Kollar, *A Foreign and Wicked Institution? The Campaign Against Convents in Victorian England* (Eugene: Pickwick, 2011).
2. The most comprehensive is Michael B. Gross, *The War Against Catholicism: Liberalism and the Anti-Catholic Imagination in Nineteenth-Century Germany* (Ann Arbor: University of Michigan Press, 2004), 157–70. See also Kollar, *Foreign and Wicked Institution*, chapter 4; Manuel Borutta, *Antikatholizismus* (Göttingen: Vandenhoeck & Ruprecht, 2010), 244–47.
3. Jean-Claude Passeron and Jacques Revel, *Penser par cas* (Paris: Éditions de l'École des hautes études en sciences sociales, 2005), 15.
4. Lauren Berlant, "On the Case," *Critical Inquiry* 33, no. 4 (2007): 663–72, at 671.
5. *Journal des Débats*, August 10, 1869.
6. *Albion, a Journal of News, Politics and Literature*, August 28, 1869.

7. *Times* (London), July 31, 1869.
8. Walter L. Arnstein, *Protestant versus Catholic in Mid-Victorian Britain: Mr Newdegate and the Nuns* (Columbia: University of Missouri Press, 1982).
9. See Britta McEwen, *Sexual Knowledge: Feeling, Fact, and Social Reform in Vienna, 1900–1934* (New York: Berghahn, 2012), 95.
10. Vernon A. Rosario, *The Erotic Imagination: French Histories of Perversity* (New York: Oxford University Press, 1997), 10.
11. In France, the first lengthy report was published in *Le Temps* and *La Liberté* on July 27, 1869, and the following day in *Le Siècle, Le Journal des Débats, Le Moniteur Universel,* and *L'Opinion Nationale.* For the United States, see *Philadelphia Public Ledger,* August 12, 1869; *Chicago Tribune,* August 13, 1869; *New York Times,* August 15, 1869; see also the *Sydney Morning Herald,* October 2, 1869.
12. *New York Times,* August 16, 1869; *Journal des Débats,* August 10, 1869.
13. Michael Warner, "Publics and Counterpublics," *Public Culture* 14, no. 1 (2002): 49–90, at 66.
14. *New York Times,* August 24, 1869; *Times* (London), August 13, 1869.
15. *Philadelphia Public Ledger,* August 12, 1869.
16. *Moniteur Universel,* July 28, 1869. Reprinted in the *New York Times,* August 15, 1869.
17. *Moniteur Universel,* August 10, 1869.
18. Warner, "Publics and Counterpublics," 62.
19. Michelet Papers, A4745, Bibliothèque Historique de la Ville de Paris. See Ford, *Divided Houses,* chapter 3, for an extended analysis of the case.
20. *The Trial of Saurin v. Star and Another: In the Court of Queen's Bench* (London: Diprose and Bateman, 1869).
21. Isaac Kelso, *Danger in the Dark: A Tale of Intrigue and Priestcraft* (Cincinnati: Moore, Anderson, Wilstach & Keys, 1854), 9.
22. Alfred Villeneuve, *Les mystères du cloître,* vol. 2 (Paris: Alexandre Cadot, 1846), 503.
23. *Tribune,* July 31, 1869.
24. *Journal des Débats,* July 28, 1869.
25. *The Convent Horror: Or, The True Narrative of Barbara Ubryk* (Philadelphia: C.W. Alexander, 1869); *Les amoureuses cloîtrées: Barbara Ubryk* (Paris: Librairie Générale, 1871); A. Rode, *Barbara Ubryk, oder die Geheimnisse des Karmeliter-Klosters in Krakau* (Munich: Neuburger and Kolb, 1869); *The Horrors of Roman Catholic Convents, Exposed in a True Heartrending Account of the Shocking Imprisonment and Sufferings of Sister Barbara* (London: n.p., 1872).
26. See, in an American context, Nina Baym, *Woman's Fiction: A Guide to Novels by and about Women in America, 1820–70* (Urbana-Champaign: University of Illinois, 1993).
27. Barbara Foley, *Telling the Truth: The Theory and Practice of Documentary Fiction* (Ithaca NY: Cornell University Press, 1986), 25–26.
28. David S. Reynolds, *Beneath the American Renaissance: The Subversive Imagination in the Age of Emerson and Melville* (New York: Knopf, 1988), esp. chapter 2.
29. *New York Weekly Herald,* August 21, 1869; *Siècle,* August 8, 1868.
30. *Les amoureuses cloîtrées,* 253.
31. Louise Michele Newman, *White Women's Rights: The Racial Origins of Feminism in the United States* (New York: Oxford University Press, 1999).
32. See Lisa Joy Pruitt, *A Looking-glass for Ladies: American Protestant Women and the Orient in the Nineteenth Century* (Macon GA: Mercer University Press, 2005).

33. *Siècle*, August 12, 1869.
34. For example, *Le Temps*, July 27, 1869.
35. Cited in Gross, *War Against Catholicism*, 161.
36. "Barbara Ubryk und das Nonnenwesen vom ärztlichen Standpunkte," *Wiener medizinische Wochenschrift* 19 (1869): 1111–13, at 1112.
37. Hector Landouzy, *Traité complet de l'hystérie* (Paris: Baillière, 1846), 186.
38. Auguste Debay, *Hygiène et physiologie du mariage* (Paris: Dentu, 1859), 17.
39. Debay, *Hygiène et physiologie du mariage*, 18.
40. Dr. Pierre Briquet, *Un traité clinique et thérapeutique de l'hystérie* (Paris: Baillière, 1859), 132.
41. Henry Maudsley, *The Physiology and Pathology of the Mind* (London: Macmillan, 1867), 210.
42. Richard von Krafft-Ebing, *Psychopathia Sexualis*, 12th ed., trans. F. J. Rebman (New York: Rebman, 1906), 8.
43. Cited in Richard D. E. Burton, *Holy Tears, Holy Blood: Women, Catholicism, and the Culture of Suffering in France, 1840–1970* (Ithaca NY: Cornell University Press, 2004), 181; Jan Goldstein, "The Hysteria Diagnosis and the Politics of Anticlericalism in Late Nineteenth-Century France," *Journal of Modern History* 54, no. 2 (1982): 209–39; Cristina Mazzoni, *Saint Hysteria: Neurosis, Mysticism, and Gender in European Culture* (Ithaca NY: Cornell University Press, 1996).
44. Peter Cryle and Lisa Downing, "Feminine Sexual Pathologies," *Journal of the History of Sexuality* 18, no. 1 (2009): 1–7, at 2.
45. "Barbara Ubryk und das Nonnenwesen vom ärztlichen Standpunkte," *Wiener medizinische Wochenschrift* 19 (1869): 1243–46, at 1245.
46. Claude Langlois, *Le catholicisme au féminin: Les congrégations françaises à supérieure générale au XIXe siècle* (Paris: Éditions du Cerf, 1984).
47. Carmen M. Mangion, "Women, Religious Ministry and Female Institution Building," in *Women, Gender and Religious Cultures in Britain, 1800–1940*, ed. Sue Morgan (Abingdon: Routledge, 2010), 72–93, at 79.
48. Mary Ewens, "Women in the Convent," in *American Catholic Women: A Historical Exploration*, ed. Karen Kennelly (New York: Macmillan, 1989), 17–47, at 21.
49. *Harper's Weekly*, February 26, 1870.
50. *The Convent Horror: The True Story of Barbara Ubryk* (Toronto: British Canadian, 1893); *The Horrors of the Carmelite Nunnery, or, The Life of Sister Barbara: The Carmelite Nun, Imprisoned for 21 Years in a Dungeon* (Sydney: Margaret L. Shepherd, 1902).
51. Michel Foucault, *The History of Sexuality*, trans. Robert Hurley, vol. 1, *An Introduction* (London: Vintage, 1990), 48.

7 The Curious Case/s of Dr. Wallace

Sexuality and the Medical File in Postwar Australia

Lisa Featherstone

The aging, hastily scrawled case files of a general practitioner from midcentury Melbourne might, at the outset, appear to be a rather dry resource for the historian of sexuality. Yet the case files of Dr. Victor Wallace (1893–1977) provide a rich and complicated archive for understanding sexuality in Australia in the 1940s and 1950s.[1] A prominent eugenicist, Wallace ran a much-needed birth control clinic in working-class Melbourne, one of Australia's largest cities. He also ran a successful private practice that provided both general medical care and contraception. Alongside these endeavors, Wallace encouraged a slow but steady clientele who sought out his self-developed form of sexual therapy. Wallace's practice proved a surprising success, in the years before either psychoanalysis or psychotherapy were well established in Australia. Between 1938 and 1954, eighty-nine men and women consulted Wallace for advice on sexual dysfunctions ranging from physical problems to psychological and social issues.

Created primarily as scientific documents, Wallace's case files allow us a nuanced consideration of how discourses on sex and sexuality were embedded into the social and medical frameworks of postwar Australia. On the surface, the case files are technologies of medicine, yet they reveal multiple intersections between sex, science, and society. This chapter considers the curious "case" of Victor Wallace himself. Wallace, as a birth controller, a eugenicist, and a sex therapist, dedicated his time to issues that other doctors considered unnecessary, unviable, and even unsavory. This chapter is also a study of Wallace's case notes on sexual dysfunction, examining how his case files inscribed medical meaning onto patients' lack of knowledge, and their illness, unhappiness, and despair. Lastly, this chapter is the story of his patients themselves. Wallace's case files offer a fragmentary glimpse of those who sought his help for a range of sexual problems. The case files, though mediated by Wallace and various protocols of medical science, suggest ways in which Australian men and women constructed ideal sexuality and their own sexual identities. The same files also offer indications about the efforts of these men and women to negotiate the specific demands of postwar sexual cultures.

I begin with a brief overview of the Wallace archive, to situate it within postwar Australian society. This is followed by an analysis of how the case files themselves might be read and understood. Case files were, and are, a very specific form of knowledge structure, bound by the conventions of medical science and practice. Nonetheless, Wallace himself frequently tested the boundaries of the case file genre. The chapter then offers a close analysis of a number of specific cases to explore the ways Wallace developed and used medical typologies to write his case files—and, by extension, to treat his patients. This study allows us to consider the plasticity of the medical case file, how it could be utilized by the individual practitioner, and the ways it simultaneously conformed to *and* defied wider medical narratives.

WALLACE'S ARCHIVE OF "SEXUAL PROBLEMS"

Dr. Victor Wallace was born and educated in Melbourne. Trained in Australia and Britain, as a young doctor he traveled widely through Europe and Asia.[2] He resettled back in Melbourne, and by the middle of the twentieth century, Wallace was most famous in Melbourne as a eugenicist. Indeed, his ideas on racial politics underscored much of his other work, and were most obviously present in his work on birth control.[3] Wallace was a founding member of the Eugenics Society of Victoria, formed in 1936, and he remained active in the society until its closure in the early 1960s. As such, he was a progressive and an activist: while eugenics rightly fell into disrepute after the tragedies of World War II, in the interwar years many eugenicists promoted social engineering as a vehicle towards a better society.[4] His 1946 book, *Women and Children First* made clear that Wallace was a humanitarian of sorts, though he considered the world through certain racialized, gendered, and nationalist frameworks. He was both sympathetic to the plight of individual women needing birth control, and critically aware of the broader eugenic implications of reproduction among the poor.[5]

It is unclear why Wallace chose to encourage sex therapy within his practice. We can speculate that this was simply an extension of his broader interests in the female body, gynaecology, and birth control. He was interested in sex education too, and gave a series of talks to adult education students in the mid-1950s, raising his profile as a doctor with an interest in sexuality.[6] That sex therapy rested at the intersection between biomedicine and social improvement may also have attracted Wallace to the area. Wallace was certainly interested in the relationship between sexuality, marriage, and divorce. He was a founding member of the Melbourne Marriage Guidance Council (1948) and the long-term Australian editor of the international journal *Marriage Hygiene*. His interest in marriage and sexuality was reflected in his patient base: nearly all of his clients were married or engaged, explicitly seeking help for a sexual dysfunction that was disrupting their marital life.

The people who sought Wallace's help were of all ages, from a handful of teens brought in by concerned parents, some very young wives (newly-weds in their late teens or very early twenties), to men and women aged in their seventies. Almost all were married; the majority were in their twenties, reflecting their age when first married. They came from all classes, and, for the era, represented an assortment of ethnicities. More than 50 percent of Wallace's clients were men.[7] His patients presented with a range of problems, including physical irregularities, a low sex drive, marital distress, or significant psychological trauma. They articulated a lack of sexual desire, or perhaps too much desire. They complained of the inability to consummate a relationship, or they came because they were simply unable to manage the mechanics of sex and/or orgasm.

These men and women shared an expectation—even a faith—that science could fix their problems connected with sexuality. And even with disparate problems, they all shared the belief that a happy sexual life was integral to life itself. They sought advice, which was expensive and most likely embarrassing, because they wanted to "fix" their sexual lives, and hence restore themselves to sexual and social normality. The men and women had often read sexology texts, and some had attended sex education lectures. Most not only understood the mechanics of sex, but also its contemporary meanings. Indeed, the majority were concerned that they were performing sex "incorrectly": too fast, too slow, too passionate, not passionate enough. This was because in Australia of the 1940s and 1950s, sex was defined in quite specific ways, drawing on wider Western traditions developed in the United States and Britain. An ideal sexuality was strictly imagined as heterosexual, penetrative, and culminating in mutual orgasm. This ideal, though originally articulated by medical science (including sexology and psychology) was popularized through myriad sex education texts and marriage manuals throughout the interwar and postwar periods.[8] The very strict ways in which sexuality was defined ensured that incalculable anxieties about sexual performance were experienced by both men and women.

Such anxieties were reflected in individuals' willingness to seek Dr. Wallace's treatment for sexual dysfunction. In doing so, these men and women were stepping outside the sexual norms of 1950s Australia, where sex was still something essentially private and hidden.[9] Though establishments such as the Church, medical doctors, and morals crusaders had begun to speak slightly more openly about sex and sexuality in the years during and after World War II, this was nonetheless a discourse of authority, and there was little public space for discussion of sex by ordinary men and women. And yet, paradoxically, while individuals were actively discouraged from speaking about sex, they were nonetheless encouraged to pursue a healthy and active sexual union—but only within the privacy of the marital home. With rising divorce rates a feature of postwar life, sex between husband and wife was seen as key to a happy marriage, and social (and political) stability.[10] Wallace's case files mirror contemporary fears about marital sexuality; the clinical notes reflect a medical genre, as well as a social expectation about the way sex was to be performed and practiced.

THE WALLACE CASE FILES AND THE CASE FILE GENRE

Historian Warwick Anderson has suggested that the case file has an historical genealogy beginning in hospitals of the late eighteenth century. In hospitals and in asylums, doctors increasingly categorized illness in terms of the individual, with the focus shifting from patients to patient, and from the disease to the individual diseased body. The case file was, as Michel Foucault indicates, an attempt to clinically discipline the body, ascribing to it a specific biomedical problem through the process of categorization.[11] The case file highlighted those ways in which an individual's body diverged from normality. Through its typology, the case file defined normality and recorded individual deviancy. Once diagnosed, the diseased body was then available for treatment and, ideally, cure. Any cure, however, was wholly dependent upon the written inscription of pathology found in the case file itself.[12]

Working in private practice, Wallace was not confined by the bureaucratic practices of the hospital, yet his case files took on many of the same generic traits of medical process. Though a general practitioner, his files were always under threat of surveillance from other medical professionals, or indeed potentially from the law. Physically, his case files represented the ideal: each patient was allocated his or her own small card/s, containing dense, handwritten notes on history, symptoms, diagnosis, and treatment. Each file was then stored in alphabetical order, with others he classified as "Sexual Problems." Wallace drew on a model system, a genre, honed through nearly one hundred years of the individual case file, and related, as Anderson suggests, to other methods used by disciplining bureaucracies, such as police files and the army service record.[13]

By the early twentieth century, the medical case file relied on "objective" means of diagnosis, such as the physical examination, the blood or laboratory test, and the x-ray. These existed, of course, in the material and the mechanistic, with the doctor able to record tangible "facts" about a patient's condition.[14] Yet Wallace only rarely called upon such clinical methods; not even simple data such as blood pressure readings are recorded. He was not, it appears, an empiricist.

What Wallace did record, however, was a raft of impressions, both physical and psychological. Throughout his case notes there is an uneasy meeting between the anatomical (the diminutive penis of one patient; the underdeveloped clitoris of another) and the psychological (the horrible childhood of one; the Oedipal complex of another). In the case files, it is the psychological that dominates, yet it does so in a way that does not implicitly embrace psychoanalysis. As in psychoanalysis, the patient was urged to be confessional, on the premise of confidentiality.[15] Yet there was not the element of "performance" that is so often found in the psychoanalytic case file. As historian Joy Damousi has suggested, Wallace did indeed embrace some notion of a talking cure.[16] Certainly, he encouraged his patients to discuss their sexual problems with him, and to perhaps gain some relief from doing so. But Wallace did not use a serious psychoanalytic framework for treatment in the manner of a handful of other Australian doctors who were his contemporaries, such as Reginald Ellery (1897–1955) or Paul Dane (1881–1950).[17] Wallace did approve of psychoanalysis—and he did refer a few of his patients to psychoanalysts—but he knew that not everyone had the finances or the time to undergo psychoanalysis. Thus Wallace largely conducted his sex counseling outside of psychoanalytic frameworks, working to a more clinical, medical model. He saw most patients only once, occasionally twice. He depended instead on a medicinal framework, where the ultimate "cure" was to come through rather dubious drug therapies. His use of medications and hormones represented an effort to treat the physical, but also a form of expediting treatment for those who could not undergo a full talking cure.

Unsurprisingly then, Wallace's case file records reflect a medical model: they define key symptoms, diagnosis, and a treatment plan. His was a system searching for efficiency. Indeed, many of Wallace's case files have a certain similarity about them: the terms "failure to orgasm" or "impotence" diagnosed generally complex physiological and psychological problems. Instead of delving into the labyrinth of meanings, however, he aimed to solve the immediate issue: through the nosological process, the disease or deviancy was rendered coherent. In his case files, Wallace was seemingly never troubled by fragmentation or inconsistency. He always offered a firm and decisive diagnosis, which he often underlined in pen or pencil, presumably to highlight its certainty.

Yet to the historian, the case files offer little clarity. First, the provenance of the case files and their archive is troubling. The case files follow medical protocols in form and function, giving a sense of Wallace's self-surveillance. If ever questioned, he could point out that his files met the public parameters of clinical practice. And yet, were the case files ever meant to be accessed or read by a public? These files—and also other records in Wallace's broader archive—reveal astoundingly intimate details of his patients' lives. Domestic violence, sexual problems, drug abuse, seemingly unmentionable desires; all of these are laid open in the files, and through the archival process, to the public. It is unclear if Wallace intended this at the time of writing. His case notes have the feel of a busy doctor in general practice, scribbling notes as a reminder of his processes and treatments. Wallace did not, to my knowledge, publish any of these case files as case studies in medical journals.[18] Probably he had not yet "realized" or imagined his public.[19] When his archive was donated to the University of Melbourne archives, however, these case files were included alongside his public writings and lectures. Although use of the case files is technically restricted (permission must be sought from the family to access the archive), and all names must be changed in publications, the twenty-first-century historian represents a new form of public that was most likely unintended.

My uncertainty over the legitimacy of reading and utilizing these case files in historical research is compounded by the fractured nature of the files themselves. Though seemingly offering coherent narratives of illness, treatment, and (ideally) cure, the case files cannot be read in such a simplistic fashion. Laura Doan has carefully articulated that, as a genre to be historicized, the sexological case study (or, in this instance, the case file) is problematic, because it tells us about "the knowledge practices of a very few, professionals in medicine and the law, the educated elite, and artistic or bohemian [types]."[20] This is certainly true of the Wallace case files, which largely record what Wallace perceived to be important. The case files are multiple constructions, layer upon layer, some of which cannot be fully unpacked. A patient sought an appointment with a doctor, and told a selective narrative, including a case history and an articulation of the so-called problem. The doctor took brief notes, following the medical protocols developed through the nineteenth century, to "construct a single narrative" of the disorder.[21] Wallace was perhaps unusual in attempting to quote verbatim from the patient: the effort to collect the patient's own words seems both an attempt to capture the client's own view and an attempt to highlight the perceived problem. The doctor observed that by taking notes, he decided what was ultimately "important" and discarded the rest. Occasionally further clinical markers were sought, but only rarely: the physical examination was far less important to Wallace than the collection of the discursive constructions. As in psychoanalysis, talking and listening were central to the medical process, and to the formation of the case file, but Wallace was hampered by time constraints and a modern model of efficiency. Of course it is unclear from the case files just how much of this "history" was a narrative articulated by the patient, and how much was a discussion with the doctor. Either way, however, it was the doctor who, in the end, built the case file itself, and left a tangible record for the historian.

Once a case history was established and scribed, Wallace would then establish a diagnosis, mapping it onto the body of the patient, and in doing so define his or her pathology. This was based on his listening to the patient, but also on Wallace's own clinical, sexological, and social knowledge. As Charles Rosenberg terms it, the diagnosis can be described as both a "ritual" and a means of communication; a dense negotiation between clinical authority of the doctor, and the lived experience of the patient.[22] In the Wallace files, it was nonetheless *recorded* by the doctor himself: diagnosis was short and sharp, a few words at most. Written diagnosis was a way of regulating the patient's unruly or uncooperative body, and rendering it formally into a system of bureaucracy, which would almost inevitably include a plan for treatment. This process of diagnosis was certainly imposed upon the body of the patient by the medical authority or expert, but in the Wallace files it was not necessarily an unwelcome imposition. The patients actively sought a diagnosis, given that it was in fact the starting point for a cure. Having diagnosed the patient, Wallace would then treat him or her, through medication, hormones, sex education or advice, or—very occasionally—surgery. All of this was carefully noted in the case file, which served the dual function of archival document and pragmatic assistant, should the patient ever return for a second consultation. Most did not return, however, and the case file remained merely a static moment; an instant that, for the historian-public, remains tantalizingly brief, and an often cursory, even formulaic construction of one element in one life.

If we turn now to the case files themselves, we can see the very specific ways in which the case file was constructed and ordered. I see the case file as an uneven negotiation between patient and doctor, but one in which power and knowledge are primarily articulated by and through the doctor. The patient's agency is in seeking advice. Wallace's patients were often very explicitly engaged with the postwar ideal of a harmonious marital sexuality: some noted quite openly that their sexual dysfunction made them fear for their marriage. In this sense, sexual modernity was ever present, but nonetheless fragmented and complex, and the case files themselves reflect these tensions between reticence and discourse, modesty and confession.

THE CASE FILE: DIAGNOSING MRS. DIANA JACKSON

In 1948, Mrs. Diana Jackson sought Wallace's advice for her problematic sexual life. On examining Diana's case file, a few simple details are revealed at the outset: her age ("31 years"); the fact that she was married with two children, aged "7 and 4.5," and that she had been fitted with a pessary four years prior. Wallace framed her problem as she herself saw it, recording, "her complaint is that she reaches orgasm before intromission." The doctor took notes on the specifics of the sexual encounter:

> Her husband stimulates her clitoris "for quite a good while" before-hand. Breasts stimulated also. Entry then takes place and lasts about 3 minutes. That is when she feels that she could scream and push her husband.

He also recorded that she "could go for 2 weeks without thinking about intercourse," although the rest of the case file is notably brief.

Wallace's diagnosis, marked at the bottom of page, was "initial over-stimulation." This is a rather more specific diagnosis than Wallace normally offered. Where he might have recorded simply "failure to orgasm," which was his general routine, he chose a more detailed, yet rather nontechnical diagnosis. In this case, it was on to treatment, both medicinal and glaringly pragmatic:

1. phenobarbital grt 1 hr before intercourse
2. cut out excessive stimulation

Phenobarbital is a barbiturate now used to stem seizures, but it also has sedative and hypnotic properties. Wallace was prescribing a depressive drug, which would slow down the central nervous system, because Diana was reaching orgasm at the "wrong" moment. Apparently Diana herself was happy enough with the results. Later the same year, she returned to Wallace, to report that she now had the orgasm after sex, albeit still with manual stimulation. It was, as Wallace carefully noted, "not yet simultaneous." Diana herself thought "things are definitely improving," and she and Wallace both seemed to look forward to a time when she would experience the appropriate feminine response to 1950s heterosex—that is, simultaneous orgasm during penetrative intercourse.

Diana's case file reveals the complex interactions between the clinical (the careful recording of case notes; the prescription of medicine) and the cultural (the very idea that an orgasm before intercourse was somehow "wrong"; the concept that scientific, medical sex counseling could "solve" the perceived problem). Medical historians have long indicated the cultural constructions of science and medicine, and the Wallace case files suggest, too, that outside of the strictures of the hospital, the potential for slippage between clinical and cultural views was even greater. In the case of Diana, the "problem," the diagnosis, the treatment, and indeed the patient's response to the treatment, were constructed around postwar expectations of gender, sex, and the social order. The case file of Diana, then, was a reflection of broader cultural capital, rather than simply a record of a medical process.

THE CASE FILE: MAISY JAMES AND SEX AS DUTY

In mid-1951, Maisy James consulted Wallace, presenting with what proved to be a common problem for his patients. The case file records that Maisy was thirty-three years old, and had given birth to three children, after which she had been sterilized. Her problem, as Wallace recorded it, was that she had "no inclination for intercourse. Does it as a duty." Wallace noted that sex left "her quite unsatisfied." Sex could be quite painful. Wallace recorded further specific details about her sex life, including that intercourse took five to ten minutes, and that she had only had an orgasm once or twice in her thirteen years of married life. Her lack of desire was probably tied to her unsatisfactory marriage: as Wallace noted, "*Husband has become very lax in telling her how much he loves her. He doesn't show it much* [underline in the original]."

Wallace diagnosed Maisy's case as an "absence of sexual satisfaction," and noted that she was also asthmatic and "nervy." This case file indicates that Wallace's approach existed at the boundaries of marital counseling, sexual therapy, and general practice. There are clearly personal issues within Maisy's marriage, and perhaps gynaecological issues too. Many of Wallace's case files reveal these complex sociomedical problems: patients were suffering not merely from biological sexual conditions, but from a raft of psychological, interpersonal, and social/cultural distresses. In Maisy's case, although there were multiple layers causing her lack of desire, she was simply treated with drugs. Wallace prescribed phenobarbital (a relaxant), Phenergan (an antihistamine with a side effect of sedation), and Hepasol compound (an iron and vitamin supplement).

It is intriguing that Maisy sought treatment: the consultation was likely embarrassing and uncomfortable for her. But by this period, sex was increasingly constructed as central to married life, and a number of Wallace's male and female patients explicitly stated that they feared their sexual problems would lead irretrievably to divorce. Maisy was treated with substantial medication to relax and sedate her, so that she too could supposedly experience the elusive orgasm. Her case file, including diagnosis and treatment plan, moved well beyond the biomedical to reveal the cultural meanings attached to female orgasm and an active sexual life within marriage.

THE CASE FILE: EDVARD BOMASIS AND THE PROBLEMS OF MEN

Wallace's case files reveal that men too were treated with a host of medications for what may have been social ills. The case file of Edvard Bomasis is illustrative. Edvard was a forty-two-year-old laborer, and an immigrant from what was then Czechoslovakia. Like many of the case files of male patients, Edvard's file is short and to the point. Generally men sought help from Wallace for two reasons: impotence or premature ejaculation. Wallace did not attempt to examine these in any great depth, suggesting that he regarded these as less interesting or less complex.

Edvard sought treatment from Wallace in 1953, after being in Australia for four years, and it is likely that he was an immigrant or displaced person at the end of World War II. Unusually for Wallace's patients, Edvard was not married, but he was nonetheless concerned about his own impotence. He had previously been able to have intercourse, and had indeed caught syphilis when younger, which had been treated in Europe with penicillin and bismuth. But by 1953, he was unable to have intercourse: "I try many times but it hangs down limply." Wallace summarized his case history very briefly, and diagnosed "impotence."

Edvard had probably suffered through multiple traumas both during and after the war. Now, as a recent migrant to a white Australia, he was still suffering, and, as Wallace noted, "says he is just a shadow of himself." Despite this allusion to broader distress, his problem of impotence was treated clinically, rather than with counseling or psychotherapy. He was given syrup of neurophosphates (a stimulant) and testosterone propionate—an injection of testosterone. This form of testosterone was short-lasting, and was very unlikely to have helped Edvard to any ongoing resolution.

As his case files reveal, Wallace tended towards a pharmaceutical response, even when there were substantial social and cultural issues at play. Sometimes he offered practical advice about sexual positions or sex education. He also gave fairly pragmatic advice to cases of domestic violence and broader marital problems. However, medication was the most important regime/solution/cure: all else was generally dispensed in conjunction with some form of serious drug therapy, including injections of testosterone for both men and women. His case notes reveal that for Wallace, sex therapy was as much about retaining hormonal balance as it was about the social and cultural aspects of sex. He was more interested in the biological than the culturally constructed factors, though of course he did himself culturally construct sex in certain specific, heterosexual ways.

THE CASE FILE: ELUDING DIAGNOSIS, MR. JIM WILSON

In March 1952, Jim Wilson, a clerk of twenty-seven years old, visited Dr. Wallace for the first time. The case file reveals his "problem," supposedly in his own words: "I'm contemplating marriage, but I have no attraction for women." Wallace took a rather substantial case history, noting that while his health had generally been good, Jim had suffered a nervous breakdown, lasting some four months. "He had no idea what brought it on." The case reveals he had been in the air force for three years, which had heightened his "nervous worrying disposition," and he was given shock treatment while in the armed forces. Neither patient nor doctor seems to have linked Jim's anxiety and breakdown to his sexuality: his mental illness was constructed merely as a part of the diligent case history, rather than as an integral part of the story of the current "problem." Only the case file itself, with its attention to chronology, hints at a connection.

According to the record, Jim had regarded himself as sexually "normal" until about five months prior to the consultation with Wallace. Although he had been in the air force from ages eighteen to twenty-one, he had not taken up any of the more obvious offers of sexual intercourse, largely because any form of petting led to ejaculation. As Wallace recorded (and underlined), *"has had no complete sexual intercourse because he just couldn't."* After this seemingly alarming confession, Wallace backtracked, and began a simple Freudian case history of the family, noting that Jim was more attached to his mother than to his father, but "was not *very* strongly attached to his mother." Wallace also noted that Jim had not had a proper sex education, and that he was not overly religious. The case file then leaps once again to Jim's present problem, that of his fiancée. While the young woman herself was "cooperative," Jim had been unable to have intercourse. This was apparently a shock to him: he had believed that he could have sex if he wanted, or if he were married. Instead, he found himself unable to get an erection "under any circumstances." Jim was concerned that he would not be able to fulfill his "sexual obligations" to his future wife.

This was a more complex case than those of most men who consulted Wallace, who were largely given drugs or hormones to treat either erectile or ejaculatory dysfunction. The case of Jim was rather more puzzling, and required a far longer case study. Again, Wallace backtracked to the sexual history. Jim did not masturbate much, but had long experienced insecurities about his body and sexuality. Wallace's notes in the case file directly contradict Jim's own statement that he had been sexually "normal." In fact, Wallace uncovered a messy rumble of sexual problems, not necessarily in any chronological order, but building to show a raft of sexual insecurities from the earliest ages. From the time he was fourteen, Jim had been afraid to undress at school; in the air force he had only associated with men; as a child he had been terribly frightened when his mother caught him masturbating, and threatened to cut off his penis. All of these histories led, slowly and indirectly, to his current problem: no sexual interest in his fiancée, or in women generally.

Through this case file, we can read the importance of the "public" in the case file, and its impact on determining diagnosis. In 1952, Jim's public was confined to one person: Dr. Wallace, who diagnosed him rather elusively with "sexual psychosis (with impotence)." A later public might have questioned this idea of psychosis—with its implications of madness—and wondered instead about the homosocial, homosexual, or asexual nature of Jim.[23] Despite his apparent interest in Jim's case, Wallace seems to have been unable or unwilling to investigate outside of the heterosexual. Perhaps this reflects the framework of Jim's presentation: he sought out medical care as a heterosexual man, unable to have sex with any women including his willing girlfriend. He had also experienced some form of sexual pleasure with women before, even if he had not had intercourse. In the case file there is no record that Jim himself thought at all outside these parameters of heterosexuality. Further, he did not disclose any dreams or desires that might have been thought of as "perversions": he was simply a man engaged to be married who was concerned he could not fulfill his marital duties to his future wife.

There is no way to know whether Jim was homosexual, heterosexual, or had desires outside of this binary system of definitions. It is more useful to consider the ways in which Wallace constructed this problematic case file. In the written record, Wallace does not even engage with the idea that Jim might not be heterosexual: heterosexuality was an assumption throughout Wallace's case histories, as articulated in the patient's own presentation, and in the doctor's assessment. This is not necessarily surprising: in Australia of the 1950s and 1960s, homosexuality was still illegal, and men were most likely reluctant to discuss their camp activities for fear of persecution or prosecution. Further, this is a period in which medicine was still negotiating the possibilities and meanings of homosexuality. World War II had highlighted the potential for homosexual activities amongst troops, and, as Garry Wotherspoon has suggested, it was no longer possible to avoid public knowledge of camp men.[24] In 1948, the American biologist Alfred Kinsey had released his sensational sexological report, which indicated that statistically, same-sex desires and actions were commonplace. The Kinsey report was widely debated in the Australian press, and again, this ensured that homosexuality was in the public imagination. As historians have shown, the 1950s represent a particularly striking moment in homosexual history, with increased policing, outraged discussions in the media, and far greater *public* debate about the deviancy of the camp man.[25]

Some of this wider context may have infiltrated medical practice. Within the court system, doctors and psychiatrists were engaged in strenuous debates over the meanings of homosexuality and the way it was marked upon the body.[26] Other doctors—including Wallace himself—would have read the extensive international sexological literature on homosexuality. The *Medical Journal of Australia* also ran a small number of articles and editorials on homosexuality in this period, engaging quite explicitly with ideas from Europe and the United States.[27] Yet little from these complex debates appears to have filtered down to this one general practitioner in Melbourne. We might speculate that this was due to his clientele. Wallace was a prominent eugenicist, concerned with building a strong and healthy white race; he is unlikely to have attracted those generally constructed as dysgenic. Wallace aimed for normality in both sex and gender roles. Through his procedures of diagnosis and treatment, he aimed to restore the abnormal to the normal.

Thus Wallace's diagnosis of Jim was unspecific, and hinted simply towards madness. Despite the seeming complexity of his diagnosis of psychosis, which might be expected to require a raft of medical interventions, his treatment plan was simple and heteronormative. Jim was to "invite his girl to produce an erection by manipulation or otherwise": Wallace, it seems, was hopeful that Jim's male hydraulic sexuality would assert itself, returning him to a normative heterosexuality. He was also given a tonic, "syrup neurophosphates," a placebo stimulant which was thought to increase desire.

Jim visited Wallace only the once, but the limitation of this doctor's medical care is quite clear. Jim was not, and could not be, imagined as anything other than a heterosexual man who was simply not being aroused in the correct fashion. There is a sense that there was some form of pathology in Wallace's clinical notation of "sexual psychosis," but the treatment that followed was no more than an attempt at social normalization, and a very limited one at that. Wallace actively avoided categorization and pathologization: he stuck to the center, looking for normality, rather than deviancy. Any hints of what might have been considered deviancy were avoided, and the patient steered back to the idealized norms of the postwar period.

THE CASE FILE: THE INCURABLE AUSTIN BRYAN

As these case files suggest, treatment by Wallace was sporadic, imprecise, and rather uncertain. He treated most clients with a medley of listening, drugs, and hormones, and with varying success. Others were simply untreatable. One such case was Austin Bryan, a manufacturing agent who sought Wallace's assistance in 1946. His case file reveals that he was forty-five years old, and had been married for seventeen years; he claimed that during this time he had never had complete sexual intercourse with his wife. She was not keen on intercourse, saying "it was a dirty habit." As retold in the case file (first by Austin and then by Wallace), "she said intercourse had nothing to do with love, and that it wasn't necessary." Instead of penetrative sex, Wallace recorded that Austin would

> satisfy himself by "getting rid of semen" by *friction between her thighs*. It was about 20 minutes to ½ an hour before ejaculation took place. He thinks that *that practice made him a nervous wreck*.

Austin originally sought treatment for his wife, as he wanted children. His wife expressed no aversion to children, but nor did she seem to actively desire any. (The case notes, of course, provide only Austin's side of the story: his wife is a passive participant in the narrative.) But it was clear that Austin was himself suffering from his own sexual problems. After eight years of marriage and intercrural intercourse, he was to experience a nervous breakdown: he was, he claimed, *"mad for complete sexual intercourse."* During this period, he attempted to rape his wife, or, as he explained it to Wallace, to "assert his marital rights." Unsurprisingly, after this she refused any sexual contact at all. He continued to try, however, to have sex, but his wife's refusal "discouraged him and disheartened him." It called into question his very masculinity, and his every desire was pathologized so that he felt as if he were "raping his own sister."

From this time onwards, Austin became totally impotent with his wife or any other woman, and his marriage was eventually annulled because it was never consummated. His inadequate sexual life resulted in the end of his marriage, and quite possibly compromised his mental health. Wallace kept no record of any treatment, which was unusual: most of the time he did offer male patients something concrete, generally drugs or hormones. But this seemed a hopeless case, with the marriage already ended, and he recorded no treatment of any kind.

CONCLUSIONS: INTERSECTIONS BETWEEN
THE SCIENTIFIC AND THE SOCIAL

The Wallace archives reflect and illustrate a key feature of the case file: its mobility. Wallace's case file operated first as a medical technology, a piece of writing in a specific genre that follows the conventions of medical protocol.

It offered a case history, diagnosis, and generally a treatment plan, derived by the doctor after consultation and some negotiation with the patient. The patient's voice, when it appears, is always mediated through the vision of the doctor. Yet just as it operated as a function of medical authority, so too the case file reflects the social and cultural discourses of the day.

The Wallace case files reflect a significant piece of postwar sexual history: the construction of an active sexual life as central to marital happiness and indeed marital success, and, within this, the centrality of the mutual orgasm. If sex was to be performed, it was to be done in certain ways—active penetration by the husband, leading to eventual mutual orgasm. While this ideal of penetrative sexuality was well recorded in marriage manuals and sex education texts, the Wallace files reveal just how clearly this idea was received, accepted, and rearticulated by ordinary men and women. Perhaps surprisingly, given their status as scientific documents, the case files of Dr. Wallace reveal the depth of the social constructions of sexuality, as they move well beyond a clinical interpretation to reveal the cultural dimensions of sex in postwar Australia.

NOTES

1. Group 17 Patient History Cards, 17/5/2, Sexual Problems, Male and Female, 1938–1954, Random ½ Box, Wallace Papers, University of Melbourne Archives, Melbourne. I would like to thank the Wallace family for permission to use these files. All names of patients have been changed to protect identities.
2. Grant McBurnie, "Wallace, Victor Hugo (1893–1977)," *Australian Dictionary of Biography*, National Centre of Biography, Australian National University, see http://www.adb.anu.edu.au/biography/wallace-victor-hugo-11943/text21405 (accessed July 16, 2011).
3. Jane Carey, "The Racial Imperatives of Sex: Birth Control and Eugenics in Britain, the United States and Australia in the Interwar Years," *Women's History Review* 21, no. 5 (2012): 733–52.
4. See Michael Roe, *Nine Australian Progressives: Vitalism in Bourgeois Social Thought* (Brisbane: University of Queensland, 1984).
5. Victor H. Wallace, *Women and Children First: An Outline of a Population Policy for Australia* (Melbourne: Oxford University Press, 1946).
6. See Group 4 Lectures, "Sex, Marriage and Family—First Series," 4/2, Wallace Papers, University of Melbourne Archives, Melbourne.
7. For a more detailed analysis of Wallace's patients, see Lisa Featherstone, "Penetrative Pleasures: A Case Study of Sex Therapy in 1940s and 1950s Australia," currently under review.
8. Lisa Featherstone, *Let's Talk About Sex: Histories of Sexuality in Australia from Federation to the Pill* (Cambridge: Cambridge Scholarly Press, 2011), chapter 9.
9. See Featherstone, *Let's Talk About Sex*, chapter 9.
10. Lisa Featherstone, "'The one single primary cause': Divorce, the Family and Heterosexual Pleasure in Postwar Australia," *Journal of Australian Studies* 37, no. 3 (2013): 349–63.
11. Michel Foucault, *The Birth of the Clinic: An Archaeology of Medical Perception* (New York: Vintage, 1994), 89.

12. Marc Berg and Geoffrey Bowker, "The Multiple Bodies of the Medical Record: Toward a Sociology of an Artifact," *Sociological Quarterly* 38, no. 3 (1997): 513–37, at 519.

13. See Warwick Anderson, this volume, for a comprehensive analysis of the "paper technology" of the case file.

14. Charles E. Rosenberg, "The Tyranny of Diagnosis: Specific Entities and Individual Experience," *Milbank Quarterly* 80, no. 2 (2002): 245–46.

15. See Joy Damousi, this volume.

16. Joy Damousi, *Freud in the Antipodes: A Cultural History of Psychoanalysis in Australia* (Sydney: University of New South Wales Press, 2005), 64–65.

17. See Damousi, *Freud in the Antipodes*; see also MS 7979, 1910–1950, Reg S. (Reginald Spencer) Ellery Papers, State Library of Victoria, Melbourne.

18. However, in his eugenic text, *Women and Children First*, Wallace did publish many revelations from his patients who sought birth control. See Lisa Featherstone, "Sexy Mamas? Women, Sexuality and Reproduction in Australia in the 1940s," *Australian Historical Studies* 37, no. 126 (2005): 234–52.

19. See Michael Warner, "Publics and Counterpublics," *Public Cultures* 14, no. 1 (2002): 49–90, at 55.

20. Laura Doan, "The Nurse, the Clerk, His Wife, and Her 'Lover': The Case Study in the History of Sexuality," (keynote address presented at the conference "Cases and their Publics: Interdisciplinary and Transnational Perspectives on the Case Study Genre," hosted by the University of Melbourne, September 26–28, 2011), 1–12, at 12.

21. Steve Sturdy, "Scientific Method for Medical Practitioners: The Case Method of Teaching Pathology in Early Twentieth-Century Edinburgh," *Bulletin of the History of Medicine* 81, no. 4 (Winter 2007): 760–92, at 775.

22. Rosenberg, "Tyranny of Diagnosis," 240.

23. In the 1952 edition of the *Diagnostic and Statistical Manual of Mental Disorders*, psychosis was defined in terms of depression and "insomnia, guilt, anxiety, agitation, delusional ideas, and somatic concerns." See American Psychiatric Association, *Diagnostic and Statistical Manual: Mental Disorders* (Washington: American Psychiatric Association, 1952), 24.

24. Garry Wotherspoon, *City of the Plain: History of a Gay Sub-Culture* (Sydney: Hale & Iremonger, 1991), 81.

25. See for example Graham Willett, "The Darkest Decade: Homophobia in 1950s Australia," *Australian Historical Studies* 28, no. 109 (1997): 120–32, and, by the same author, "From 'Vice' to 'Homosexuality': Policing Perversion in the 1950s," in *Homophobia: An Australian History*, ed. Shirleene Robinson (Sydney: Federation Press, 2008), 113–27; Garry Wotherspoon, "'This nest of perverts': Policing Male Homosexuality in Cold War Australia," *Working Papers in Australian Studies* 52 (1990): 1–21.

26. Yorick Smaal, "'It is one of those things that nobody can explain': Medicine, Homosexuality, and the Australian Criminal Courts in World War 2," *Journal of the History of Sexuality* 22 (2013): 501–24.

27. See, for example, Editorial, "Homosexuality," *Medical Journal of Australia*, February 7, 1948, 175; "Sexual Psychopathy," *Medical Journal of Australia*, September 9, 1950, 420.

8   Sexuality and the Public Case Study in the United States, 1940–65

Joy Damousi

In his pioneering article "Thinking in Cases," John Forrester describes how psychoanalysis created

> a new way of telling a life in the 20th century, a new form for the specific and unique facts that make that person's life their life; and at the same time, it attempts to render that way of telling a life public, of making it scientific. The bridge between these two aims is the case-history.[1]

Shaped on the basis of a life history in the search for origins, case histories formed through psychoanalysis are distinguished from other case studies primarily by two aspects: confidentiality, and the intersection between internal and external worlds. The "public" narrative that emerges through the confidential psychoanalytic relationship involves the excavation of the self—bringing to light origins, personality structures, patterns of behavior and conflict—and an examination of the self in the world. As Timothy G. Ashplant observes, there is "the detective-story aspect of some of his case-histories as [Sigmund Freud] strives to uncover the primal scene concealed by a screen memory."[2] What makes this kind of case study unlike other cases (legal, literary, medical, military) is that its public audience involves only one other person, namely the analyst, and it is affected by transference and the analytic relationship.

In this chapter I analyze the mid-twentieth-century psychoanalytic case study through the notes of New York psychoanalyst Viola Wertheim Bernard. In doing so I consider the form, structure, and dynamics of the psychoanalytic case study in relation to sexuality. As we shall see, the approach adopted within the psychoanalytic case study differed from case studies adopted in other fields during the mid-twentieth century. Despite their individual differences, psychoanalytic case histories such as those collected by Bernard were bound by the adoption of a certain language and understanding of sexuality.

Viola Bernard was a leading analyst in New York from the 1930s until her death in 1998, and a fervent champion of expanding psychiatry for the benefit of social causes. Born in New York City in 1907, she graduated in

medicine in 1936 from Cornell University. She undertook psychiatric studies at the New York State Psychiatric Institute, and postgraduate work in
psychoanalysis at the New York Psychoanalytic Society, from where she
graduated in 1942. Throughout her career, Bernard tirelessly campaigned
for African Americans to be admitted to medical courses, and she wrote
constantly of the need to have them included within the medical, psychiatric, and psychoanalytic professions. She was a supporter of the People's
Press, a trade-unionist news service that was attacked as a Communist
front organization; she testified before the House Un-American Activities
Committee, obliged to answer questions about her political views and her
activism.[3]

In the case under consideration—that of her patient "Grace Hamilton"
(a pseudonym)—I argue that Bernard's case notes reveal how a particular narrative concerning sexuality was shaped through the interaction of
patient and analyst. It is significant that other case studies within the fields
of literature, medicine, science, and journalism also drew on the experience
of sexuality in the postwar period. Mary McCarthy (1912–89), the novelist and writer of short stories, discussed sexuality in new ways through
her literary writing, some of which touches on psychoanalysis. Alfred C.
Kinsey (1894–1956) defined a public discourse of a very different nature
through his research on the sexual practices and experiences of American
men and women, based on extensive interviews. Following Kinsey, the
research undertaken by William Masters (1915–2001) and Virginia Johnson (1925–2013) from the late 1950s constitutes a further example, derived
from experimental observations, of how the use of case studies of sexuality
and sexual behavior created an especially powerful discourse and knowledge about sexuality. Finally, Betty Friedan (1921–2006) formulated the
"problem with no name"—that is, among middle- and upper-class women,
a profound lack of fulfillment in their destiny as housewives. Friedan examined this by interviewing college classmates fifteen years after they had
graduated from Smith College, considering the role of sexuality in their predicament. These writers took remarkably different approaches to the task
of writing about sexuality through case histories. But each was propelled
into the public arena, becoming a high-profile celebrity.

In the United States after World War II, the psychoanalytic case study
is distinguished from the approaches of the aforementioned writers by the
relationship between the analyst and the patient, which produces a particular kind of narrative. Importantly, the relationship between analyst
and patient is confidential. This fact, coupled with transference and countertransference in the psychoanalytic relationship, produces a distinctive
"public," and allows for the possibility of unconventional behavior to be
articulated, analyzed, and examined. The singular contribution of the psychoanalytic case study is the way in which it explores the individual subjective experience, thereby opening up new knowledges about sexuality. With
this in mind, I now turn to a short history of the confessional form, as a

way of contextualizing and historicizing these observations about the mid-twentieth-century psychoanalytic case study.

SEXUALITY AND SUBJECTIVITY

In his *History of Sexuality*, Michel Foucault traces the idea of the confessional form from the ancient Greeks. He considers the practice of regimen in the discipline of dietetics, and its connection to the emergence of secrecy associated with the Christian confession. Foucault observes that regimen, with its emphasis on repetition and form, is replaced by technologies of secrecy such as the confession, the inquisition, the meditation, and the autobiography. In the course of the latter phenomenon, an intimate interiority emerges—in sharp contrast to other practices of regimen, which involve *external* acts, and are defined by public performance.

During the nineteenth century, as attempts were made to move the theory and practice of mental health towards rationality and science, the individual subject became central. Among the middle classes in the latter part of the nineteenth century, emphasis was placed on the self as a source of knowledge and meaning, rather than the doctor alone. With the shift to the individual, to self-reflection, and the rise of the autobiographical text, the language and speech of those classified as ill began to be recognized and legitimated as part of the patient's subjectivity.[4]

Outside the field of mental health, and before the advent of the "talking cure," it was the genre of autobiography that expressed the inner life of the Victorians in Australia, Britain, and the United States. Freud's biographer Peter Gay states that the Victorian period was marked by the "ascent of inwardness." Autobiography, he claims, served as the means of confession during that period, expressing emotions and passions as "a kind of therapy." The nineteenth century spawned far more autobiography than ever before, characterized by a heightened form of memory and nostalgia.[5]

The novel was the other cultural form that became the way in which "the story of private people expressed the general experiences of society." Through reminiscences and confessions, according to Peter Gay, the private self of Victorians was on public view. While these texts employed clichés and plagiarisms—"usually disappointing guides to the inner dimension"— their confessions were "enshrined [in] an authentic feeling." Another popular form of enunciating one's private self that predated these methods was the Catholic confession. In Gay's view, Freud distinguished his method from these confessional techniques by introducing a means of interpretation that recognized the need to analyze the confessional scientifically.[6] In contrast, John Forrester describes psychoanalysis as a "new form of accounting for the self in 20th-century scientific and popular discourses."[7] This was especially true in the United States.

In 1939, when Grace Hamilton approached Viola Bernard to undertake treatment, psychoanalysis had already made an impact on American psychiatry. The psychodynamic approach, which emphasized psychological and social factors as the cause of anxiety and psychoses, began to supersede models based on assumptions about heredity and neurology. The limited success of these older approaches, and the lack of other successful psychological theories that might have replaced psychoanalysis, had narrowed the field. "Psychoanalysis gradually became the major American medical psychology," argues Nathan Hale, "and there were increasing claims for the effectiveness of psychoanalytic treatment, even in the psychoses." For the period preceding Hamilton's therapy, Hale estimates an increase in demand for psychiatric services. It is difficult to be certain why there was such an increase—whether it was simply a result of wider awareness of "nervous and mental" disorders, or due to the success of mental hygiene campaigns—however, it is clear that a rise in the use of services and the labeling of patients did occur. In New York City in 1929, "some 30,000 patients sought psychiatric treatment in 67 clinics, while some 7,500 of these were diagnosed as psychoneurotics." By 1939, within the medical fraternity, the specialist field of psychoanalysis had made considerable inroads as an explanation for nervous and mental disorders.[8]

SEXUALITY AND USES OF THE CASE STUDY

Psychoanalysis was a form of therapy favored by various groups during the interwar years, including those in artistic, upper-, and middle-class circles. Writer Mary McCarthy recreates the scene in a therapist's room in her short story "Ghostly Father I Confess," first published in *Harper's Bazaar* in 1942, in which the protagonist visits her analyst. As McCarthy's biographer Frances Kiernan affirms, no work of fiction can be taken as straightforward autobiography, but in her view "Ghostly Father I Confess" seems to be "coming uncomfortably close to real life," and mirrors many details of McCarthy's own torments and troubles. Like the reality, the fiction, Kiernan observes, "makes painful reading." Certainly, McCarthy would have used the writing process to reflect on her own life, as she would have used her experience of therapy itself.[9] Kiernan argues that psychoanalysis provided the support that allowed McCarthy to write.[10] But in terms of McCarthy's personal relationships, Kiernan's assessment is more ambivalent: psychoanalysis, the biographer contends, may have perpetuated the hold on McCarthy of Edmund Wilson, her second husband. By the summer of 1945 McCarthy did not wish to have anything further to do with psychoanalysis. She felt she had no need for it. "To justify her wholesale rejection of its precepts and methods, [McCarthy] would eventually argue that it fostered in patients a most unattractive self-pity."[11] "Ghostly Father I Confess" combines a literary form with a medical paradigm; it reveals an intersection of the psychological with the social. Tellingly, psychoanalysis becomes the place where the protagonist can conduct the type of conversations that she cannot have with others.

> One reason, it occurred to her suddenly, that she continued to go to Dr. James long after she had admitted that he could do nothing for her was simply, if the truth were acknowledged, that she had no one else to talk to. Her conversation had become official conversation—the war, the Administration, the Managerial Revolution, Van Wyck Brooks, Lewis Mumford, the latest novel by a friend. . . . Dr. James was the Outlet, paid for by the month, the hygienic pipe line that kept the boiler from exploding.[12]

Also from this era, the Kinsey reports comprise a second example of published texts that explore the intersection between the case history and sexuality, raising pertinent points regarding the methodology of the case study during the mid-twentieth century. The issues that preoccupied novelists such as McCarthy and analysts such as Bernard found expression in the so-called Kinsey report on male sexuality, published as *Sexual Behavior in the Human Male* in 1948, and the report on female sexuality published as *Sexual Behavior in the Human Female* in 1953. Both reports were multiauthored volumes produced by Kinsey and his research team at Indiana University.[13]

The Kinsey scale (also known as the Heterosexual–Homosexual Rating Scale), attempted to chart an individual's sexual activity and behavior over a period of time. The aim was to develop a scale that would accurately capture homosexual and heterosexual behavior:

> The world is not to be divided into sheep and goats. It is a fundamental of taxonomy that nature rarely deals with discrete categories. . . . The living world is a continuum in each and every one of its aspects. While emphasizing the continuity of the gradations between exclusively heterosexual and exclusively homosexual histories, it has seemed desirable to develop some sort of classification which could be based on the relative amounts of heterosexual and homosexual experience or response in each history. . . . An individual may be assigned a position on this scale, for each period in his life.[14]

Employing this "count and catalogue" approach, Kinsey drew from a large number of cases that were based on interview and note-taking techniques, aimed at capturing the interviewee's sexual life.[15] The Kinsey scale was designed to measure a range from 0 to 6, where 0 denoted "exclusively heterosexual" and 6 denoted "exclusively homosexual"; "asexual" was assigned a rating of X. Such a scale may seem ludicrous today, but at the time it was considered radical, subversive, and highly controversial.

The material on homosexuality in particular shocked the readership of the Kinsey reports: the studies reported that 50 percent of interviewees acknowledged erotic responses to their own sex; over one-third had had a postadolescent homosexual experience; and homosexuals were to be found throughout the entire community. What was earlier perceived as a fringe, deviant group suddenly became identified as a group spread through mainstream society.[16]

A major theme of the Kinsey studies was sexuality and marriage, and women's sexual experiences especially. Kinsey concluded that there had been an increase in women reaching orgasm, and that the younger generation experienced greater variety in lovemaking. Even a behavior as "taken for granted" as nudity for sex had changed: one-third of the women born before 1900 usually remained clothed during sex, in contrast to 8 percent of women born between 1900 and 1920. Kinsey did not present marriage as a sexual haven, and he drew attention to different expectations of men and women. Women preferred intercourse less frequently than men, and were far more likely to refuse to have sex, while men more often than their wives acknowledged a desire for extramarital affairs. Husbands were having intercourse less frequently than they desired, while women achieved orgasm only about three-quarters of the time. Yet in general, the authors concluded, the studies showed that the potential for sexual satisfaction was greater than it had been earlier in the century.[17]

The case study methodology employed by Kinsey, and its reception—its publics—point to several historically significant developments. John D'Emilio and Estelle Freedman describe how the most strident challenge to sexual reticence in the public realm emerged not from the "pornographic fringe" but from "the respectable domain of science." Kinsey's studies "propelled sex into the public eye in a way unlike any previous book or event had done. Whether bought, read, debated, or attacked, the Kinsey reports stimulated a nationwide examination of America's sexual habits and values."[18] The studies revolutionized public discourse about sexuality, and created a celebrity in Kinsey. Both volumes of the Kinsey reports became bestsellers, each selling almost a quarter of a million copies. "Kinsey," notes D'Emilio, became a household name, signifying the liberation of sexuality from the restraints of earlier periods.[19]

Kinsey's work also inspired the 1962 film *The Chapman Report* directed by George Cukor, and distributed by Warner Bros. Pictures. Starring Shelley Winters and Jane Fonda, the film explores four cases of "abnormal" sexual behavior of upper-middle-class women who become the focus of a psychologist's team of investigators. According to A.H. Weiler's contemporary review in the *New York Times*, the film depicts "a frigid type, a nymphomaniac-alcoholic, a confused, bored mother and a gay, flighty intellectual"; the film itself is "disjointed," and "makes little point except the obvious."[20]

While Kinsey developed the interview method as a form of case study, William Masters and Virginia Johnson developed another approach that was also controversial, attracting much attention and vociferous criticism. More radically than Kinsey, Masters and Johnson developed a laboratory-centered methodology that was based on observing couples copulating and masturbating. They began their research into sexual responses in 1954, as well as the treatment of "sexual disorders" and "dysfunctional" sexuality. Their initial project from 1957–65 comprised a study of 382 women and 312 men, mostly married couples. This study especially dispelled myths around female sexual arousal. Masters and Johnson wrote two texts that revolutionized the field of sexuality: *Human Sexual Response* (1966) and *Human Sexual Inadequacy* (1970).[21] Whereas Kinsey's research was based on personal interviews, Masters and Johnson aimed to examine the psychology and physiology of sexual behavior by measuring masturbation and sexual intercourse. Critics of this methodology argued that it was incorrect to assume that people's behavior under laboratory conditions was consistent with their behavior in their own home. Supporters of Masters and Johnson argued that by looking for the first time at the physiological responses to sexual arousal the researchers gave agency and primacy to women's sexuality; that, as a result, women's sexuality could no longer be considered a reflection of male sexuality, but should be attributed a key role in studies of human sexual behavior.[22]

Paul Robinson has observed that Kinsey and Masters and Johnson held different views on the purpose of their research and its value. Kinsey was not interested in the therapeutic value of his findings; rather than focus on individual cases and curing patients, he saw his findings as a contribution to assisting the entire society.[23] There were also differences in terms of their respective positions as scientists and as clinicians. Masters and Johnson, Robinson has argued, were "clinicians first" and scientists second—revealed by the therapeutic aspect of their research, which explicitly stated that "the greatest handicap to successful treatment of sexual inadequacy was a lack of reliable physiological information in the area of human sexual response."[24] Robinson contends that this difference explains why Masters and Johnson were "methodologically more radical" but at the same time "substantially more conservative" than Kinsey. As Robinson observes, the "therapist tends to accept the established order and seeks to adjust his patient to it. The pure scientist, on the other hand, is free to imagine a better order."[25]

Although representing two differing approaches to case studies, Kinsey and Masters and Johnson shared the instant celebrity status that resulted from the popularization of their studies. Like Kinsey, the findings of Masters and Johnson attracted huge publicity, and their published works were an instant commercial success, including translation into thirty languages. The public expressed an insatiable appetite for their work, and they became overnight sensations. Such publicity, however, proved to be a mixed blessing. In his biography of Masters and Johnson, Thomas Maier describes how the American media instantly seized upon the findings of their works and generated heated debates around them.[26] The political arena was another area where the results of Kinsey and Masters and Johnson were adopted and discussed. Feminists embraced the findings of Masters and Johnson, especially their claim that female sexuality was not a pale "replica" of male sexuality, and indeed that "female sexuality [was] superior to that of men, and . . . women express their sexuality in many varied forms."[27]

The research conducted by Betty Friedan in the late 1950s was based on surveys she had undertaken of fellow alumni, as well as a number of case studies. It culminated in her iconic work *The Feminine Mystique*, published in 1963. Friedan's method constituted a unique way of gathering and disseminating knowledge about sexuality at that time. She began *The Feminine Mystique* as a survey conducted in 1957 at a college reunion, finding that all the women she interviewed were unhappy as housewives. She ends the book with several case studies of women challenging the feminine mystique. Today *The Feminine Mystique* is always discussed in retrospect—with reference to "the beginning of the women's movement." Yet to view it in its historical context opens the work to another reading, showing how experiential studies such as Friedan's were beginning to provide a further source of knowledge about sexuality for a public with a ready appetite for such knowledge.[28] Rather than solving women's dissatisfaction, Friedan argued that sexuality had become a way for her interviewees to explain a fundamental lack of fulfillment. The women she spoke to

> would often given me an explicitly sexual answer to a question that was not sexual at all. I would ask about their personal interests, ambitions, what they did, or would like to do, not necessarily as wives or mothers, but when they were not occupied with their husbands or their children or their housework. The question might even be what they are doing with their education. But some of these women simply assumed that I was asking about sex. Was the problem that has no name a sexual problem, after all?[29]

There was a "false note," observed Friedan, when her respondents spoke about sexuality—"a strange, unreal quality about their words." In her view, the apparent "sex hunger" of American women documented by Kinsey and others had reduced women to sex creatures, and sex had become a joyless national obsession.[30] It is notable that 1963 also saw the publication of *The Group* by Mary McCarthy; this best-selling novel traces the lives of eight young, educated, middle-class women, and deals with the same themes explored by Friedan in *The Feminine Mystique*. *The Group* features such frank descriptions of sexuality that it was banned in some countries, including Australia.[31]

THE PSYCHOANALYTIC CASE STUDY

The celebrity status that elevated all of these writers in the public arena was missing in the confidential confines of psychoanalytical therapy. Tackling therapeutic solutions to questions of sexuality through analytic practice was based on individual case studies. Yet analytic practice also differed from the case-study-based explorations of sexuality undertaken in other contexts due to its interrogation of subjectivity and subjective experience. What binds particular stories by McCarthy with the work of Kinsey, Masters and Johnson, Friedan, and psychoanalysts from the period 1940–65, despite their specific styles and methodologies, is the emergence of a particular sexual modernity that predates the so-called sexual revolution of the 1960s. Of all these approaches, the psychoanalytic case study is the least documented.

In the psychoanalytic case study the role of the analyst is crucial in framing questions, responding to the answers, and directing the analysis. The relationship between analyst and patient is paramount. The narrative emerges in the shape that it does through the transference and countertransference exchange. Grace Hamilton's case is distinctive, in that it involves a female patient and a female analyst, when more usually such cases involve a male analyst and a female patient. This distinctiveness raises particular questions in relation to transference and countertransference, especially when the focus of the discussion is same-sex relationships. As documented by Viola Bernard, the case captures a period that predates the Kinsey reports, while its testimony points to many themes that Kinsey would subsequently address, including homosexuality, orgasm, pleasure, identity, and social constraints in marriage and relationships.

Kinsey's findings pointed to the "hidden" world of sexual experience, which did not match that of social and cultural norms.[32] However, importantly, Hamilton's testimony was never intended for an audience beyond one witness—her therapist, Bernard. In this sense, the psychoanalytic case study under Bernard's direction works in very different ways to the cases of Kinsey and Masters and Johnson; for example, it is less concerned with trying to conform to a fixed categorization or typology. The free association of the therapist contrasts with the categorization and labeling that characterize the approach of Kinsey and Masters and Johnson, and through which their studies fixed identity, positioned it within a rigid framework, and made it digestible to a mass audience. As such, of the various case writers examined here—the novelist (McCarthy); the scientist (Kinsey); clinicians (Masters and Johnson); the journalist (Friedan), and the analyst (Bernard)—it is the latter who allows for less definitive views about sexuality and the self to be articulated. Bernard's work, as a consequence, offered the greatest possibility for change. The case of Grace Hamilton demonstrates a fluid engagement with the self and the social—with internal and external experience—framed around the confidential and the confessional procedure of analysis: these themes I will now explore.

GRACE HAMILTON

Who was Grace Hamilton? We are introduced to her through Bernard, as a

> 20-year-old young woman, of medium height and weight, black, bobbed wavy hair, and well-shaped features. The cheeks are flushed, and complexion clear and the throat unusually full. . . . She is neatly dressed in a sweater and tailored tweed suit, wearing pearl earrings. Her voice is extremely low-pitched, and masculine in type, to such an extent that this is the most conspicuous element is the first impression one gains of this patient. She entered the office with some degree of swagger, and immediately swung into voluble discussion about herself.[33]

In her case notes, Bernard develops a narrative about this seemingly confident, strident, and striking young patient:

> This young woman is apparently intelligent. She employs a good vocabulary, liberally besprinkled with profanity when she wants to emphasize her point. Her use of these terms enhances the masculine flavor of her talk, and one suspects is also used to test the physician's attitude and possible likelihood of being shocked or startled. The patient's manner was one of almost exaggerated self-assurance and lack of inhibition in discussing intimate matters with minimal eliciting on the part of the examiner. There was a good deal of undue smiling while reciting these self-revelations, which may be a defensive display of casualness to conceal the true associated anxiety. . . . One is inclined to feel, however, that there was considerable façade of bravado behind which lay apprehension.[34]

The focus of Hamilton's analysis is the issue of her masculinity—how to handle it, understand it, and, ultimately, change it. As part of this process, there is an explicit attempt to discuss Hamilton's masculinity, largely because of her difficulty with sexual relationships with men, and the uncomfortable and confronting attraction she expresses towards women.

The tension between Hamilton's heterosexual and homosexual desire is apparent, and Bernard attempts to draw out her behavior, which, in her assessment, her patient attempts to negate.

> Her frequent changes in residence during the past couple of years have been chiefly due to being forced to leave because of compromising behaviour with men. Thus, this steady boy friend . . . lived in the same boarding house with the patient, and they were both forced to leave when discovered in bed together. The patient had to leave her last address under rather embarrassing circumstances when discovered by

the janitor in intensive petting on the stairs. With some resentment, the patient states she is forced into these humiliating circumstances by the fact that she cannot afford a suitable place in which she may invite her men friends. Thus, she had difficulties last year when living at a hotel for women.[35]

Bernard's assessment of this narrative is that Hamilton was not entirely innocent of how she behaved:

> It would look as though perhaps the patient desired in a certain way, perhaps unconsciously, to bring about the very situations she deplores. Thus, why choose a hotel for women only, when one wishes to invite men to one's rooms? Perhaps being caught in apparently heterosexual situations is a means of advertising to others, and, therefore, herself, that she leads an active heterosexual life to abundantly drown out the whisper of her inner humiliating sense of non-heterosexuality.[36]

Unlike some of Bernard's other patients, Hamilton does actually pursue her same-sex sexual desires, by venturing into the various subcultures of bohemian New York:

> The patient has attempted and experimented with Lesbianism. This she did because she knew herself to be unpopular with boys. She effected a mannish dress at night, going down to Greenwich Village and trying to act like a Lesbian, frequenting restaurants patronized by such individuals. Although several made advances to her, she found the actual physical practices repellent. It is not clear just what experiences she underwent and she was not questioned. On these Greenwich Village jaunts the patient would further attempt to imitate Lesbianism by purposely forcing her voice deeper. She seems to be of the impression that her voice is within normal feminine range, except when she so purposively distorts it. This is not true.[37]

Hamilton seeks clarification regarding how she should "handle" her attraction to women, and whether her attraction could be anything more than a passing phase.

> Recalls that a week ago she became *very sexually aroused when seeing a Hawaiian woman dancer*. Attended this with her 54 year old "feminine" woman friend to whom she feels protective as she does to her mother. She envied the woman's brown well-shaped body and wished her own was similarly curved. She phantasised she'd dance as this woman was doing, in front of her boy-friend. She wonders if her becoming sexually aroused was akin to Lesbianism as it was excited by another woman.[38]

Hamilton's own interest is also an intellectual and academic one:

> At Columbia when she started at 17, she took a course in psychology which interested her greatly and lead to her reading a good deal of Kraft-Ebbing, Freud, Adler and Havelock Ellis. It is her interest in the writings of these men that indirectly lead her to seek our assistance in the hospital now.[39]

Hamilton is also incredibly secretive about these details, and wishes to keep the medical and the psychiatric implications separate and independent of one another. "One problem," notes Bernard, is the desirability "of integrating the endocrine and psychiatric aspects[,] as there appears to be a disturbance in both, mutually interrelated." But Hamilton is determined to keep them distinctive.

> Her desire to retain her anonymity in her contact with us militates against her wishing her own physician to know of her connection here, thus restraining us from consulting with him as to past medical history and present treatment. On the other hand, she makes it clear she is satisfied with her physician and we assume she would not wish us to take over his function.[40]

Hamilton is unpopular, and feels that her unpopularity gets in the way; this feeling, at its heart, relates to questions around femininity and masculinity. She finds sexual activity difficult with men, and is certainly not at ease about her sexuality, speculating constantly about whether or not she is a lesbian.

> Started talking immediately of attraction to a fragile helpless innocent-looking girl on a bus which she felt with feeling of protectiveness towards her. Finds it paradoxical that though she usually despises feminine types preferring masculine-type women, she found this "virginal sweet girl" so attractive. Thinks this is evidence of her Lesbian component and probable "bisexual make-up." Likens the feelings aroused as similar to those aroused in her by Hawaiian dancer referred to in earlier interviews.[41]

Sexuality was not the only reference to her biological self that she tried to conceal.

> Also patient won't buy sanitary napkins, asking her mother to do so, and refusing to walk with her mother on street were latter carrying a box of wrapped sanitary napkins, lest they be recognized. Recognized justice of mother's mild ridicule of this. Has overcome her exaggerated avoidance of menstrual subjects to such an extreme degree.[42]

Matters of secrecy in relation to sexuality are, of course, very much a part of the history of lesbian desire. As Martha Vicinus so accurately points out,

> we have too long assumed that women in the past *could not name* their erotic desires, rather than recognizing their *refusal to name* them. Because of this, it remains difficult to trace same-sex love among women. . . . The consequences of speaking or acting too openly about physical desire could be dangerous in a world that insisted upon women's respectability. Women wrote in code, warned each other to conceal or burn letters, and used metaphors or allusion. Far better, most women felt, to remain quiet or to speak only to trustworthy allies.[43]

While lesbians in working-class communities in New York frequented bars and house parties, and may have experienced some sense of belonging or community, individuals with very little connection to these communities found that same sex desires or fragmented sexual subjectivity could be a lonely, isolated, confusing, and frustrating experience. Hamilton's narrative resembles that of several other women whom Bernard psychoanalyses. These women are typically middle or upper class, and not part of a lesbian subculture; indeed they would feel uncomfortable in such a subculture. Hamilton's predicament also puts her at the edge of historical research: because women like her had no visibility, they are lost to the historical record. Many professional women at this time found expression of their lesbian identity through business and professional women's groups, and friendship groups that provided and sustained a lesbian identity for the first time.[44]

As mentioned above, the question of masculine or feminine gender is at the core of Hamilton's narrative. Her masculine-sounding voice gives her some concern, while her own femininity is contested, especially by her father.

> Father's irritation at her deep voice—at 14 he was angered at her speaking in restaurant—attitude made her feel like a "freak" and afraid to speak. Till now *he upbraids her masculine habits*—urges her to dress more femininely. I'm afraid to be feminine—I feel protected when dressed "mannishly." I'm afraid of men—if I look alluring men may be attracted to me whereas deep voice and tailored clothes defend me by hiding that which attracts them. (pause).[45]

This paternal censure becomes a constant threat and theme in her narrative.

> Used to be proud of her hairy legs—as hairy as his (her father's). Now shaves legs. At 14, when she declaimed to him how she hated feminine women he'd reply she shouldn't talk so, or she'd be thought a Lesbian. She blames him for such a statement to a developing girl.[46]

Hamilton comes to Bernard with a specific problem, "because she feels her personality stands in the way of her securing employment. Potential employers do not like her because of certain personality traits which[,] therefore[,] for economic reasons as she needs a job, she feels she should alter."[47]

Bernard discusses the specifics of her patient's life story, but Hamilton retains a secrecy about her past.

> The patient came to this country at the age of four with her parents from Hungary. Her mother is Hungarian, her father Russian. She is an only child. The mother is described as a submissive, feminine type; the father as an intellectual, dominating, thoughtful man. . . . While the patient is remarkably forthright in personal matters . . . she shows striking reluctance to give any specific, identifying information, apparently desirous of maintaining an anonymity essential to her sense of freedom of expression. This was respected and no effort made to elicit specific material where such was withheld. . . . Her entire school life was characterized by unpopularity with her classmates, with what she considers a compensatory turning of her energies to scholastic achievement, with the result that she always led the class and was liked by her teachers because of her excellence in her work. She had no friends and, consequently, much leisure for reading which she did avidly.[48]

Bernard focuses on her father especially, who looms large in this account:

> Her father took considerable pride in her intellectual accomplishments, considering her a "potential blue stocking," a term to which the patient often returns, describing this opinion others have had of her, apparently enjoying the irony of this in contrast to her actual unconventionality and "over-sexedness." The patient resented the father's methods in the home and they had many battles because "I'm just like him." When she was about 13 she created something of an ideal for herself out of a woman friend of her father's, who was associated with him in business. This woman was a "regular blue-stocking" and extremely intellectual. The father liked meek, feminine women "whom he could boss around." Two years ago the parents were separated and the mother is working in Canada as an artist in some theatrical enterprise, sending the patient a small allowance on which she is at present dependent.[49]

Bernard adopts the view that it is indeed Hamilton's masculinity that points to her struggle with her father, a figure Bernard finds intriguing and fascinating as a case study in masculinity:

> On the basis of our first contact we would thoroughly agree with the patient's self-diagnosis that she has a "masculine protest." However,

her insight stops short at that point. Superficially it would seem that the patient has reacted to her father by sadistic aggression motivated by her jealousy of the masculinity which he possesses and she lacks. Her battle with her father is repeated with all other men. To insure the victory she only goes with weaker men whom she can dominate. The possibility of intercourse arouses so much anxiety she cannot tolerate it, confirming as it would her lack of the penis she envies, and representing the submission which she dreads. On the other hand, her masquerading as a man is incomplete and she has not abandoned adherence to the standard of feminine behaviour current in our culture. It is because of this partial nature of her adaptation that we find evidence of repression and distortion of which the patient is unaware.[50]

What would be the outcome of this therapy? Bernard was not sure. "What is the therapeutic goal in a case of this kind?," Bernard asked. "How accessible can the patient be to any therapeutic plan in view of her powerful and articulate desire to retain her symptoms?" On the other hand, Bernard could more easily identify the benefit of a case such as Hamilton's for her own professional interest.

Presents many challenging features and should be instructive towards this doctor's understanding of such problems. It is relatively rare that patients' worst symptomatology is in such overt form [when they] come to the psychiatrist for treatment, thus affording us an opportunity for study.

Therapy, for Hamilton, became a confessional forum for sexual exploration and discussion:

Patient brings along the book of erotic poetry she's reading at present (George Viereck, '31). Was reminded of her preference above all others as a friend of a sexless, brilliant, cultured woman. Feels men want to "use women in a boudoir" but they prefer men for companions—"they like women at night but men in the daytime." Patient again lay on couch with the last few buttons of her tunic open, exposing her pink satin slip. As she talked she (apparently unawares) opened the tunic entirely, lying in negligé—then without comment, still talking, she buttoned herself up. Her talk centred about her lover's lack of sexual need for her Saturday so that she accepted invitation to meet two very cultured Chinese women (21 and 24), sisters, both studying for M.A. degrees, introduced by her elderly woman friend, mentioned often before. Patient fascinated by the elder Chinese girl who seemed to reciprocate so that after 4 hours patient felt elevated on leaving and pleased that she hadn't spent the day with her lover, feeling the new female friend was worth 10 times him—said to herself, "a woman of this type fascinates me more than any man." "I have much of the Lesbian in make-up potentially—this woman a diamond compared to the rhinestone of a man."[51]

As for the protagonist in Mary McCarthy's story "Ghostly Father I Confess," the analyst's room was the only place in which Hamilton could discuss these desires and anxieties, and Bernard was the only person to whom she could open up. I have argued elsewhere that, paradoxically, while the "talking cure" was ostensibly intended to "cure" women like Hamilton of same sex desires, in fact it simply served to bring these desires to the forefront, and allow for more exploration.[52] The case study examined here serves this same purpose: to encourage further discussion of and discourse around sexuality, and yet also to attempt to contain it. Unlike other discussions and case studies in public circulation during this period, the approach adopted by Bernard from the 1940s onwards allowed for the investigation and analysis of less conventional practices of sexuality, rather than their dismissal. In *The Feminine Mystique*, Betty Friedan, for example, tended to dismiss or belittle homosexuality, linking women's lack of fulfillment—their lack of personal commitment in education and work—with the development of excessive mother-son devotion, which would lead to an increase in latent or overt homosexuality.[53] Male homosexuals, she noted, are "Peter Pans, forever childlike, afraid of age, grasping at youth in their continual search for reassurance in some sexual magic."[54]

* * *

Timothy G. Ashplant considers the relationship between the internal and external worlds that shape the psychoanalytic dynamic by observing that psychoanalysis itself began with a consideration of the forces of the external reality—sexual trauma—impinging on patients. In the reverse—where the psychic life of the patient interprets the wider world—this includes consideration of relationships with family members, and of the intersections between the social and psychic. These elements are evident in Grace Hamilton's story as documented by her psychoanalyst, characterized as it is by the confessional form and the confidential mode. But here the transference relationship between patient and analyst creates a distinctive psychoanalytic case study.

The 1940s to the early 1960s in the United States was an extraordinary period when literary, medical, journalistic, and psychoanalytic case studies opened new perspectives on the links between the case study form, sexuality, and public culture. In relation to Mary McCarthy, Alfred C. Kinsey, William Masters and Virginia Johnson, and Betty Friedan, this created a sensation in public life, through interest from the popular media, journalists, political groups, and emerging social movements. By contrast, psychoanalysis was not conducted in the public arena in this way. Knowledge about sexuality was confined to the individual case, and was communicated in private. For this reason analysts like Viola Bernard did not "make headlines" or become celebrities. However, Bernard's methodology was no less transformative. While she did not assume a public or celebrity status, it could be argued that at an individual level, as in the case study of Grace Hamilton, her approach had more explanatory power than studies undertaken on a larger, less personalized, and wider public scale.

NOTES

1. John Forrester, "If *p*, then what? Thinking in Cases," *History of the Human Sciences* 9 (1996): 1–25, at 10.
2. T.G. Ashplant, "Psychoanalysis in Historical Writing," *History Workshop Journal* 26 (1988): 102–19, at 106.
3. For Bernard see Joy Damousi, "Viola Bernard and the Analysis of 'Alice Conrad': A Case Study in the History of Intimacy," *Journal of the History of Sexuality* 22 (2013): 474–500.
4. Michel Foucault, *The History of Sexuality*, trans. Robert Hurley, vol. 1, *An Introduction* (London: Vintage, 1990), 10–13, 69–73.
5. Peter Gay, *The Bourgeois Experience: Victoria to Freud*, vol. 4, *The Naked Heart* (London: Fontana, 1998), 111.
6. Gay, *The Naked Heart*, 111.
7. Forrester, "If *p*, then what? Thinking in Cases," 13.
8. Nathan G. Hale, *The Rise and Crisis of Psychoanalysis in the United States: Freud and the Americans, 1917–1985* (New York: Oxford University Press, 1995), 157–59.
9. Frances Kiernan, *Seeing Mary Plain: A Life of Mary McCarthy* (New York: Norton, 2000), 177. I am grateful to Professor Desley Deacon for this reference.
10. Kiernan, *Seeing Mary Plain*, 213.
11. Kiernan, *Seeing Mary Plain*, 230.
12. Mary McCarthy, "Ghostly Father, I Confess," one of the interlinked stories comprising her debut novel *The Company She Keeps*, 2nd ed. (London: Weidenfeld and Nicholson, 1957), 199–246, at 231–32.
13. Albert C. Kinsey, Wardell B. Pomeroy, Clyde E. Martin, *Sexual Behavior in the Human Male* (Philadelphia: Saunders, 1948); Albert C. Kinsey et al., *Sexual Behavior in the Human Female* (Philadelphia: Saunders, 1953).
14. Kinsey et al., *Sexual Behavior in the Human Male*, 639.
15. John D'Emilio and Estelle B. Freedman, *Intimate Matters: A History of Sexuality in America* (New York: Harper and Row, 1988), 286.
16. D'Emilio and Freedman, *Intimate Matters*, 291–92.
17. D'Emilio and Freedman, *Intimate Matters*, 269–70.
18. D'Emilio and Freedman, *Intimate Matters*, 285.
19. John D'Emilio, *Sexual Politics, Sexual Communities: The Making of a Homosexual Minority in the United States, 1940–1970* (Chicago: University of Chicago Press, 1983), 34.
20. A.H. Weiler, "Screen: 'Chapman Report': Adaptation of Wallace Novel Opens Here," October 18, 1962; see www.nytimes.com/movie/review?res=9E05EEDB123CE63ABC4052DFB6678389679EDE (accessed February 5, 2014).

21. William H. Masters and Virginia E. Johnson, *Human Sexual Response* (Boston: Little, Brown, 1966); and by the same authors, *Human Sexual Inadequacy* (Boston: Little, Brown, 1970).

22. See Larisa Kerrigan, "Masters and Johnson," *Psychological History of Women*, http://psychistofwomen.umwblogs.org/sexuality/post-kinsey/masters-and-johnson/ (accessed February 5, 2014).

23. Paul Robinson, *The Modernization of Sex: Havelock Ellis, Alfred Kinsey, William Masters and Virginia Johnson* (New York: Harper and Row, 1976), 121.

24. Robinson, *The Modernization of Sex*, 121.

25. Robinson, *The Modernization of Sex*, 121.

26. See Thomas Maier, *Masters of Sex: The Life and Times of William Masters and Virginia Johnson, The Couple Who Taught America to Love* (New York: Basic Books, 2009).

27. Robinson, *The Modernization of Sex*, 153.

28. See Stephanie Coontz, *A Strange Stirring: The Feminine Mystique and American Women at the Dawn of the 1960s* (New York: Basic Books, 2011).

29. Betty Friedan, *The Feminine Mystique: 50 Years*, intro. Gail Collins (New York: Norton, 2013), 306.

30. Friedan, *The Feminine Mystique*, 310.

31. Elizabeth Day, "*The Group* by Mary McCarthy," *The Observer*, November 29, 2009; see www.theguardian.com/books/2009/nov/29/the-group-mary-mccarthy (accessed February 5, 2014).

32. D'Emilio and Freedman, *Intimate Matters*, 286.

33. November 30, 1939, Outpatient Interview, Box 294, Folder 7, Series 12, Clinical Files, Viola Wertheim Bernard Papers, 1918–2000, Archives and Special Collections, A.C. Long Health Sciences Library, Columbia University, New York City. All references to Bernard's notes and other manuscripts are to materials in this collection.

34. November 30, 1939, Outpatient Interview, Clinical Files, Viola Wertheim Bernard Papers.

35. November 30, 1939, Outpatient Interview, Clinical Files, Viola Wertheim Bernard Papers.

36. November 30, 1939, Outpatient Interview, Clinical Files, Viola Wertheim Bernard Papers.

37. November 30, 1939, Outpatient Interview, Clinical Files, Viola Wertheim Bernard Papers.

38. January 22, 1940, Outpatient Interview, Clinical Files, Viola Wertheim Bernard Papers (emphasis in original).

39. November 30, 1939, Outpatient Interview, Clinical Files, Viola Wertheim Bernard Papers.

40. November 30, 1939, Outpatient Interview, Clinical Files, Viola Wertheim Bernard Papers.

41. April 19, 1940, Outpatient Interview, Clinical Files, Viola Wertheim Bernard Papers.

42. April 15, 1940, Outpatient Interview, Clinical Files, Viola Wertheim Bernard Papers.

43. Martha Vicinus, *Intimate Friends: Women Who Loved Women, 1778–1928* (Chicago: University of Chicago Press, 2004), xix.

44. D'Emilio and Freedman, *Intimate Matters*, 291.

45. February 1, 1940, Outpatient Interview, Clinical Files, Viola Wertheim Bernard Papers (emphasis in original).

46. April 5, 1940, Outpatient Interview, Clinical Files, Viola Wertheim Bernard Papers.

47. November 30, 1939, Outpatient Interview, Clinical Files, Viola Wertheim Bernard Papers.
48. November 30, 1939, Outpatient Interview, Clinical Files, Viola Wertheim Bernard Papers.
49. November 30, 1939, Outpatient Interview, Clinical Files, Viola Wertheim Bernard Papers.
50. November 30, 1939, Outpatient Interview, Clinical Files, Viola Wertheim Bernard Papers.
51. April 15, 1940, Outpatient Interview, Clinical Files, Viola Wertheim Bernard Papers.
52. See Damousi, "Viola Bernard," 500.
53. Friedan, *The Feminine Mystique*, 328.
54. Friedan, *The Feminine Mystique*, 328.

Part III
Literary Circulations

9 Female Sex Murders and Literary Case Writing
Alfred Döblin's *Die beiden Freundinnen und ihr Giftmord* (1924)

Alison Lewis

During the interwar period of the Weimar Republic, the reading public's appetite for lurid crime stories found a new focus in an obsession with female criminal types. Of all such types in literature and the media, readers were possibly most fascinated by the figure of the female poisoner (*Giftmischerin* or *Giftmörderin*), who poisons her husband. Women, one could be mistaken for thinking, had a virtual monopoly on the crime of murder by poisoning, usually arsenic poisoning. And this crime came to channel diffuse postwar anxieties about women's sexuality and power through the prism of discourses of perversion and criminality.[1] Especially striking about this public interest in female perpetrators was the symbiotic relationship that developed between real cases and fictional cases. In the interwar period particularly, the crime fiction stories that were printed in magazines and serialized in daily newspapers, or packaged in popular crime fiction series, borrowed unashamedly from real crime cases. The worlds of the criminal court and its cases, which were opened to the public, helped to feed this hunger for tales about female criminality—as did, albeit rather less obviously, new scientific developments in psychiatry, psychology, medicine, and psychoanalysis. As we shall see, specialist and popular discourses both contributed substantively to the classification of knowledge about the female criminal, while they participated in making this knowledge more widely known to the literate classes.

In the first two decades of the twentieth century, a number of German and Austrian authors, some of whom were trained as medical doctors, took up the themes of violent crimes and sexual psychopathology via the literary case study. In this way they contributed to the formation of knowledge about sex crimes, specifically female sex crimes, and to the dissemination of this knowledge to an educated, lay audience. Expressionist, naturalist, as well as modernist writers of the time shared a similar fascination with female violence and sexually motivated crimes. Some literary creations were based on real court cases, like Austrian writer Robert Musil's character Moosbrugger, who, in the epic three-volume work *Der Mann ohne Eigenschaften* (*The Man without Qualities*, 1930–43) murders a prostitute. Ernst Weiß's story of 1924, *Der Fall Vukobrankovics* (The case of Vukobrankovics), about a woman who has poisoned her employers, was likewise based on a real court case. Others, like the child murderer in Gerhart Hauptmann's play *Rose Bernd* from 1903, and the child murderer Marie Farrar in Bertolt Brecht's ballad "Von der Kindesmörderin Marie Farrar," from 1922, were loosely based on real events and characters.

Public access to information about murder cases grew through the diversification of literary markets and print media in Weimar Germany, and a new, literate, middle-class, and petit bourgeois public emerged to consume these shocking stories. Authors with a background in the law or medicine, such as Erich Wulffen and Alfred Döblin, whose professional engagement brought them into close proximity with real-life criminal cases, found themselves with an advantage when writing for these publics, since graphic source material for their literary endeavors could be readily obtained through their professional associations. State Prosecutor Erich Wulffen used a variety of different media and genres to expound his ideas about the law and criminality. By contrast, Alfred Döblin chose as his preferred medium not the burgeoning new forms of journalism and print media of the day, nor the many psychoanalytic or medical journals of the time, but that timeworn mode of communication, middlebrow literature.

It will be suggested here that literature provided Döblin and others like Brecht and Wulffen with a heterogeneous and flexible space; one with its own ready-made and enlightened reading public that was sufficiently distinct from other, competing publics such as newspaper readers. Literature, in particular the so-called objective, empirically based literature produced by writers associated with the movement of "New Objectivity" (*Neue Sachlichkeit*), opened up a safe discursive space that enabled writers to borrow insights and even methods from the empirical human sciences, without apparent predetermined limits. In many ways, literature became a competitor with the life sciences—a "Lebenswissenschaft," to use Ottmar Ette's term, delineated not so much by its difference from other disciplines, but by mimicking, copying, and borrowing, sometimes to a baffling extent, from real-life cases.[2]

Yet, as I hope to show, this experimental zone, permeable as it was to other "life discourses," both scientific and nonscientific, both specialist and lay, was deeply unstable. Or, as Ottmar Ette argues with regard to literature in general, it was an "experimental dynamic space [*Bewegungsraum*], in which and from which we can test the fractures and aporias of our 'knowledge-of-living-together' [*ZusammenLebensWissens*]."[3] Under siege from competing directions—especially from the life sciences—literature was under pressure to innovate. This meant that writers were concerned to experiment with literary forms, which they did with carefree abandon, and to engage with, and even incorporate, the latest findings from a whole host of life disciplines; ones as disparate as medicine, psychiatry, sexology, neurology, criminology, the law, and psychoanalysis. Like much else in the aftermath of the Great War, a state of shock characterized the literary sphere, and writers and readers were deeply unsure of literature's identity. In this rapidly changing field, the case study genre became, as I will argue, anxious, if not neurotic about shoring up its epistemological foundations, even to the point of becoming unreadable.

A MODERNIST CASE STUDY?

Alfred Döblin's novella *Die beiden Freundinnen und ihr Giftmord* (Two girlfriends commit murder by poison), which he published in 1924 as part of a new literary series on crime, offers an intriguing example of literary case writing.[4] Based on the widely publicized Klein-Nebbe murder trial of 1923, the work belongs to a much older tradition of European crime writing.[5] Notably, with its focus on the criminal, *Die beiden Freundinnen und ihr Giftmord* is typical of much of the newly emergent crime writing from the second half of the nineteenth century onwards.[6] It is a case study that offers a "Beispiel," or a specific example of a general aspect of the human condition, in this instance, a scandalous, rare example of female criminality and sexuality, rather than an "Exempel," or an exemplar of a rule, a moral or legal norm.[7]

In many ways, *Die beiden Freundinnen und ihr Giftmord* might be considered a concretization of the simple form of the *Kasus*, which, according to André Jolles, is a universal form that discusses a criminal event in the context of a deviation from accepted moral behavior. Its function in Jolles's schema of simple narrative forms is to pose questions and weigh up norms of social behavior.[8] Rather like the riddle, which is a question that begs an answer, the *Kasus* poses a moral question via the crime. Often the question can be answered only partially, frequently by asking further questions. In addition, the *Kasus* appears to have much in common with legal and medical case writing, namely a concern with the relationship between the specific and the general, although the precise modality of this relationship can vary across case studies. In inductive case forms, the general can be inferred from the specific example; in deductive forms, the general exists prior to presenting the specific—or both exist simultaneously when interpretation and representation of the case happen to coincide.[9] The literary case study, especially the romantic, realist, and modernist cases of the nineteenth and twentieth centuries, gives preference to the inductive method over the deductive.[10] Further, it appears to place less weight on the general than on the specific instance.

Altogether, *Die beiden Freundinnen und ihr Giftmord* represents a curious, even anomalous, instance of case writing. The work is based on careful empirical research Döblin conducted into the case of the murder of the carpenter Klein by his wife Ella Klein and her accomplice Margarete Nebbe. Döblin fictionalizes this crime mainly by changing the names of the accused (but not the plot). Although following an inductive method, Döblin appears unsure of what general rule or conclusions he should draw from his meticulously researched and documented representation of the murder case. It is no surprise to find that his finished work is made up of a bricolage of different, discrete text types. The actual story of the murder is supplemented by other nonliterary and paraliterary components, which have largely perplexed critics. At the end of the narrative of the case there is a short epilogue, which is followed by two illustrated one-page analyses of each of the women's handwriting, "Zu Ellis Handschrift" (On Ellis's handwriting) and "Zu Margaretes Handschrift" (On Margarete's handwriting). At the very end of the volume of the first edition in 1924, and only in this edition, Döblin added an unusual psychoanalytic addendum to his narrative. Unbound from the text of the novella, and inserted in an envelope glued inside the back cover, the addendum presents a series of psychoanalytic diagrams to illustrate and comment further on the case. The diagrams are printed in color on ten A4-sized pages (or, to use the German measurement of the day, the page size is DN 476). The author calls this addendum, which comprises seventeen visualizations and two graphs, "Räumliche Darstellung der Seelenveränderung" (Spatial representation of the changes to the soul).

Some have read *Die beiden Freundinnen und ihr Giftmord* as a "strange hybrid of medical and literary writings," as a "trial report," or a "medical case history," while others have stressed it ought to be read as a "crime novel" or a "short story."[11] Most convincing is Todd Herzog's diagnosis of the work as a modernist case study.[12] The experimental spirit of modernism is in evidence in the "remarkable epilogue," in which Döblin comments on the poetological implications of his own case writing.[13] But the psychoanalytic addendum or supplement at the end of the work has puzzled readers the most, and has continued to defy attempts at classification. The series of circular Venn-like diagrams could be seen as presenting an additional narrative about the case in a different mode. Indeed, these diagrams may have served to sharpen Döblin's focus on the case. Rather than concentrating on events and circumstances, they foreground the psychic disposition of the three main characters in relation to one another over the course of the crucial years in which the crime was committed. Above all, they take up the themes of the women's homosexuality, of sadomasochism and perversion. Thus Döblin's addendum offers not merely a scientific commentary—it is also a painstaking analysis of the diachronic dimensions of the case in relation to the sexual pathology of the main protagonists.

Even so, strangely, this supplement does little to illuminate Döblin's literary account, neither reinforcing the overall coherence of the case nor elaborating on it in any greater depth. Its specialist discourse does not appear to shed any more light on the crime than does the story itself; nor does the addendum introduce additional, attenuating factors to the case that are not apparent from its fictionalized version. Instead it serves to overdetermine the plethora of evidence in circulation about the case; it provides a type of expert commentary, which is itself a type of case study, a psychoanalytic case, in which Döblin reframes his case in the fashionable and new language of psychoanalysis. In foregrounding the psychological determinants in the case, say, over the social or physiological motivations for murder, the addendum would therefore appear to lend legitimacy to newly emerging psychoanalytic epistemologies about sexuality and perversion. By the same token, it does so without substantially affecting the literary case study, which, as I hope to show, has the capacity for greater granularity of analysis than Döblin's pseudomedical addendum.

TRANSFORMING CRIMINAL CASES INTO LITERATURE THROUGH PSYCHOANALYSIS

Die beiden Freundinnen und ihr Giftmord presents the famous Klein-Nebbe murder case, still well known to the Weimar public when Döblin wrote the novella, only a year after the trial took place in Berlin. Arguably, Döblin borrows his material from the trial to explore the complexity of the female psyche and sexuality, turning the court case into a medical, psychiatric, and sexological case about the scandalous new type of female criminal, the "female poisoner." The trial of Ella Klein and Margarete Nebbe for attempted murder by poisoning their husbands with arsenic touched a raw nerve with readers of the time, whose fears and anxieties about female sexuality and power had already been amply nurtured by publications such as Richard von Krafft-Ebing's sexological study *Psychopathia Sexualis* (1886); Oskar Panizza's satire *Psichopatia Criminalis* (1898); and Erich Wulffen's handbooks for lawyers and doctors, *Das Weib als Sexualverbrecherin* (1923) and *Psychologie des Verbrechers* (1908 and 1913). The Klein-Nebbe case, which was heavily sensationalized in the print media and taken up by the international press as well, had the added intrigue of female homosexuality, or inversion, along with another modish topic of the day, the "perversion" of sadomasochism.

At first glance, despite its fictionalizing aspects, Döblin's case study most closely resembles legal and medical-forensic case reporting of the time, particularly in relation to murder cases by poisoning. Forensic case reporting first emerged in the eighteenth century, as part of a new "forensic dispositive" that was grounded in pharmacological and medical discourses, and made possible by new administrative structures and testing possibilities that were then deployed as forensic evidence in trials.[14] In the medical-forensic reports written by experts for courts, the fields of medicine, policing, and criminal justice were closely interlinked in the creation of expert knowledge about crime. Early case reports often served a didactic function, and their writers were keen to extrapolate the general lesson from the specifics of the case, with specialist readers in mind.[15]

Increasingly throughout the nineteenth century, specialist medical knowledge was presented in forms and media specifically aimed at a general reading public. During the eighteenth century, the Pitaval tradition of crime writing had already made sensational criminal court cases accessible to a lay reading public, and, as middle-class publics expanded in the course of the nineteenth century, so did the level of awareness about criminality and pathology, as well as competency in reading such cases. This was partly due to the fact that, after 1850, legal trials were opened to the public, and newspapers were able to report cases of general interest with greater fidelity, and in a more realistic style. Literary writers, too, were able to ground their crime narratives in more reliable sources of empirical evidence, such as material presented at trials, as well as expert witness statements.[16] With the advent of psychoanalysis and sexological theories about "deviant" sexual behavior in the twentieth century, the forensic dispositive came to focus on the criminal and her state of mind. By the time of the Klein-Nebbe trial in 1923, the courts deployed state-of-the-art medical evidence, often from competing areas within the same discipline; from all branches of forensic medicine, neurological psychiatry, sexual medicine, and psychology. Of all the branches of psychiatry it was, however, psychoanalysis—the least "disciplined" of the new medical disciplines—that was least well represented in court cases.[17] This lack of presence during trials is symptomatic of the difficulties surrounding the institutional acceptance of psychoanalysis.[18]

As far as we know, Döblin was not an expert witness at the Klein-Nebbe court case, nor was he present during the trial of the 23-year-old Ella Klein, whom Döblin calls Elli Link, and her accomplice Margarete Nebbe, whom he calls Grete Bende. Instead, Döblin draws on the comprehensive newspaper coverage of the trial, which lasted five days in March 1923, but which was reported in the morning and evening issues of virtually every national and regional newspaper. Furthermore, we know that through professional contacts Döblin possessed a copy of the senior public prosecutor's indictment (*Anklageschrift*) from the Berlin County Court, summarizing the court proceedings. Döblin was also familiar with the three medical expert witness statements; these had been made by sexologist and psychiatrist Magnus Hirschfeld, the psychiatrist Otto Juliusberger, and psychiatrist and neurologist Friedrich Leppmann.[19]

From an analysis of much of the available source material it is apparent that Döblin tried to remain faithful to his empirical sources. In this sense his literary case study appears to be a good exemplar of the modernist aesthetics of New Objectivity, which aimed to move literature away from conventional psychology and into closer proximity to the human and empirical sciences. This meant that literature became more documentary in style, what Döblin was to call a form of "Tatsachenphantasie," or "factual imagination/fantasy."[20] If greater objectivity was only to be obtained at the price of greater attentiveness to interdisciplinarity, then this was, according to Döblin, a price he felt able to pay. In terms of Döblin's own development as a writer, *Die beiden Freundinnen und ihr Giftmord* is a transitional work, representing a pivotal moment in the evolution of Döblin's concept of epic prose, and of the montage technique of later works such as *Berlin Alexanderplatz*.[21] The 1924 novella also marks a transition from a reliance on psychology to a growing awareness of the value of psychoanalysis.[22]

DÖBLIN'S EPILOGUE: COMPLEXITY IN LITERARY CASES

In terms of the genre of the case study, Döblin's story *Die beiden Freundinnen und ihr Giftmord* is significant for what it can tell us about the *literary* case study and its public at a crucial stage of its development. More specifically, this instance of a literary case study can assist us with delineating the value added by a literary treatment of the topic of sexually motivated crime. Does the literary medium offer, for example, a privileged space for case studies—a home with a broad, heterogeneous public for a nomadic genre that had, by the 1920s, become fiercely contested? Or does the experimental nature of Döblin's case writing suggest instead that while the public may have become more competent—medically, sexologically, legally, and psychoanalytically—to deal with greater complexity in literary texts, literature struggled as a medium to cope with this complexity?

In the epilogue to *Die beiden Freundinnen und ihr Giftmord* Döblin has provided a number of answers:

> When I cast my eye over the entire thing, it seems like it was in the story: "and then the wind came and tore down the tree." I don't know what type of wind it was and where it came from. The whole is a carpet which consists of many individual bits, of cloth, silk, metal pieces as well as lumps of clay. It is stitched together with straw, wire, yarn. In some places the parts are only loosely connected. Other fragments are connected by glue or glass. And yet it is all seamless and bears the mark of truth. And this is the way it happened: even the actors think so. But it could as easily not have happened this way.[23]

With his metaphor of a carpet, woven out of cloth and silk, but also metal and clay, Döblin has found a powerful image for his multidisciplinary creation. Unsurprisingly, he is not entirely convinced that the heterogeneity of methods used has created an integrated whole. That some sections of the carpet are woven out of glass, rope, straw, and clay—that is, out of material that is normally extraneous to rug weaving—is an admission that he is not happy with the coherence of his work. To be sure, if we look at its odd structure, the image of a patchwork is no exaggeration. Indeed, more than a carpet, the case could be seen to resemble a garment or a coat, even an overcoat; the body woven out of literary fabric, while the rest is made of other disciplinary material. This overcoat could be thought to have, for instance, graphological sleeves from the two analyses of the accused's handwriting included after the epilogue. The same woven overcoat has an added frame or fringe in the epilogue, and, at the back, a secret gusset, tucked away out of sight, in the ten unbound leaves containing the psychoanalytic emplotment of the case.

The metaphor of a patchwork carpet or coat aptly captures Döblin's keen sense of the multiple causal factors at play in this intriguing case. Yet he is clearly baffled and bewitched by its complexity. As the patchwork shows, this complexity is unwieldy and irreducible; the coherence of the case is not so much enhanced by the multiple perspectives as undermined by them. Döblin, it seems, balks at the disciplinary richness and determinism of the case—a response all the more perplexing given that he was an expert in most of the specialist discourses included in *Die beiden Freundinnen und ihr Giftmord*.

TOWARDS LITERATURE AS A LIFE SCIENCE

Like many of his literary forebears, Döblin was a practicing doctor. Trained in neurology and psychiatry, he worked in large psychiatric clinics before setting up private practice in Berlin. Around the same time he became interested in psychoanalysis, training after World War I as an analyst in the Berlin Psychoanalytic Institute under Ernst Simmel.[24] Notwithstanding his expertise in medicine and the humanities, Döblin always felt an uneasy tension between his work as a doctor and his work as a writer. In two curious essays of 1927, cast in the form of a dialogue, "Der Nervenarzt Döblin über den Dichter Döblin" (The nerve doctor Döblin on the writer Döblin) and "Der Dichter Döblin über den Nervenarzt Döblin" (The writer Döblin on the nerve doctor Döblin), he wrote about the odd relationship between the two different aspects of his life. Here, Döblin the doctor claims to barely "know" Döblin the writer, and maintains that his literary works "are completely foreign to me and I am also completely indifferent to them."[25] The doctor side of himself does not share the political views or the tastes in literature of his writer self. Döblin the writer, however, appears to have a far better relationship to his namesake in Döblin the doctor; he is at least curious to learn more about the life of a doctor, and even to exploit it, if only to find source material for use in his writing.

In these dialogues, the split between Döblin's two passions in life is presented less in psychological than in sociological terms, and offers a commentary on the increasing specialization of knowledge in the modern world. The writer is an individualist and a generalist, while the doctor is nothing out of the ordinary, a "grey soldier in a quiet army," and a specialist.[26] Nonetheless, Döblin the writer has an inferiority complex with regard to Döblin the doctor: "I have defects, probably complexes, and the practiced doctor probably sensed something."[27] Despite the writer's greater fame, he feels defensive towards the doctor, as if intimidated by the knowing gaze of the psychiatrist, whereas Döblin the doctor is unashamed of his ignorance of literature.

From this exchange, it is not hard to adduce the crisis of dominant literary systems of knowledge in the face of increasing specialist knowledge from the life sciences—or, to borrow from Ottmar Ette, from the "other" life sciences. The doctor possesses a qualitatively different type of knowledge from the writer, a superior perspective on life that intimidates the writer. The writer, by contrast, must look further afield for inspiration, and draw on the doctor's experience for material. Furthermore, the writer's crisis is fuelled by an economic difference between the two forms of knowing in Döblin's life. In an essay about the viability of writing literature, titled "Ökonomisches aus der Literatur" (Economic observations from the literary sphere), Döblin complained bitterly that despite publishing ten books and selling 6,200 copies, he had barely managed to earn 400 reichsmark per month in the year of 1924 alone.[28]

In *Die beiden Freundinnen und ihr Giftmord*, both this existential crisis of the writer and the crisis of literature in general find themselves echoed in Döblin's epilogue to the case, which in turn underscores his perceptions of the limitations of literature as a medium. Instead of summarizing his findings on the court case, the epilogue ends up negating the value of definitive diagnoses altogether: "And this is the way it happened: even the actors think so. But it could as easily not have happened this way."[29] That is, the epilogue undermines the epistemological basis of applied case writing. Paradoxically, it serves to distinguish the difference that literature makes, as a form of case writing, and to negate the ability of the literary case study to make definitive judgments about cases. At the same time, Döblin suggests in his epilogue that the literary case can be defined by the fact that it problematizes what other genres cannot know. It may also be the place where skeptics of other genres reside.

Döblin's literary case writing in *Die beiden Freundinnen und ihr Giftmord* offers, I suggest, an instance of overdetermination. By overdetermination I mean the identification of multiple causal factors, any one of which would have been a sufficient condition to produce the motivation and give rise to the crime. My usage lies somewhere between Sigmund Freud's use of overdetermination in dream theory, and Louis Althusser's adaptation of the notion to investigate the necessary social contradictions needed for change.[30] *Die beiden Freundinnen und ihr Giftmord* overdetermines the actual Klein-Nebbe murder case on a number of levels. The literary section borrows furiously from newspaper reports, court materials, expert witness statements, and Döblin's own vast theoretical and practical knowledge of the subject. Döblin's literary analysis is already overdetermined in the way it points to various causes—such as the lesbian relationship between Elli and Grete; their violent and loveless marriages; the choice of poison; the psychology and pathology of the characters—each one of which could have been sufficient to produce the crime of murder. Further, Döblin has overburdened his case study in formal, aesthetic terms as well. By embroidering on the literary case, first by adding his fringe, then his sleeves, and finally the hidden gusset of his carpet-overcoat-like creative work, Döblin deliberately overstates his case. Or, rather, he stages the overdetermination of the case genre in several discrete acts.[31]

In each of these acts, Döblin tries to elucidate the etiology of the crime, with the help of distinct discursive formations. The first chapter of the narrative recounts the story of Elli Link and her abusive relationship with her husband; the second chapter tells of the lesbian relationship between Elli and Grete, and their plot to kill their husbands; and finally Döblin concludes with a summary of the findings of the trial. In the literary sections Döblin provides his own etiology of the case, stressing similar causal factors such as infantilism, homosexuality, and the brutality of Elli's husband.[32] But unlike the court reporting, Döblin is at pains to offer a sympathetic and impartial account, which he achieves mainly through censoring much of the original evidence produced at the trial. The court transcripts are full of explicit statements taken from the six hundred letters exchanged by the accused, and include repeated references to Klein/Link as a "Schwein" (pig).[33] By contrast, Döblin's accounts are tempered by the use of focalized narration, and by references to Elli's suffering. These mitigating circumstances point to an important functionality of the literary mode, which is to humanize the criminal rather than diagnose him or her.

At the level of plot, the narrative is preoccupied with the psychosexual dynamics of the marriage between Link and Elli—described from both perspectives—and the plan to murder Link, while the trial and Elli's time in jail are given little coverage. The language used throughout is literary in the broadest sense, neither medical nor psychoanalytical, yet it is replete with allusions to common psychoanalytical terminology of the day. For instance, when referring to the work of the unconscious, Döblin uses the word *unterirdisch* (subterranean).[34] While the behavior and actions of his characters are clearly viewed through the lens of medical knowledge, Döblin's craft is purely literary.

HOMOSEXUALITY IN THE LITERARY CASE AND IN THE PSYCHOANALYTIC ADDENDUM

In this final section I take an example of one knowledge dispositive, and examine the ways in which Döblin's treatment of this in *Die beiden Freundinnen und ihr Giftmord* differs in two different parts of his patchwork. Specifically, I compare the collection of psychoanalytic diagrams that make up the addendum with the literary treatment of the case. In the literary case, Döblin alludes in general terms to that which Döblin the doctor would probably call the unresolved Oedipal complexes of Elli and Grete. Elli's infantile sexuality and her homosexuality beg to be read, it seems to me, in conjunction with a famous psychoanalytic text that also appeared in 1924, namely Freud's essay "The Dissolution of the Oedipal Complex."[35] Read alongside Freud's groundbreaking text, which Döblin was doubtless familiar with, Elli's sexuality can be interpreted as a regression to an earlier phase of Oedipal development, or even as a homosexual resolution.

In Döblin's story, Elli, who is characterized as "light-hearted and funloving," naively marries Link because of his similarity to her father. Döblin mentions that Link even has the same profession as Elli's father.[36] Grete also appears to have strong libidinal ties to one parent, that is, to her mother: "Under the close attachment to her mother Grete had remained unfree."[37] During the courtship between Elli and Link, Elli is described as attempting to substitute Link for her father—in what seems a normal, if not extremely belated dissolution of the Oedipal complex in classic Freudian terms. However, she is hindered by Link's slavish attachment to her, which sparks off her hatred of him. This turning point is described in pseudopsychoanalytic terms as a "subterranean disappointment" ("unterirdische Enttäuschung").[38] A "normal" transference of desire from the father to the husband becomes impeded, and Elli regresses to an earlier stage of sexual development in which she views men as presexual playthings. Significantly, all these terms are similar to terms used by Freud when describing the trigger for a girl's abandonment of affection for her mother, and its transference to her father during the Oedipal phase. Disappointment with the mother (because she is castrated) is a key plank of Freud's psychoanalytic theory, part of regarding the mother as the cause of the girl's lack of a penis; of course feminists have taken issue with these interpretations.[39] Freud considers disappointment important because, in contradistinction to the little boy who stays fixated on the mother and finds a mother-substitute, disillusionment with the mother provides the trigger for the girl to abandon her mother as love object, "tak[e] her mother's place and . . . adopt . . . a feminine attitude to her father," and hence a heterosexual object choice.[40] According to Freud, this precedes the onset of the incest taboo, and the final dissolution of the Oedipal complex, in which the girl transfers her affections from her father to a father-substitute. In Döblin's text, a disappointment is clearly at the source of the marital problems soon encountered by Elli and Link, and this triggers Elli's regression. Ultimately, disappointment also leads to her homosexuality. For if a disappointment with the mother is the trigger for a heterosexual object choice in Freud, with Döblin it is disappointment with a father-substitute that sets in motion a homosexual object choice. Döblin's account, although somewhat different from Freud's, is clearly framed in Freudian terms of the day.

If we take Döblin's attempt at creating a psychoanalytic case, namely his addendum or supplement in the hidden gusset of our textual coat, we find that this reading of an Oedipal conflict is reinforced but not enriched in any substantial way. Elli's psychic disposition is described throughout this addendum as dominated by two main complexes—these complexes are represented by the two circles inside the Venn diagram of Elli's personality, and they are depicted in "Phase 1" by "parental love" ("Elternliebe"), and sexuality.[41] In Döblin's representation of Elli's psyche, these complex-circles are shown overlapping at the beginning of the story, and at the end after the crime has been committed; that is, throughout all seventeen depicted phases. The effect of this overlap, which is reminiscent of mathematical set theory, is to suggest that the *aim* of Elli's desire and the *object* of her desire are both connected to parental love—as indeed they are in Freud's theory of the Oedipal complex.[42] The interconnection also points to Elli's arrested, infantile sexuality. However, Döblin's imagery for the complexes, which he possibly took from his mentor, the psychiatrist Alfred Erich Hoche, is strangely one-dimensional.[43] The complex-circles, although dynamic, possess neither the depths of the unconscious as described by Freud and Carl Gustav Jung, nor the added dimension of the superego.[44] In addition, Döblin makes no distinction between mother and father, and the diagram does not explore the key moment of disappointment. Hence it identifies little development from beginning ("Phase 1") to end ("Phase 17").[45]

In the addendum, homosexuality is likewise depicted as a complex that emerges first in Grete in "Phase 10," as an offshoot of her sexuality and "motherly love."[46] Elli's homosexuality (which also splits off from her sexuality) first appears spontaneously in "Phase 11," as a mechanistic response to Grete's already activated homosexuality complex.[47] The complex then wanders off in "Phase 12" towards the periphery of the psyche in the direction of Grete, where it meets up with Grete's complex.[48] The emergence of homosexual desire is thus presented in psychological terms in relation to parental love, as with Freud's Oedipal complex—but here not specifically in relation to the unconscious. Döblin also presents homosexual desire as having social or circumstantial origins in Elli's abusive marriage to Link, and in her friendship with Grete, which is borne out by the story. The psychoanalytic diagrams make no clear distinction between active and passive subjects of desire; they portray both women with certain masculine traits at various times. Interestingly, Döblin does not depict the homosexuality of the women as a perversion.

However we read the addendum, this topography of the souls of the three main characters, and the seventeen diagrams and two graphs are a curiosity. What does this supplement add to the case? Does it provide an alternative etiology of the crime, or reinforce the same causality proposed by the literary section of the case? I maintain that, first and foremost, for the audience of the first edition of *Die beiden Freundinnen und ihr Giftmord*, the psychoanalytical diagnosis added a layer of specialist terminology, which was at least gratifying to the trained reader. Did Döblin's addendum help the educated public of the 1920s to unlock the unconscious motives for the crime?[49] Or did it merely allow the writer to display his expert knowledge and his cultural capital? Undoubtedly this singular material evidences Döblin's familiarity with Freud's topographical model of the soul; Alfred Adler's physiological models; Hoche's theory of complexes, and Jung's. It also displays Döblin's vast knowledge of current psychological and psychoanalytical ideas.

THE LABORATORY OF LITERATURE AND THE OPEN CASE

The addendum stresses epistemological complexity and diversity. This complexity presented one of the greatest challenges to modernist literature, and to the artists and writers of the New Objectivity movement in particular. That in 1924 Döblin felt compelled to blur the boundaries between the literary and the psychoanalytic case, and to encumber his literary treatment of the Klein-Nebbe murder with extra scientific "bells and whistles," is testament to this crisis in aesthetics. For Döblin the medical practitioner who was a part-time writer, the aesthetic dilemmas were mirrored by the real existential crisis of the 1920s writer, who could not live from literature alone. The compromised, hybrid form of the case study that Döblin devised for *Die beiden Freundinnen und ihr Giftmord*, and which he abandoned in subsequent works, thus underscores his personal crisis of faith in literature, and in its traditional alliances with psychology and criminology. Rather than consider literature an "interdiscourse" adept at mediating between other forms of knowledge, Döblin desired literature to be more like the other life sciences, with a greater "access to the facts."[50] In the epilogue to *Die beiden Freundinnen und ihr Giftmord*, he compares the inferior methods of novelists with those of the chemist, remarking that that "no chemist would work with such impure materials" as the novelist.[51] According to Hania Siebenpfeiffer and Jürgen Link, it is the role of interdiscourses such as journalism and literature to "despecialize" specialist discourses, and not to mimic them.[52] Arguably, Döblin lost sight of this mediating role for literature when writing the transitional work *Die beiden Freundinnen und ihr Giftmord*. Moreover, he seems to have overlooked the fact that literary creations can and do replace real-world clarity and pertinence with ambivalent and open-ended messages. Ambivalence does not destabilize literature, and only enriches it: literature specializes in exploring life's complexities in nonspecialist language. From this perspective, in the first edition of *Die beiden Freundinnen und ihr Giftmord* Döblin may have made a case for literature's obsolescence.[53]

* * *

Die beiden Freundinnen und ihr Giftmord reflects the multidisciplinarity of the case genre of the interwar period, and the openness of the literary case, in particular, to external influences. Reading as an anxious, unruly, and overdetermined case, his study in *Die beiden Freundinnen und ihr Giftmord* is at the extremes of intelligibility—and was an experiment he was not to repeat. *Die beiden Freundinnen und ihr Giftmord* does not present the female criminal as a specific instance of a general rule for disciplinary action or prevention. Instead, in the laboratory of literary culture, the exception or deviation from the normal is normalized as a possible modality of the human. Even so, this laboratory functions best when it remains an inexact science. Hence the topographical diagrams of the addendum, which were never republished in editions after the first, seem out of place in a literary work, even today. For writers and artists with a commitment to New Objectivity, the solution to the crisis of literature was to reground literary communication about sexuality and female criminals in the empirical life sciences, only to realize, perhaps too late, that literature had a much more sympathetic complement in psychoanalysis. And yet, as contended above, the mere *addition* of psychoanalytic models after the close of the narrative cannot necessarily improve readers' understanding of sex crimes. The interdiscourse of the literary does not gain from the authentication strategy of "tacking on" a scientific addendum—although to Döblin the literary account given in *Die beiden Freundinnen und ihr Giftmord* must have seemed deficient enough to require further, expert padding. As a result, in this instance, the case study genre became so overdetermined by extraliterary discourses, so overwhelmed by disorder and sheer complexity, that it threatened to separate into its constituent parts altogether. This is indeed what Döblin's patchwork creation did over time, insofar as the hidden gusset of the coat disappeared from public view into the archive. Meanwhile, his literary case survived to the present day, in the public domain, to be republished as part of all subsequent editions of the work.

NOTES

1. See Hania Siebenpfeiffer, *"Böse Lust"*: *Gewaltverbrechen in Diskursen der Weimarer Republik* (Cologne: Böhlau, 2005), 95.
2. See Ottmar Ette, ed., *Wissensformen und Wissensnormen des ZusammenLebens: Literatur—Kultur—Geschichte—Medien* (Berlin: Walter de Gruyter, 2012), and Ottmar Ette and Wolfgang Asholt, eds., *Literaturwissenschaft als Lebenswissenschaft: Programm—Projekte—Perspektiven* (Tübingen: Narr, 2010).
3. "Ein experimenteller Bewegungsraum, in dem und von dem aus wir die Brüche und Aporien unseres ZusammenLebensWissens gleichsam testen können," in Ette, "Vorwort," in *Wissensformen und Wissensnormen*, vi.
4. Döblin's novella was one of the first in a new series called "Außenseiter der Gesellschaft: Die Verbrechen der Gegenwart" (Outsiders in society: Today's crimes), edited by Rudolf Leonhard, and published by the newly established publishing house Verlag Die Schmiede in Berlin.
5. Joachim Linder, "Sie müssen das entschuldigen Herr Staatsanwalt, aber es ist so: Wir trauen Euch nicht . . .," in *Erzählte Kriminalität: Zur Typologie und Funktion von narrativen Darstellungen in Strafrechtspflege, Publizistik und Literatur*, ed. Jörg Schönert (Tübingen: Niemeyer, 1991), 533–570, at 534.
6. Linder, "Sie müssen das entschuldigen Herr Staatsanwalt, aber es ist so," 535.
7. André Jolles, *Einfache Formen—Legende, Sage, Mythe, Rätsel, Spruch, Kasus, Memorabile, Märchen, Witz* (Tübingen: Niemeyer, 1968), 178–79.
8. Jolles, *Einfache Formen*, 191.
9. Johannes Süßmann, "Einleitung: Perspektiven der Fallstudienforschung," in *Fallstudien. Geschichte—Theorie—Methode*, ed. Gisela Engel, Susanne Scholz, and Johannes Süßmann (Berlin: Trafo, 2007), 7–27, at 20.

10. Medical cases ranged from the *consilia* offering medical advice in the Middle Ages; cases focused on therapies in the *curationes*; reports on deformities and strange diseases; to autopsy reports of deaths by poisoning, which retrospectively diagnosed the patient: see Michael Stolberg, "Formen und Funktionen ärztlicher Fallbeobachtungen in der Frühen Neuzeit (1500–1800)," in *Fallstudien. Geschichte—Theorie—Methode*, ed. Gisela Engel, Susanne Scholz, and Johannes Süßmann (Berlin: Trafo, 2007), 81–96). Medical case writing produced reports that could be used either to illustrate medical theories, or to show how medical knowledge should be applied to specific cases. In modern medicine, which has a long tradition of using case reporting of different kinds, the relationship between the specific and the general remains similar.

11. For a summary of the main interpretations in the research see Todd Herzog, "Crime Stories: Criminal, Society, and the Modernist Case History," *Representations* 80, no. 1 (2002): 34–61, at 50.

12. See Todd Herzog's extensive discussion of the work in terms of a "modernist case history" which "takes the modernist crisis of narrative as its starting point in order to depict a larger crisis of faith in the legal and social order," Herzog, "Crime Stories," 54.

13. Herzog, "Crime Stories," 51.

14. Bettina Wahrig, "Erzählte Vergiftungen: Kriminalitätsdiskurs und Staatsarzneikunde 1750–1850," in *Fallstudien. Geschichte—Theorie—Methode*, ed. Gisela Engel, Susanne Scholz, and Johannes Süßmann (Berlin: Trafo, 2007), 97–111, at 98.

15. Wahrig, "Erzählte Vergiftungen," 104–6.

16. Siebenpfeiffer, "*Böse Lust*," 73–74.

17. Wolfgang Schäffner, *Die Ordnung des Wahns: Zur Poetologie psychiatrischen Wissens bei Alfred Döblin* (Munich: Wilhelm Fink, 1995), 8.

18. Sarah Winter, *Freud and the Institution of Psychoanalytic Knowledge* (Stanford: Stanford University Press, 1999), 131ff.

19. Hirschfeld also wrote an article for the media about the case, see Magnus Hirschfeld, "Die Giftmischerinnen," *Die Weltbühne* 19 (1923): 358.

20. Alfred Döblin, "An Romanautoren und ihre Kritiker: Berliner Programm," in *Schriften zu Ästhetik, Poetik und Literatur*, ed. Erich Kleinschmidt (Olten: Walter Verlag, 1989), 119–23, at 123.

21. Devin Fore, "Döblin's Epic: Sense, Document, and the Verbal World Picture," *New German Critique* 99 (2006): 171–207, at 175.

22. See Schäffner, *Die Ordnung des Wahns*, 11.

23. "Überblicke ich das Ganze, so ist es wie in der Erzählung: 'da kam der Wind und riß den Baum um.' Ich weiß nicht, was das für ein Wind war und woher er kam. Das Ganze ist ein Teppich, der aus vielen einzelnen Fetzen besteht, aus Tuch, Seide, auch Metallstücke, Lehmmassen dabei. Gestopft ist er aus Stroh, Draht, Zwirn. An manchen Stellen liegen die Teile lose nebeneinander. Manche Bruchstücke sind mit Leim oder Glas verbunden. Dennoch ist alles lückenlos und trägt den Stempel der Wahrheit. Es hat so sich ereignet; auch die Akteure glauben es. Aber es hat sich auch nicht so ereignet." See Alfred Döblin, *Die beiden Freundinnen und ihr Giftmord* (Düsseldorf: Artemis und Winkler, 2001), 79 (unless otherwise noted, all translations into English are my own).

24. While training as a psychoanalyst under Ernst Simmel, Döblin joined Karl Abraham's reading group, and came into contact with some of the great psychoanalysts of the time in Erich Fromm, Wilhelm Reich, and Melanie Klein (see Veronika Fuechtner, "'Arzt und Dichter': Döblin's Medical, Psychiatric, and Psychoanalytical Work," in *A Companion to the Works of Alfred Döblin*, ed. Roland Dollinger, Wulf Köpke, and Heidi T. Tewarson

(Rochester: Camden House, 2004), 111–37, at 119–20). Döblin shared the social and political concerns of the Berlin Psychoanalytic Institute, and became a member of the "Verein Sozialistischer Ärzte" through which he came into contact with the work of Magnus Hirschfeld's Institute for Sexual Science.

25. Alfred Döblin, "Der Nervenarzt Döblin über den Dichter Döblin," in *Autobiographische Schriften und letzte Aufzeichnungen* (Olten: Walter Verlag, 1980), 33–34, at 33.
26. Döblin, "Der Dichter Döblin über den Nervenarzt Döblin," 34.
27. Döblin, "Der Dichter Döblin über den Nervenarzt Döblin," 34.
28. Alfred Döblin, "Ökonomisches aus der Literatur," in *Schriften zu Leben und Werk* (Olten and Freiburg im Breisgau: Walter Verlag, 1986), 77–78, at 78.
29. Döblin, *Die beiden Freundinnen*, 79.
30. Mikko Lahtinen, *Politics and Philosophy: Niccolò Machiavelli and Louis Althusser's Aleatory Materialism*, trans. Gareth Griffiths and Kristina Köhli (Leiden: Brill, 2009), 33ff.
31. My argument here is similar to that advanced by Hania Siebenpfeiffer, who argues that the sections of the work be understood not as a text-paratextual relationship, but as individual components of a narrative whole which comment upon and complement each other in their truth claims (see Siebenpfeiffer, "*Böse Lust*," 132).
32. Siebenpfeiffer, "*Böse Lust*," 122.
33. Alfred Döblin, "Anklageschrift Klein-Nebbe" (copy of the court's indictment), Alfred Döblin Papers, Deutsches Literaturarchiv, Marbach am Neckar, HS 1997.7.100/2, 1–61, at 27.
34. Döblin, *Die beiden Freundinnen*, 7.
35. Sigmund Freud, "The Dissolution of the Oedipal Complex" (1924), in *The Penguin Freud Library*, vol. 7, *On Sexuality: Three Essays on the Theory of Sexuality and Other Works*, trans. James Strachey, ed. Angela Richards (Harmondsworth: Penguin, 1977), 314–22.
36. "War leicht und lebenslustig": Döblin, *Die beiden Freundinnen*, 5.
37. "Unter der engen Anhänglichkeit an die Mutter war Grete unfrei geblieben": Döblin, *Die beiden Freundinnen*, 17.
38. Döblin, *Die beiden Freundinnen*, 7.
39. See, for example, Irene P. Stiver, "Beyond the Oedipus Complex: Mothers and Daughters," in Judith V. Jordan et al., *Women's Growth in Connection: Writings from the Stone Centre* (New York: Guilford Press, 1991), 97–121, at 101–7.
40. Freud, "The Dissolution of the Oedipal Complex," 321.
41. Alfred Döblin, *Die beiden Freundinnen und ihr Giftmord* (Berlin: Die Schmiede, 1924), unnumbered folio under Phase 1—henceforth referenced as Döblin, *Die beiden Freundinnen* (1924 edition).
42. See Veronika Fuechtner, *Berlin Psychoanalytic: Psychoanalysis and Culture in Weimar Republic Germany and Beyond* (Berkeley: University of California Press, 2011), 54–55.
43. Fuechtner, "Arzt und Dichter," 114.
44. Fuechtner argues that the main contribution of Döblin's topography of the soul lies in the "relational dynamics" between the characters, which distinguishes him from Adler, Jung, and Freud: See Fuechtner, *Berlin Psychoanalytic*, 55.
45. Döblin, *Die beiden Freundinnen* (1924 edition), unnumbered folio under "Phase 17."
46. Döblin, *Die beiden Freundinnen* (1924 edition), unnumbered folio under "Phase 10."

47. Döblin, *Die beiden Freundinnen* (1924 edition), unnumbered folio under "Phase 11."
48. Döblin, *Die beiden Freundinnen* (1924 edition), unnumbered folio under "Phase 12."
49. Siebenpfeiffer argues that the main innovation of Döblin's version of the court case was his addition of the dimension of the unconscious. While this holds true for the narrative, it does not appear to hold for the psychoanalytic diagrams comprising the addendum, which seem more indebted to Hoche's symptom complexes than to theories of the unconscious. See Siebenpfeiffer, "*Böse Lust,*" 121.
50. "Zugang zu den Tatsachen": Döblin, *Die beiden Freundinnen,* 80.
51. "Kein Chemiker würde mit solchen unreinen Stoffen arbeiten": Döblin, *Die beiden Freundinnen,* 80.
52. Siebenpfeiffer, "*Böse Lust,*" 72, and Jürgen Link, *Versuch über den Normalismus: Wie Normalität produziert wird* (Göttingen: Vandenhoeck and Ruprecht, 2006), 40f.
53. See Ette, "Vorwort," in *Wissensformen und Wissensnormen,* vi.

10 The Lunatics of Love
Armand Dubarry's Psychopathological Novels and Their Publics

Jana Verhoeven

In 1896 veteran French journalist and popular novelist Armand Dubarry (1836–1910) took on an unprecedented task: he started to produce a series of "psychopathological novels" based on sexological case studies. The series, entitled *Les déséquilibrés de l'amour* (The lunatics of love) turned out to be a great success, and resulted in twelve novels, many of which went through dozens of reprints. The themes and style of these novels are representative of a large body of texts produced in France during the late nineteenth century and variously concerned with the medicalization of sexuality. Alternatively called medico-erotic literature, *romans des mœurs*, or psychopathological novels, these "middlebrow" texts point to specific sociocultural developments linked to the emergence of new publics for such literature, and to associated questions of middle-class respectability and its increasing relationship to medical science.[1] Over the past twenty years Peter Cryle, Michael Finn, Vernon Rosario, Gabrielle Houbre, Michael L. Wilson, and others have contributed important insights to our understanding of the interplay between medical discourse, fiction, and sexuality in fin-de-siècle France.[2] This chapter contextualizes Dubarry's series of novels in order to better understand the interrelated dynamics of sexology, the fictionalization of cases, changing readerships and forms of address, and the "respectable" limits of eroticism in this period. Specifically, I argue that Dubarry, basing his writing on Richard von Krafft-Ebing's collection of case studies of sexual "perversion," *Psychopathia Sexualis* (1886), used medical discourse in a very deliberate manner, in order to claim respectability for his particular brand of "middlebrow" erotic literature. In doing so, he explicitly addressed a less educated and less exclusively male "public" than that which made up the typical readership of sexological texts.

The following analysis is based on twelve novels published between 1896 and 1902.[3] *Le fétichiste* (The fetishist, 1896), the first novel of Dubarry's series, describes the unsuccessful conspiracy between a fetishist and his nymphomaniac wife to cheat a young orphan out of her inheritance. In the second novel, *Les invertis: Le vice allemand* (The inverts: The German vice, 1896), a sexually "inverted" woman (that is, a same-sex desiring woman) tries to pressure the wife of her likewise "inverted" brother into a homosexual relationship, while the effeminate brother pursues the former fiancé of his young, virginal wife. The third book, *L'hermaphrodite* (The hermaphrodite, 1896), traces the adventurous voyage from Europe to South America of a young woman afflicted with a penis and a sexual desire for women—which ends in her suicide. *Hystérique* (Hysteric, 1897), the fourth installment of the *déséquilibrés*, narrates the case of a hysterical but calculating young girl who wrongly accuses one of her father's employees of rape. The fifth "deviant," the main protagonist of *Coupeur de nattes* (Braidcutter, 1898), acts in tandem with a fellow fetishist, a handkerchief thief, to hassle a young working-class girl and her mother. *Les flagellants* (The flagellants, 1898) are a group of upper-class debauchees who conspire to withhold the inheritance of a returning young soldier. *Le vieux et l'amour* (The old man and love, 1898), the seventh of the series, adapts the actual criminal case of a senile erotomaniac millionaire who falls victim to a greedy and murderous couple. The eighth novel, *Les femmes eunuques* (The eunuch women, 1898) puts on trial feminists who undergo voluntary sterilization in order to escape motherhood. *Mademoiselle Callipyge* (Miss Beautiful Buttocks, 1900) describes how perverts who specialize in anal intercourse plot the murder of an innocent heiress. I have been unable to access the tenth novel, *Lourdes, amoureuse et mystique* (Lourdes, enamored and mystical, 1900). *Le plaisir sanglant* (The bloody pleasure, 1901), the eleventh installment of the series, discusses the cases of two sadistic Englishmen; one murders, disembowels, and rapes young girls, while his brother stabs women's bottoms for sexual pleasure. The twelfth and final novel, *L'abbe écornifleur: L'inceste* (The scrounger priest: Incest, 1902), was actually written before the series took shape. Consequently, neither the lecherous priest nor the unhappy young wife who falls in love with her stepson qualify as sexually "deviant" in the sense of the other *déséquilibrés* portrayed by Dubarry. Nevertheless, they furnish occasion to incorporate into Dubarry's series a sexological discourse of incest.

Dubarry, I suggest, used these novels about sexual "deviance" to make sexological findings available to a broader reading public that encompassed lower-middle-class male readers and also, explicitly, women. Whereas openly pornographic books were circulated clandestinely during this period, the present chapter demonstrates that Dubarry managed to convince *the* public and *his* public that, despite the openly sexual themes of his books, it was not an act of immorality to read them.[4] *The* public, in Michael Warner's sense of a social totality, refers here to French fin-de-siècle society as a whole, including institutions of censorship, whereas *his* public—"the kind of public that comes into being only in relation to texts and their circulation" is constituted by the readers of Dubarry's books.[5] I demonstrate how, in order to appear inoffensive to *the* public, and to enforce the claim to respectability for his books and *his* reading public, Dubarry employed a pseudoscientific discourse that was also openly nationalistic and xenophobic.

CLASSIFYING SEXUAL PERVERSION

Dubarry was certainly considered a respectable author in fin-de-siècle France. By 1896, when the first of the *déséquilibrés* novels appeared, Dubarry, an active member of the prestigious writers' society *Societé des gens de lettres*, was at the height of a prolific and successful journalistic and literary career. Born in 1836, he had been the Italian correspondent for various French pub-lications during the 1860s. The earliest entry for Dubarry in the catalogue of the French national library is the title *Un vétéran d'Arcole à l'Italie, ode aux peuples allies* (1859), a statement of solidarity with the Italian people fighting for their independence and national unity. Back in France after the Franco-Prussian War, Dubarry took the post of editor of illustrious and respectable periodicals such as *Le Pays* and *Le Figaro*.[6] He published across many genres, but was most prolific in the field of travel adventures, which were often given exotic locations such as the Congo, Turkey, or Australia. The long list of Dubarry's book publications also includes titles such as *Service des mœurs* (Vice squad) and *Délire des sens* (Delirium of the senses), which indicates a penchant for risqué material; the sheer number of titles makes it probable that he employed ghost writers for some of these.[7] That he published twelve novels in the *déséquilibrés* series within the space of seven years, each of them over three hundred pages long, certainly supports this speculation.

In the preface to the first book in the series, *Le fétichiste*, Dubarry explains that reading the French translation of Krafft-Ebing's *Psychopathia Sexualis* inspired him to fictionalize that which Krafft-Ebing had taxonomized as sexual "perversions."[8] In the subsequent titles, Dubarry presents the above-mentioned variations of sexual perversion in a manner that echoes the taxonomizing impulse of early sexology. Although Dubarry based several of his novels on French criminal and medical cases, his attempt to transform medical cases from the realm of German sexology into *romans des mœurs* stands out by its sheer scope. To fictionalize the greatest possible number of sexual perversions in a series of middlebrow literary texts was an ambitious undertaking, and often necessitated the attribution of several perversions to a single character. In this section I investigate the specific manner in which his works transformed cases from the medical to the fictional domain, creating an enlarged reading public for sexological knowledge. This discussion of Dubarry's books as a series with a distinct underlying pattern contributes to a more thorough understanding of the uses of medical knowledge at the fin de siècle, of its transformation across genres, as well as of the role of cases in this particular author's oeuvre.[9] Reading Dubarry's texts gives a modern reader the impression that they were written primarily to titillate his fin-de-siècle audience; the relative lack of character or plot development nourishes this impression. At the same time, Dubarry's crude grafting of medical discourse onto his literary nar-ratives is puzzling at first glance. Only by considering these narrative and stylistic choices as deliberate components of a larger authorial agenda can we apprehend their purpose, especially considering Dubarry's own good social standing. Dubarry's specific handling of the case study, I argue, provides the bridging element between two seemingly irreconcilable concepts: that of erotic literature, which graphically depicts acts of sexual transgression, and that of bourgeois respectability.[10]

Dubarry provided each novel of his series with a preface in which he justifies his project. In the preamble to *Le fétichiste* he states his purpose as follows: by fictionalizing scientific cases of sexual aberrations, he wants "to provoke reflection, compassion, to unveil the wretchedness and infirmities which can be relieved when they cannot be cured." The aim of the book is not, he insists in the same sentence, "to arouse lewdness."[11] Rather, the author claims that the series will make medical cases accessible to a public hitherto excluded from their reach. Dubarry also points us to what, for him, makes a case: he calls it "une déviation du sens génésique"—a deviation of the reproductive senses.[12] This characterization of the case can be linked to the definition of the *Kasus* (case) given by André Jolles in 1935, as a deviation from the norm, a crime, or a deformation.[13] In the context of late nineteenth-century morals, the norm of "proper" bourgeois sexuality is violated in Dubarry's novels by *déséquilibré* or "lunatic" characters that, on account of their specific sexual leanings and practices, represent such a "deviation."

The opening novel introduces the specific manner in which Dubarry transforms cases into fiction, or what might be termed "case stories." The actual sexological case was probably taken from the eighty-first observation in the French translation of Krafft-Ebing's *Psychopathia Sexualis*, which presents the son of a general who was interested only in blonde women who wore a certain costume.[14] The fetishist in the novel, Frédéric Genlis, similarly has very distinct ideas about the women to whom he is capable of being attracted. A scheming widow who is trying to extract a fee for her role as procuress introduces him to a lower-class girl, who corresponds to his particular type.

In *Le fétichiste*, Dubarry institutes a number of character constellations and plot developments that recur throughout the series. First, the *déséquilibrés* are almost invariably both sexually "deviant," and criminal; in this novel, Genlis cheats a young girl out of her inheritance. Second, the *déséquilibrés* usually exhibit multiple perversions: Genlis has a fetish for young women who dress and behave in a certain way, but he also has masochistic leanings. Third, Dubarry's *déséquilibrés* almost never act alone; they belong to a larger group of mentally ill and morally corrupt men and women. It is thus possible to extend to these characters Michael L. Wilson's argument that fictional "pederasts"—a common nineteenth-century term for men who practiced cross-generational homosexual behavior—"are invariably involved with criminality, primarily blackmail and prostitution; . . . that pederasts form a hidden network—a sort of freemasonry."[15]

Another feature linking the "deviant" characters in this novel is a lack of character development. Krafft-Ebing and other sexologists presented cases as narratives that included childhood experiences, traumatic events, and attempts to explain the cause of their subject's perversion. Dubarry, however, took little interest in the biography or psychology of the *déséquilibrés*. Despite proclaiming his wish to arouse sympathy for these medical subjects, he presents them as sick, criminal "freaks of nature" with a tendency to be drawn towards others like themselves. They can be easily dismissed as the deviant, evil "Other," for the writer's moralizing tone is unmistakable, and represents an attempt to reach out to his readers on a basis of common values.

At the same time, Dubarry compensated for the superficial portrayal of his "deviant" protagonists by presenting positive counterparts who engage in the kinds of struggles and development characteristic of the nineteenth-century novel. These young, unmarried (or married but virginal) men and women represent the sexually and socially normal, and the morally strong. In *Le fétishiste*, for example, the young Emma Divonne has just lost her father. Only following long struggles is she able to recover his fortune, which has been unjustly withheld by the fetishist. Her regained wealth enables her to marry her fiancé, a penniless officer, providing a conventional "happy ending." However, Divonne does not meet the fetishist in person; she recuperates her rights only with the help of intermediaries. This is typical of Dubarry's series, where the narrative plot involving the "normal" protagonist is usually kept separate from the plot involving the *déséquilibrés*. In order to maintain the virginal heroine's purity of body and soul there is no direct contact between her and the pervert. In this first novel, Divonne is kept out of the "dirty" sexual business of the plot. At no point is she confronted with erotic scenes, and her connection to the fetishist is only through a subplot entirely concerned with money.

Other installments in the *déséquilibrés* series likewise involve an innocent young girl and her manly protector who together struggle against a criminal activity—a withheld inheritance, theft, blackmail, slander, even attempted murder—and who are rewarded with financial and marital security at the end of the novel. These parallel plots serve several purposes: first, they present the readership with repeated reinforcements of a normal, moral object of identification. Furthermore, the inclusion of a conventional romance plot represents an explicit attempt by Dubarry to address the female members of his intended readership (an aspect to which I return below), for women were the foremost consumers of the *roman à l'eau de rose*, the sentimental novels in which the protagonist overcomes multiple obstacles and is rewarded at the end with matrimonial happiness and prosperity.[16] Above all, however, presenting a positive alternative to sexual deviance was premised upon a claim to respectability. As George Mosse argues, the "distinction between normality and abnormality was basic to modern respectability; it provided the mechanism that enforced control and ensured security."[17] In Dubarry's series, the positive male protagonist is invariably endowed with "love of work and fatherland, goodness and integrity," providing a "normal," respectable bourgeois counterpart to the "abnormal" *déséquilibrés*.[18]

GRAFTING MEDICAL DISCOURSE ONTO LITERATURE

This dichotomy of the "normal" versus the "abnormal" is played out on different levels: socially, sexually and, of course, medically. Peter Cryle and Lisa Downing demonstrate how, during the nineteenth century, physicians and scientists were increasingly preoccupied with the "anomalous, the excessive and the defective."[19] The medical profession had claimed for itself the authority to establish the difference between normalcy and abnormality. The realization of this authority leads to a dazzling structural choice in Dubarry's novels: an abrupt insertion of medical discourse. Roughly halfway through the plot development, the author exits the narrative to give a historical overview of the particular perversion from antiquity to the late nineteenth century, followed by an exposé of the latest scientific findings on the topic. The narrative is thus interrupted, and a crude switch from the textual mode of literary fiction to that of pseudoscience occurs. These abrupt inserts, I suggest, served as a device which allowed Dubarry to claim respectability for his texts. As Peter Cryle argues, the "second-hand authority of science is offered as a guarantee that this work will never descend into pornography."[20] In some cases the pseudoscientific material seems to be incorporated in an almost arbitrary fashion: in *Le fétishiste*, for instance, instead of discussing fetishism per se, Dubarry introduces the reader to historical occurrences of masochism. He stops at the figure of the Marquis de Sade to explain the latter's perversion in more detail, and then cites a recent example of the criminal case of a sadistic murderer known as Lesteven, who had been tried in Paris in 1894.

Dubarry was surely no scientific expert, but he had acquired vast experience in the popularization of scientific texts, having succeeded Jules Verne as the popular science writer for the periodical *Le musée des familles*. His superficial treatment of sexological matters points to his intended public: readers with little previous experience of scientific discourse—including women, who generally had less exposure to such material than men. It is also noteworthy that Dubarry did not make the effort to weave the medical discourse into the fabric of the narration—as had, for example, Émile Zola in his series *Les Rougeon-Macquart* (1871–93), a cycle of novels depicting the social and physical decadence of a family with specific emphasis on the effects of heredity and the environment. Yet this lack of subtlety was, I argue, quite a deliberate strategy: Dubarry's abrupt grafting was not only economical in terms of the rapid production of texts; it also served as an easily discernible signal of his intention to disseminate medical knowledge, and thereby appropriate respectability for his work.

It seems, however, that in some instances Dubarry did have a genuine interest in medical discourse, especially when this was linked to the practical implications of mental illness, and the asylums in Paris in particular. Dubarry was fascinated by these institutions, and passionate about their social repercussions; he also used them to establish his credentials as a writer with a social conscience. In his second novel he quotes Benjamin Ball, psychiatrist at the Sainte-Anne hospital in Paris and author of *La folie érotique* (Erotic insanity, 1888); he also quotes Alfred Binet's 1887 article, "Le fétichisme dans l'amour," which appeared in the *Revue Philosophique*.[21] Dubarry's interest in mental illness was shared by many of his contemporaries. Formerly used as a place to contain the "mad" and deranged, and to isolate them from society, mental asylums had become hotspots of science, due especially to the late nineteenth-century growth of psychiatry as a "respectable" medical discipline.[22] The medical management of mental illnesses, or even their possible cure, moved physicians and lay observers alike. Similarly, the names of Parisian hospitals such as Sainte-Anne, la Salpêtrière, Villejuif and Bicêtre—all used as settings in the *déséquilibrés* series—as well as those of famous psychiatrists like Jean-Martin Charcot (1825–93), were highly evocative well beyond the immediate psychiatric profession.

In the *déséquilibrés* series the mental asylums serve a double purpose. First, they provide the background against which Dubarry can demonstrate his credibility as a social observer, and showcase his series as an expression of a socially progressive agenda. These discussions of the asylums are the only instances where the writing moves away from case stories or medical discourse and refers to public institutions of fin-de-siècle France, discussing their usefulness and their effects on the population's well-being. Dubarry attributes his close attention to mental institutions to the clarity with which they reveal modern developments in psychiatry: "it is in the asylums that one sees best the fragility of the human machine and the vanity of the science of the alienists."[23] He goes on to condemn as particularly counterproductive the medical hierarchy in the asylum of Villejuif.

Second, mental asylums serve as the place of final punishment for a number of his protagonists. In the first of Dubarry's novels, the fetishist, his nymphomaniac wife, and her exhibitionist lover all end up permanently shut away in the Sainte-Anne hospital. This puts into doubt Dubarry's prefatory protestation of merely wishing to "unveil the miseries and infirmities which might be alleviated if not cured, and not to light up lechery."[24] His claims of wanting to incite understanding for the problems of the *déséquilibrés* are contradicted by his plots. The sexually "deviant" are positioned as the agents of evil, blocking the way to happiness for the "normal" protagonists. Consequently, they must be isolated from society, either by being permanently confined to a mental institution, or by suffering a horrific death—a denouement typical of the fin-de-siècle psychopathological novel according to Cryle.[25]

HOMOSEXUALITY AND NATIONALISM

Dubarry's second book in the *déséquilibrés* series, *Les invertis: Le vice allemand*, deals with "inversion," or homosexuality, both male and female.[26] In this novel, the "deviant"/"invert" protagonist is ultimately attacked by an eagle and falls off an alpine cliff, leaving the young, "normal" couple in the parallel plot to enjoy their subsequent marital love in financial security. To maximize plot efficiency, Dubarry presents "the inverts" of the title as brother and sister, Adolphe de Champlan and Florine de Morangis. Their respective love interests are the "normal," positive protagonists, whose own path to a love relationship is blocked by the siblings' perverse desires. As in all of his psychopathological novels, Dubarry portrays the "inverts" as cases, in the sense described by Jolles above: as an instance of the abnormal, but, at the same time, an example of a wider social phenomenon. The effeminate, "invert" brother and his masculine, "invert" sister serve as cases and types through which to construct otherness—particularly when juxtaposed with their two objects of desire: the heterosexual, "normal," virginal girl and her hardworking but not-yet-rich lover. The fact that Dubarry chose death as the punishment of "the inverts" (and not sequestration in an asylum), points to the particular problem faced by fin-de-siècle morality: although homosexuality was widely considered immoral, abnormal, and vicious, it could no longer be straightforwardly classed amongst the perversions regarded as mental illnesses.[27] Dubarry himself admits that homosexuality did not necessarily stand in the way of greatness, and cites the historical examples of alleged inverts such as Alexander the Great or Frederick the Great of Prussia. Furthermore, he must have been aware of recent developments in sexology, whereby homosexuality had begun to be considered neither a disease nor a crime.

The case story of the homosexual siblings Adolphe and Florine also highlights how notions of "nation" and "perversion" were linked. *Les invertis* is notable for its specifically anti-German bias, already indicated in the subtitle, *Le vice allemand,* or "the German vice." In his customary insertion of medical discourse midway through the book, Dubarry discusses homosexuality as more prevalent outside France, including in other European countries.[28] He proclaims that "nowadays the English and the Prussians are the leading European pederast movement," and adds that even the French word *prussien*, which designates the lower back of the body, is indicative of the relative prevalence of homosexuality in the German lands of Prussia.[29] In making this claim, Dubarry cites several factors. First, he notes that homosexuality first became an important object of scientific discussion in Germany, and quotes from Krafft-Ebing and other leading German sexologists such as Albert Moll (1862–1939); he also cites Oswald Zimmermann's 1885 discussion of sadomasochism, *Die Wonne des Leids* (The joy of suffering, 1885). In Dubarry's view, the fact that

German sexologists played a pioneering role in the discussion of homo-sexuality was proof that the vice was far more widespread in that country than elsewhere.[30]

Apart from noting the origins of the sexological discourse of homosexu-ality, Dubarry also points to the existence of a homosexual scene in Ger-many, quoting from a German newspaper that reported on a homosexual masked ball in the social column, a degree of public exposure unfathomable in France.[31] French historian Julian Jackson has argued that, in reaction to the criminalization of homosexuality in Germany, homosexuals in that country, much more than in France, let their voices be heard, such that an openly homosexual journal, *Der Eigene*, was published from as early as 1899.[32] In *The History of Sexuality*, Michel Foucault argues that the con-cept of homosexuality, and the identity of the homosexual, was a product of social, juridical, and most importantly, medical discourse.[33] In line with this argument, the concentration of sexological literature in German surely contributed to the perception of Berlin as the center of "invert" activities from the mid-nineteenth century, or, as Robert Beachy writes in a recent article, to the "German invention of homosexuality."[34]

Dubarry links the perceived prevalence of homosexuality in Germany to the country's strong militarism. However, his presentation of the mil-itary as the hotbed of "pederasty" (Dubarry's term) points to another dimension in such claims. While Dubarry's adamant attribution of the modern source of homosexuality to the Germans was due, in part, to a more generalized perception in France of a heightened visibility of homo-sexuality in Germany, his indignation also had clear patriotic undertones. For Dubarry, like many of his French readers, the memory of the traumatic defeat of France at the hands of the Prussians during 1870–71 remained strong. In *Les invertis*, this explains his insertion of an episode related neither to the narrative nor to homosexuality, in which he recounts how he witnessed Bavarian soldiers pillaging a train store during the Franco-Prussian War.[35] Dubarry uses the motif of homosexuality to conclude that the barbarians who had overrun his beloved fatherland were nearly all sodomites. Here, again, he tries to make a link between sexual deviance and criminal greed.

By treating homosexuality in a pseudoscientific manner, and situating it in a historical and geopolitical context—here with a strong anti-German bias—the *invertis* in this second novel demonstrate the close link between nationalism and claims to respectability. George Mosse has argued that nationalism "absorbed and sanctioned middle-class manners and morals and played a crucial part in spreading respectability to all classes of the popula-tion."[36] The fifth novel in the *déséquilibrés* series, *Coupeur de nattes* (Braid cutter) takes up the nationalistic theme once more by attributing English origins to two fetishists; one who cuts braids from female strangers, and another who steals handkerchiefs. In the wake of the recent trial of Oscar

Wilde in 1895, Dubarry endows the fetishists with attributes evocative of English aesthetes:

> Robert Guildford and Sosthène Stroud were childhood friends, of the aesthete kind, worthy of each other, . . . of English origin. . . . After some university studies and obtaining bachelor diplomas, both, born lazy, instead of embracing regular careers, devoted themselves to decadent literature, . . . they were internationalists and booed their fatherland France.[37]

The worst part of their anti-French diatribes involve "lambast[ing] the immorality of the French and magnify[ing] the virtues of the Germanics [*germanique*], from whom they had taken onanism, sodomy and other sexual aberrations."[38] Dubarry completes the social circle of the anglophile aesthetes with a German spy, also a "pervert" with homosexual leanings. Similarly, in the eleventh novel, *Le plaisir sanglant*, the sadistic killer is a puritan English pastor. Before this killer, his sadistic wife, and his bottom-stabbing brother are unmasked, the righteous normal protagonist, who is French, puts the English in their place by explaining why there is no need for an *entente cordiale* between the two countries:

> The English, persisted Voutenay, are the Pharisees of politics and the robbers of the planet. Egoistical, fallacious, positive, cupid, solemn, imperious, hypocrite, more immoral than those they denigrate, they are the object of everybody's aversion, because they have oppressed, hurt and injured everybody, and never given help to anyone.[39]

These xenophobic portrayals help Dubarry to again point to the allegedly foreign origins of sexual perversion, and to counterattack the widespread stereotype of French immorality.

L'hermaphrodite

Only one book of the series, *L'hermaphrodite*, is told from the perspective of the "deviant." The parallel plot of conventional romance is missing, and the reader's sympathies are directed towards the *déséquilibré*: Brigitte Lambert is constructed as an object of pity rather than horror or indignation. Furthermore, Dubarry chose to structure this novel as a travelogue rather than a *roman Parisien*. This is clearly due to the material on which Dubarry based his novel: the case of Herculine Barbin (1838–68), who left a long autobiographical narrative detailing the life of a woman who was gradually becoming conscious of her masculine sexuality. Completed before her suicide, Barbin's autobiography was excerpted for publication by the physician Auguste Ambroise Tardieu (1818–79). Barbin's case attracted the attention of several notable physicians of the day, and also that of several literary figures beyond French borders. A further middlebrow novel, *L'hermaphrodite au couvent* (The hermaphrodite in the convent), by a certain Dr. Caufeynon, was published in 1905, while German master of provocation Oskar Panizza also took up the subject, and in 1893 published a short story entitled *Ein skandalöser Fall* (*A scandal at the convent*).[40]

Foucault presents Herculine Barbin as a case illustrating his approach to the textual genre of the case more broadly, first in a French edition of Barbin's memoirs published in 1978, and then in an English edition.[41] As in his other case presentations, such as that of Pierre Rivière (1973), Foucault explains that he considers a case as a "'dossier,' that is to say, a case, an affair, an event that provided the intersection of discourses that differed in origin, form, organization and function."[42] Both the case of Pierre Rivière and that of Herculine Barbin are viewed from a variety of angles: Foucault presents the perspective of the representatives of institutions, such as physicians and the bishop, but also a first-person narrative by the subject of the case. Together, these testimonials can be seen as the discourses that, in turn, constitute sexuality. In each of these two case presentations, Foucault lets the discourses of textual sources stand for themselves. No final truth or explanation is offered. The case reveals itself in the intertextuality of the different documents comprising the dossier, with the different narratives and institutional voices completing or challenging each other.

The same is not true for Dubarry's approach in the *déséquilibré* novels: like others writing stories on pathological themes at this period, Dubarry does not question medical authority, since it is the doctor who proclaims unalterable truths.[43] The final words in *L'hermaphrodite* come from the autopsy of the *suicidiaire*, whereby genital attributes were used to confirm belonging to one sex—the male one. This conclusion reflects Foucault's finding that, until recently, a person was obliged to have only one true sex, either male or female.[44] Throughout the nineteenth century, the figure of the hermaphrodite raised complex questions about the makeup and role of gender, the attribution of fixed criteria, and the justification of male hegemony.[45] In Dubarry's novel, the doctor's pronouncement of a single sex defuses the potential challenge embodied in the hermaphrodite.

Dubarry remains true to his bric-a-brac narrative structure in *L'hermaphrodite*. He attributes the protagonist's biological "dysfunction" to the dramatic events of her genesis, by grafting a criminal case onto the beginning of the novel. This case was inspired by that of the real rapist and murderer Lesteven, who had already appeared in the first novel of the series. Having been raped and almost killed by this bloodthirsty "erotomaniac" (known as "the terror of la Villette"), the mother gives birth to Brigitte, only to die in an anarchist bomb attack a few years later. The hermaphrodite then embarks on a voyage to South America, facing volcanoes, murderous Indians, crocodiles, vampire bats, and jaguars. This blatant deviation from Barbin's autobiography, and from the conventions of Dubarry's own series, results in a travelogue slightly more entertaining than the other novels. The travelogue seems to have been the genre in which Dubarry was most comfortable, since most of his published books were classified in that category. The psychological and erotic introspection offered by Barbin's original narrative, however, are discarded in favor of repeated voyeuristic rape scenes, graphically described. As Magali Le Mens argues, rather than showing real interest in the situation of hermaphrodites, *L'hermaphrodite* is more revealing of the author's erotic fantasies.[46] The remaining nine novels of the *déséquilibrés* series repeat these established textual structures, such as linking sexual deviance with criminal activity; the triumph of the normal; punishment for the *déséquilibrés*; and the crude grafting of medical discourse onto fictional material. Other novels in Dubarry's series reveal broader social concerns specific to their day, such as anxieties about depopulation or the rise of feminism. In *Les femmes eunuques*, number eight of the series, Dubarry's condemnation is accordingly directed less toward sexual deviance and more toward debates about the role of women in the professional sphere, and about patriarchy as the foundation of society.

DUBARRY'S PUBLICS

Dubarry's very particular way of presenting cases, and the very idea of creating a series of sexual-pathological case stories, give indications about the sort of education, class, and ideological leanings of his readership. Obviously, his readers were not part of the educated elite, but nor would they have been the usual consumers of cheap adventure or pornography novels aimed at the uneducated masses. The number of editions for each volume of the *déséquilibrés* series indicates that these reading publics were many; there were even translated versions, including into Portuguese. Judging from its list of publications, the publishing house Editions Chamuel seems to have specialized in this field of risqué and sometimes shocking erotic literature. As argued above, the weaknesses in structure, language, and character development indicate that the series was not written for a highly educated audience, but for an audience that was nonetheless anxious to claim respectability.[47] The novels contain passages that most likely would have been classified as pornography at the time. Yet the author succeeds in creating a varnish of pseudoscientific decorum by justifying the necessity of such passages in the prefaces; by inserting medical discourse; and by his proclamations of a socially progressive agenda, such as his concerns over the management of mental institutions, and his halfhearted support of the afflicted.[48]

To better grasp the sociocultural composition of an audience, Warner points to temporally structured forms oriented towards the circulation of texts, such as advertisements, reviews, or other intermediaries between the author and the reader, which engage in "the reflexive circulation of discourse."[49] The novels were reviewed, for example, in the Parisian magazine *Le monde artiste*, an illustrated magazine dedicated to the theatre, music, and fine arts.[50] Although the texts about each new installment of the series present generic advertisements rather than critical reviews, their inclusion in these publications indicates that Dubarry's target audience included reasonably educated middle-class men and women, consumers of the wide array of mainstream cultural activities offered in fin-de-siècle Paris. A very clear indication that Dubarry included women among his intended audiences can be found at the end of the preface to *Le fétichiste*, where the author addresses his public directly, expressing his hope that this book will induce the "lecteurs et lectrices," the male *and female* readers, to be interested in the remainder of the series. That is, Dubarry expressly uses the masculine and feminine form of the noun "readers," although the French masculine plural would have sufficed to indicate a general audience.

A few passages in the texts themselves represent a direct address by Dubarry to an intended readership that encompassed the lower middle class; in these he expresses solidarity with simpler tastes. Dismissing the decadent and elitist cultural leanings of more highly educated groups, he calls, for example, on the worship of the decorative in everyday life. One of his "normal" and "positive" protagonists, the painter Silvère Voutenay, is thus

> convinced that the role of the artist does not exclusively consist in brushing vague paintings which will be hung in more or less illuminated places, that the art of embellishing the dwelling, the furniture, the kitchen, the garden, enters into practical life, to make it more amenable, and to naturally develop the taste for beauty, refine the soul and improve education.[51]

Dubarry's strategy is to engage a complicity of shared values with his intended readership—of sexual morality, middle-class culture, and patriotism—in order to declare it acceptable to consume fiction with openly sexual content. I suggest that his readers, like Dubarry himself, were titillated by the erotic passages in his books, and gladly took up the offer (made through the inserted medical discourse) to justify their reading on moral grounds. The shortcomings of the narrative and style point to an audience without great aesthetic expectations, while the awkward reproduction of medical discourse indicates that the intended readership was not assumed to possess extensive experience with scientific texts.

CONCLUSION

Dubarry's sloppy grafts and juxtapositions of the results of modern sexology suggest that he was eager to include as much "deviant" sex as possible in his books. His personal interest in sexology does not seem to have gone far beyond the desire to titillate; there is no attempt to provide his "deviant" characters with psychological depth. I suggest that sexological literature was gladly taken up as an excuse to portray "deviant" practices, and erotic or sexual practices more generally, in Dubarry's middlebrow fiction. His series of novels demonstrates an effort to claim respectability for erotic fiction and its consumers at the fin de siècle. His structural borrowings from the sexological case study, which had achieved prominence with Krafft-Ebing's *Psychopathia Sexualis*, his grafting of medical discourse onto otherwise conventional melodramatic fiction, and his strong nationalistic tone indicate that he engaged in a deliberate discussion with *his* lower middle class reading public—and that he did so to forestall any accusations of lewdness on the part of *the* public, namely, French fin-de-siècle society.

NOTES

1. "Medico-erotic literature" is the phrase used by the Goncourt brothers in Edouard and Jules de Goncourt, *Journal: Mémoires de la vie littéraire*, vol. 2 (Paris: Éditions Robert Laffont, 1989), 1142.
2. See Peter Cryle, "Foretelling Pathology," *French Cultural Studies* 17, no. 1 (2006): 107–22; Michael Finn, "Female Sterilization and Artificial Insemination at the French Fin De Siècle: Facts and Fictions," *Journal of the History of Sexuality* 18, no. 1 (2009): 26–43, and *Hysteria, Hypnotism, the Spirits, and Pornography: Fin-De-Siècle Cultural Discourses in the Decadent Rachilde* (Newark: University of Delaware Press, 2009); Vernon A. Rosario, *The Erotic Imagination: French Histories of Perversity* (New York: Oxford University Press, 1997); Gabrielle Houbre, "The Bastard Offspring of Hermes and Aphrodite: Sexual 'Anomalies' and Medical Curiosity in France," in *Sexuality at the Fin De Siècle: The Makings of a "Central Problem"*, ed. Peter Cryle and Christopher E. Forth (Newark: University of Delaware Press, 2008), 61–73; Michael L. Wilson, "'The Despair of Unhappy Love': Pederasty and Popular Fiction in the Belle Epoque," in *Sexuality at the Fin de Siècle*, ed. Cryle and Forth, 109–23.
3. The titles forming the series are as follows: Armand Dubarry, *Les déséquilibrés de l'amour 1. Le fétichiste* (Paris: Chamuel, 1896); *Les déséquilibrés de l'amour 2. Les invertis: Le vice allemand* (Paris: Chamuel, 1896); *Les déséquilibrés de l'amour 3. L'hermaphrodite* (Paris: Chamuel, 1897); *Les déséquilibrés de l'amour 4. Hystérique* (Paris: Chamuel, 1897); *Les déséquilibrés de l'amour 5. Coupeur de nattes* (Paris: Chamuel, 1898); *Les déséquilibrés de l'amour 6. Les flagellants* (Paris: Chamuel, 1898); *Les déséquilibrés de l'amour 7. Le vieux et l'amour* (Paris: Chamuel, 1898); *Les déséquilibrés de l'amour 8. Les femmes eunuques* (Paris: Chamuel, 1899); *Les déséquilibrés de l'amour 9. Lourdes, amoureuse et mystique* (Paris: Chamuel, 1900); *Les déséquilibrés de l'amour 10. Mademoiselle Callipyge* (Paris: Chamuel, 1900); *Les déséquilibrés de l'amour 11. Le plaisir sanglant* (Paris: Chamuel, 1901); *Les déséquilibrés de l'amour 12. L'abbe écornifleur: L'inceste* (Paris: Chamuel, 1902).
4. Despite the passing of an 1881 law stipulating the liberty of the press and the book, such publications were vulnerable to laws concerning the offence of affront to public decency. However, the application of the public decency

laws is qualified by scholars as "passably liberal": Bernard Joubert, *Anthologie érotique de la censure* (Paris: Éditions de La Musardine, 2001); see also Annie Stora-Lamarr, *L'enfer de la IIIe République: Censeurs et pornographes, 1881–1914* (Paris: Imago, 1989).

5. See Michael Warner, "Publics and Counterpublics," *Public Culture* 14, no. 1 (2002): 49–90, at 49, 50.

6. Rosario, *The Erotic Imagination*, 181.

7. For the period between 1861 and 1902, there are more than fifty new book titles to Dubarry's name.

8. For the sake of readability I will use the terms "pervert" and "perversion" henceforth without quotation marks, reflecting their use by Dubarry and contemporaries; no value judgment is implied. Dubarry read Krafft-Ebing in the translation of 1895: Richard von Krafft-Ebing, *Étude médico-légale: Psychopathia sexualis, avec recherches spéciales sue l'inversion sexuelle*, trans. Émile Laurent and Sigismond Csapo (Paris: Georges Carré, 1895). Laurent and Csapo translated the eighth German edition of *Psychopathia Sexualis* from 1893.

9. Of the existing scholarship on Dubarry's work, Peter Cryle's analysis of the way in which the use of psychosexual science functioned as a protection from accusations of frivolity in *Les invertis* (Cryle, "Foretelling Pathology") has been particularly helpful for my argument. Specific books of the series have also been discussed by Michael Finn and Mark S. Micale, see: Finn, "Female Sterilization"; Mark S. Micale, *Approaching Hysteria: Disease and Its Interpretations* (Princeton: Princeton University Press, 1995), and *The Mind of Modernism: Medicine, Psychology, and the Cultural Arts in Europe and America, 1880–1940* (Stanford: Stanford University Press, 2004).

10. On what constitutes pornographic and erotic literature see Peter Cryle, *Geometry in the Boudoir: Configurations of French Erotic Narrative* (Ithaca NY: Cornell University Press, 1994).

11. Dubarry, *Le fétichiste*, 7. Translations are mine.

12. Dubarry, *Le fétichiste*, 6.

13. André Jolles, *Einfache Formen: Legende, Sage, Mythe, Rätsel, Spruch, Kasus, Memorabile, Märchen, Witz* (Tübingen: Niemeyer, 1974), 179.

14. Krafft-Ebing, *Étude médico-légale: Psychopathia sexualis*, 221.

15. Wilson, "The Despair of Unhappy Love," 112.

16. On women as readers of novels see Martyn Lyons, *Readers and Society in Nineteenth-Century France: Workers, Women, Peasants* (New York: Palgrave, 2001), 81–83.

17. George L. Mosse, *Nationalism and Sexuality: Respectability and Abnormal Sexuality in Modern Europe* (New York: H. Fertig, 1985), 10.

18. Dubarry, *Coupeur de nattes*, 45.

19. Peter Cryle and Lisa Downing, "The Natural and the Normal in the History of Sexuality," *Psychology & Sexuality* 1, no. 3 (2010): 191–99.

20. Cryle, "Foretelling Pathology," 112.

21. Dubarry, *Les invertis: Le vice allemand*, 261–62.

22. See Jan Goldstein, *Console and Classify: The French Psychiatric Profession in the Nineteenth Century* (Chicago: University of Chicago Press, 2001), and Cryle, "Foretelling Pathology," 113–14.

23. Dubarry, *Les invertis: Le vice allemand*, 261–62.

24. Dubarry, *Le fétichiste*, 6.

25. Cryle, "Foretelling Pathology," 120.

26. For an in-depth discussion of the way in which the term inversion is used in *Les invertis: Le vice allemand* see Erin G. Carlston, "German Vices: Sexual/

Linguistic Inversions in Fin-de-Siècle France," *The Romanic Review* 3 (2009): 279–305, at 279.

27. See Robert Beachy, "The German Invention of Homosexuality," *The Journal of Modern History* 82, no. 4 (2010): 801–38, at 805, and Heike Bauer, *English Literary Sexology: Translations of Inversion, 1860–1930* (New York: Palgrave Macmillan, 2009), 21–42.

28. Dubarry also believed that homosexuality was even more rampant in Muslim countries, where he considered it already inscribed in the Koran: see Dubarry, *Les invertis: Le vice allemand*, 93.

29. Dubarry, *Les invertis: Le vice allemand*, 122.

30. Dubarry, *Les invertis: Le vice allemand*, 131.

31. Dubarry, *Les invertis: Le vice allemand*, 127.

32. Julian Jackson, *Living in Arcadia: Homosexuality, Politics, and Morality in France from the Liberation to Aids* (Chicago: University of Chicago Press, 2009), 25 and 30.

33. Michel Foucault, *Histoire de la Sexualité* (Paris: Gallimard, 1984), 58.

34. Robert Beachy, "The German Invention of Homosexuality," 801–38.

35. Dubarry, *Les invertis: Le vice allemand*, 130–31.

36. Mosse, *Nationalism and Sexuality*, 9.

37. Dubarry, *Coupeur de nattes*, 29–30.

38. Dubarry, *Coupeur de nattes*, 33.

39. Dubarry, *Le plaisir sanglant*, 120.

40. A modern translation of Panizza's story was published in Foucault's casebook of Barbin, cited below.

41. Herculine Barbin, *Herculine Barbin dite Alexina B., présenté par Michel Foucault* (Paris: Gallimard, 1978); Herculine Barbin and Michel Foucault, *Herculine Barbin: Being the Recently Discovered Memoirs of a Nineteenth-Century French Hermaphrodite* (New York: Pantheon Books, 1980).

42. Michel Foucault and Blandine Kriegel, ed., *I, Pierre Rivière, Having Slaughtered My Mother, My Sister, and My Brother . . . : A Case of Parricide in the 19th Century*, trans. Frank Jellinek (New York: Pantheon, 1975), 11.

43. See Cryle, "Foretelling Pathology," 116.

44. Foucault, *Herculine Barbin*, vii.

45. Houbre, "The Bastard Offspring," 63.

46. Magali Le Mens, "L'hermaphrodite dans le cabinet du médecin, de la fin du XVIIIe au XXe siècle," *Face à face* 8 (2006), see http://www.faceaface.revues.org/233?lang=en (accessed November 5, 2013).

47. See Anne-Marie Thiesse, *Le roman du quotidien: Lecteurs et lectures populaires à la Belle Epoque* (Paris: Le Chemin Vert, 1984).

48. See Dubarry, *Le Fétichiste* and *Les invertis: Le vice allemand*.

49. Warner, "Publics and Counterpublics," 62.

50. See, for instance, "Bulletin bibliographique," *Le monde artiste*, July 19, 1896, 458; July 27, 1896, 830; January 15, 1899, 46; June 24, 1900, 396; June 29, 1902, 412.

51. Dubarry, *Le plaisir sanglant*, 33.

11 Making a Case for Castration
Literary Cases and Psychoanalytic Readings

Christiane Weller

This chapter seeks to address three sets of interrelated questions regarding literature, psychoanalysis, and the reading publics of each field. First, why does psychoanalysis read literature; what kind of audience or public does psychoanalysis present for literature; and *how* does psychoanalysis read literature?[1] Second, when Sigmund Freud reads literature—here the short story "The Sandman" by E. T. A. Hoffmann—how does he construct a case?[2] More specifically, how is this interpretation heard within his own field, by other psychoanalysts, in this instance by Jacques Lacan, who answers with another case, another literary text that responds to the "Sandman" text?[3] Third, in which way is this exchange between literature and psychoanalysis an open process; and how does the psychoanalytic interpretation impact on any subsequent reading of a literary case—or, for that matter, on any subsequent reading of a clinical case?

Since its inception psychoanalysis has been in constant dialogue with literature. Through literature psychoanalysis accesses myths, motifs, topoi, linguistic/textual material, and the biographies of its producers.[4] Admittedly, interpretation of the latter, the psychobiography of authors, has become a somewhat problematic undertaking. But the insistence of psychoanalysis on referencing literature raises the question of what kind of knowledge literature has to offer. Peter-André Alt argues that literature, like psychoanalysis, sets in motion transformation processes by which meaning as well as subject positions become unstable. In psychoanalysis, signification becomes polyvalent, producing a tension between conscious and unconscious.[5] Binary logic is dissolved by continuous mirroring and duplication; identity is given up in favor of a structure of differentiation.[6] Alt suggests that Freud makes use of literature by focusing on uncovering its depth structure, which supposedly opens up the unconscious dimension of the text. But by doing so Freud, according to Alt, apparently "underestimates" the text's fictionality or constructedness.[7] Freud is therefore in danger of falling victim to the "treachery" of literature.

Jochen Hörisch approaches this problem by way of Niklas Luhmann's binary distinctions. According to Luhmann, the various social discourses or "social systems" must respond to binary propositions or paradoxes that are particular to them. The discourse of science, for example, must answer to the paradox of true/false. Aesthetics—with its binary codes of conclusive/inconclusive (*stimmig/unstimmig*), beautiful/ugly, interesting/boring, and so forth—differs markedly from science, since it keeps alive the improbable, counterintuitive, marginal, and highly doubtful theses (for example in canonical works).[8] Psychoanalysis, cunningly, in Hörisch's view, makes use of this fact; therefore it is not naïve as Alt suggests.[9] But since literature is "immune to negation" (that is, we cannot fit literature into the scientific true/false paradox) it is precluded from entering the scientific sphere. Accordingly, having wedded itself to the principles and processes of literature, psychoanalysis is equally separate from science.[10] Like literature, psychoanalysis is not "pure," and Hörisch refers to Friedrich Kittler when he contends that psychoanalysis has to do with "'Abfall' in every sense of the word" (*Abfall* can be translated as "waste" or "garbage," but also as "apostasy" or "defection").[11] This suggests that psychoanalysis is making something of what is otherwise regarded as abject, by simultaneously instituting a method of inquiry that undermines any master narrative. Like literature, psychoanalysis understands language as "impure" or "contaminated."[12] But while psychoanalysis is aware of this fact, literature, apparently, is not.[13] Following Hörisch, psychoanalysis therefore becomes literature's counterbalance (*Widerlager*); one might say that psychoanalysis becomes literature's ideal audience or public. Psychoanalysis operates according to the same principles as literature, but adds a layer of self-reflection that is always suspicious of its own means, always problematizing these means—namely, language itself.[14]

Some of Freud's key concepts are derived from literature, including those of the Oedipus complex, narcissism, masochism, or the uncanny. Yet not only does psychoanalysis develop its concepts by way of literature, it also constitutes itself by way of literary forms. The "family romance" (*Familienroman*), for instance, is first mentioned by Freud in a letter to Wilhelm Fliess (1858–1928) of June 20, 1898. As later defined in the 1909 essay "Der Familienroman der Neurotiker" (translated by James Strachey as "Family Romances"), it is the fantasy of the neurotic, a transposition of the family drama into a fiction of wish fulfillment.[15] The case study too—in German, *Fallgeschichte* (*Geschichte* meaning both "story" and "history")—suggests a literariness that makes it a "story" more than a "history." Freud's case studies (*Fallgeschichten*) have, in turn, become narratives worthy of interpretation by literary scholars. For the practice of psychoanalysis, however, they still serve as templates with which to model the presentation of clinical cases. For Freud the distinction between the clinical case and the literary case is somewhat obscured. In his investigation of neurotic and psychotic pathologies the study of Fräulein Anna O., "Dora," the "Rat Man," the "Wolf Man," and "Little Hans" is readily complemented by the study of Daniel Paul Schreber's memoirs, and by the analysis of literary fiction such as Hoffmann's "The Sandman," Wilhelm Jensen's "Gradiva," or William

Shakespeare's *The Merchant of Venice*.[16] Freud is interested in foregrounding the structure of a particular pathology, be it in the patient speaking
from the couch, in the writing of the paranoid schizophrenic (Schreber's
testimony of his own madness), or in the literary text that explores the subject's positioning. Freud's interpretative act, either of the patient's speech
or the fictional text, constructs a story and a history, as well as a phyloge-
netic or an ontogenetic trajectory. On this basis, pathology is read. Freud's
clinical case studies might at first seem more instructive for the practice of
psychoanalysis. Yet I would argue that his work on literature enables him
to better capture certain concepts, such as castration, in their complexity
and differentiation, thanks to the inherent complexity, reflexivity, and open-
endedness of literature itself. This is not to say that the patient's speech is
not complex or open-ended. Even so, arguably, in its constructedness, literature, and hence the literary case, might constitute a dialogue partner on a
par with psychoanalysis, since it presents both (literary) material and theory
(of literature, of reading) *at the same time*—very much in the way that psychoanalytic case studies tie the (pathological) material to the psychoanalytic
interpretation and, in turn, to the theorization of psychoanalysis.

INTERVENTION AS INTERPRETATION AND CUT

Freud's work on literary as well as clinical cases is shaped by his understanding of what an interpretation must "do." In the cases of the "Rat Man,"
the "Wolf Man," "Little Hans," and so forth, Freud's interpretative act is
not just a retrospective literary or textual analysis, but also an intervention
within the process of the respective clinical analysis. The effects of these
interventions are then taken up in the overall interpretation and presentation of the case. Freud's interventions and interpretations (*Deutungen*) are,
like their material, open-ended, since—as Alt observes—psychoanalysis deals
with overdetermined texts; that is, the speech of the patient or the literary
text will always open up to a new and different understanding. Freud nevertheless tries to read coherence into the text, attempts to establish meaning
and decode the symptom. Jacques Lacan, in his linguistically framed "return
to" or reappraisal of Freud, questions Freud's approach to interpretation,
and hence Freud's working of the case.[17] The Freudian interpretation, Lacan
argues, domesticates the pathology in its reliance on the sexual. The sexual
conflict that Freud locates at the heart of the neurotic, psychotic, or perverse
structure is read as a cause that sets in motion a certain history, the history of
the subject, which is then retraced in the analysis by way of interpretation.

When Lacan in his psychoanalytic writing engages with Freud in a conversation about literature and the clinic, he does so by way of reconceptual-
izing the interpretative act. For Lacan, the intervention as "interpretation"
that aims at sense must be replaced by the intervention as a "cut." The
intervention conceived of as "cut" or rupture interrupts the "making of

meaning," and therefore, one might say, it interrupts the domestication of the analysand's complaint. In this cut—the cutting of the analysand's discourse, or the cutting of the text—something is produced, a knowledge that acquaints the analysand with something beyond the day-to-day chatter, an uncanny moment in which something is designated, named, recognized; something constitutive of the subject. Therefore, a case—or, better, the narration of the case—interprets not only the Oedipal conflict (the subject's position in reference to castration); it also points to the cut in, or cutting of, the (analysand's) discourse. The case study as *Fallgeschichte* by its very name suggests that something is cut or "falling away." The fall denotes the anxious, uncanny moment in which the split between subject and object arises.

FREUD'S CASE

In the following I would like to address the question of how Freud and Lacan approach literature and thereby formulate their respective theories concerning castration. The two *Fallgeschichten* examined here—both literary, both concerned with the Oedipal situation—are Freud's analysis of Hoffmann's story "The Sandman" in his article "The Uncanny" (1919) and Lacan's "Introduction to the Names-of-the-Father Seminar" (1963). The latter offers an analysis of a biblical text from Genesis 22:1–19, which tells of the binding of Isaac, known in the Jewish tradition as the Akedah.[18] Freud first approaches the problem of the uncanny by way of an etymological analysis. The word uncanny, in German *unheimlich*, is the antonym as well as the synonym of the word *heimlich*, which can mean "belonging to the house, not strange, familiar, tame, intimate, friendly," as well as "concealed, kept from sight . . . withheld from others."[19] Freud contends, therefore, that the German word points to an ambiguity, the feeling of unease. Hence the uncanny is produced by something that is most familiar at heart or most intimately known. The meaning of the word *heimlich* slides or shifts, according to Freud; it "develops in the direction of ambivalence, until it finally coincides with its opposite, *unheimlich*."[20] Freud refers to the German psychiatrist Ernst Jentsch (1867–1919), who, in his 1906 paper on the psychology of the uncanny, had already noted the "rather fortunate formation" of the word *unheimlich* in German.[21] Like Jentsch, Freud takes Hoffmann's "The Sandman" story to illustrate this point. In his investigation of the uncanny Jentsch satisfies himself, in the main, with listing the various objects and occurrences that can be experienced as uncanny. By contrast, Freud suggests that these are structurally linked. Although the automaton, the *Doppelgänger*, the loss of eyes or a limb, or the idea of being buried alive can be uncanny, Freud points out that all such objects or occurrences present either the return of something believed to have been overcome or transcended (for example, animism; a belief in the omnipotence of thought; the double as an insurance against death), or that which has been repressed (castration for example, or the desire/fear to return to the womb). Anxiety here is the affect attached to these returns or recurrences. The story of "The Sandman" plays with several of these elements, but the element that Freud deems most uncanny is tied to the figure of the Sandman itself.

In Hoffmann's story, the fairytale figure of the Sandman steals the children's eyes and feeds them to his offspring in the moon; the Sandman is identified with the lawyer Coppelius. He demands the eyes of Nathanael, the protagonist, and while Nathanael's father pleads successfully for his son's eyes, Coppelius "unscrews" Nathanael's limbs instead.[22] Sometime later, in a nightly encounter between Coppelius and Nathanael's father, the father is killed. The loss of the eyes, the nightly secret encounters, the child Nathanael observing alchemistic experiments from his hideout, the threat of losing his eyes, the "unscrewing" of limbs, and the eventual death of the father all establish the castration complex, according to Freud. The revival of this scenario is brought about by the appearance of Coppelius's *Doppelgänger*, the optician Coppola, many years later. (Hoffmann, of course, begins his story with this second scene, which brings back the memories of the childhood trauma—the first, or primal scene, the *Urszene*). In Freud's view the trauma of castration is reproduced in various forms: in the doubling or pairing of fathers who have produced Nathanael (the biological father and Coppelius), and also of the fathers who later produce the automaton Olimpia (these fathers being Spalanzani, who is also Nathanael's physics professor, and Coppola). The duality of the good and the bad father momentarily merges into one character, when, for example, the biological father, while experimenting over the stove, shows a distorted face identical to that of Coppelius. Furthermore, Coppelius and Coppola merge not just in Nathanael's imagination, but also in a slip of the unreliable narrator: when Olimpia is torn apart by Spalanzani and supposedly Coppola, the narrator calls him, at one point, Coppelius.

Hoffmann's Olimpia is for Freud Nathanael's feminine complex, representing Nathanael's libidinal relation to the father. At the same time Olimpia is Nathanael's narcissistic mirror image. The fathers of both Nathanael and Olimpia seek to destroy their offspring. The castration is also reproduced in Nathanael's writing: here, the bond between Nathanael and his fiancée Clara is obstructed by Coppelius (the bad father), who first castrates Nathanael (by taking his eyes) and then Clara, at least according to Nathanael's skewed perspective (Nathanael notes her dead eyes, her "tote Augen").[23] One might add here that while one pair of siblings is produced and then castrated by the fathers (Nathanael and Olimpia), another pair of siblings (Clara and her brother Lothar) escapes the wrath of their father; their father or family is dead: in other words, they have successfully "killed" the father. Nathanael's confused and mad ravings that accompany the scenes of anxiety, of castration, and annihilation are given as "hui Holzpüppchen" (hurry up wooden doll), "sköne oke" (beautiful eyes) and "Feuerkreis, dreh dich" (ring of fire, spin about). One could read the term "Holzpüppchen" as a reference to the lifeless, wooden doll that cannot be animated by man; "sköne oke" might—in line with the Oedipus story—evoke the idea of the phallus, with "Feuerkreis" standing for the mad, ecstatic animation of the subject. The last recurrence of castration or mutilation in Hoffmann's story is Nathanael's fall from the tower, a building reminiscent of the phallus; a fall from, or away from, the phallus. For Freud, the "Sandman" story exemplifies the functioning of castration. The nursemaid's fairytale of the Sandman, in conjunction with the "fathers'" threat to mutilate the child, occasion a trauma that, according to Freud, results in the mental breakdown of the protagonist.

With his interpretation of "The Sandman," Freud described the pathological effects of an unresolved Oedipal conflict. But I would like to suggest that Freud, in a short footnote, also introduces a further case—that of the author E. T. A. Hoffmann himself, whose history seems intricately linked to that of Nathanael. Gerhard Kurz quite rightly points out that Freud's analyses of literary texts tend to replace the author's name with the generic term "der Dichter," meaning "the author" or "the writer." Freud, Kurz suggests, is acutely aware that in relation to the literary text, the generic term "Dichter" is inevitably a product of the literary process.[24] In his article "The Uncanny," Freud again favors the term "Dichter." Thus the inclusion of the footnote about Hoffmann breaks in some way with that habitual reference. In that footnote, Freud tentatively mentions that Hoffmann suffered on account of his parents' divorce early in life. He was only three years old when the parents separated, and the relation to the father was "eine der wundesten Stellen" (one of the most tender wounds).[25] In this way, and by way of Freud's words, Nathanael's castration appears to be prefigured by Hoffmann's own injury.

CASTRATED BODIES AND CASTRATING LANGUAGE

As can be seen in Freud's analysis of "The Sandman," his idea of castration is tied to and inscribed in the body; the threat of castration is still the threat of a mutilated body, something that is at once visceral as well as hallucinatory. In his reworking of the problem of castration Lacan takes another interpretative leap, and reads castration as cut. The constitutive cut becomes possible in and through language. Language is already structured by cuts since one signifier is marked by its difference to another signifier.[26] In poetic or literary terms one could also say that language entails stressed and unstressed material, silences and sounds; a rhythmic structure and meter that can be defined as scansion. Subscribing to language, to a system where something can be said—albeit in a particular way—and where something cannot be said, demands at the same time a subscription to the cutting or castrating effects of language. Lacan makes use of this castrating effect of language in the analytic setting. The notion of scansion, as scansion in and of language, is transferred onto the analytic situation or speech of the analysand, which is cut, interrupted, or terminated by the analyst. This scansion in and of speech confronts the analysand again with the effects of castration. Castration can therefore move from the body (as Freud has it) into language (as Lacan suggests). Still, for both Freud and Lacan, castration organizes the subject by way of curbing its desire and demanding renunciation. When Lacan replaces the notion of interpretation within the analysis with the notion of a cut, he suggests that what is required is not another layer of meaning added to the neurotic's attempt to make meaning, but rather a halt to the incessant and overdetermined process of "making meaning."

For Freud "The Sandman" story also presents the reader with the concept of a trauma neurosis: this is what Nathanael, according to Freud, is afflicted with. In his 1920 paper "Beyond the Pleasure Principle," Freud concludes that the memory of trauma is a repetition (a *Wiederholung* in German), and the onset of the trauma neurosis is tied to a return of the primal scene.[27] This is so fittingly developed in Hoffmann's story, where the primal scene only reappears in retrospect, with the onset of Nathanael's mental breakdown. The same *Wiederhólen* (here meaning "repetition," with the stress on the third syllable) can also be read as a *Wíederholen* (here meaning "a fetching again," with the stress on the first syllable), as apparently staged by Freud's grandson in his "fort-da" game with a cotton reel ("fort" meaning "gone," "da" meaning "there"), a cotton reel that he throws and retrieves whenever his mother leaves him on his own.[28] One might say that for Freud, this repetition is already an interpretation, an attempt to make sense of and to master what provokes anxiety, although in the case of Nathanael it seems to achieve little success.

Contrary to Freud's view, Lacan believes that repetition in trauma neurosis is not the attempt to master a painful event. The subject here is resisting its disintegration or dissolution. The repetition is in the act.[29] The trauma or the phantasm is bound up with the real, and repetition is not symbolic or symbolizing; it is not the repetition or reproduction of signs, nor a reenactment of memories. Instead, the repetition, this *Wiederholung*, occurs "by accident." The encounter that the repetition seeks to capture is always a missed encounter, it is unattainable. Hence in Lacan's view, repetition of the traumatic experience does not assume a mastery of the situation. When the child plays the "fort-da" game following his mother's disappearance, he is not, according to Lacan, symbolizing her disappearance and her return subject to his will or mastery. Lacan writes that the cotton reel thrown away and retrieved represents the subject; the subject as mutilated, castrated, or cut. Therefore Lacan concludes that castration, or better castration anxiety, presents a rupture, a cut, a trauma that will henceforth organize the development of the subject. As such one could conclude that in the case of "The Sandman," the repetitions in the trauma neurosis of Nathanael, and Nathanael's own writing of his delusional phantasies, are not so much an attempt at mastery, but the attempt to graft the subject (as mutilated) onto the existential and basic structure of castration.

LACAN'S CASE

Introducing his seminar "On the Names-of-the-Father," Lacan rereads Freud's interpretation of "The Sandman," and his concept of the uncanny, by exploring the interconnection between castration, desire, and anxiety.[30] Lacan reads this not with reference to clinical material, but with reference to another literary, or rather, biblical case.

If castration or the cut organizes the relation between subject and Other, then anxiety, the feeling of unease, is the marker for this existential gap or "essential breach."[31] "In anxiety, the subject is affected by the desire of the Other," Lacan writes.[32] At this point he brings into play another variable, which he calls "objet petit a."[33] While the relation between subject and Other is in good part regulated and contained within the field of the symbolic, something escapes this, something is not absorbed by the symbolic; a rest or remainder that for the subject keeps the notion of the Other's threatening desire virulent, or real. This object *petit a* is indebted to various ideas. It can be thought of as an imaginary part-object separable from the body, or, as Lacan says in his introduction to "On the Names-of-the-Father," it is the object that falls from the subject, thereby embodying castration, and pointing to the lack of the subject.[34] In a metonymic shift it can be conceived of as a scopic object, or as an invocatory object. As scopic object the object *petit a* is tied to the gaze, thus, as in "The Sandman," to the eyes. As invocatory object it is presented by the voice, something Lacan proceeds to develop in reference to the Akedah and the voice of the father or of God. In general one could say that this object *petit a* supports the function of desire. In other words, desire—of which the subject is consciously most acutely aware, or which can be experienced most intensely—is inextricably tied to the object *petit a.*[35] But when, for example, the object *petit a* establishes itself at the level of the scopic, equating the phallus (or the castrated organ) with the eye, it also most importantly exposes the subject to a voyeuristic gaze, in which the world and the subject within are pure spectacle, and in which the subject becomes a victim or sacrifice.[36] The subject is duped, and believes itself to desire because it sees itself as desired, without recognizing that the Other desires the subject's regard or gaze, and therefore, by extension, its castration: this is Lacan's well-known formulation of the transitivism of "the mirror stage."[37] If this mirroring, make-believe, or deceit that identifies one's own desire with the desire of the Other fails, the uncanny emerges. Lacan contends that every time the subject encounters its own image in the Other devoid of its own (the subject's) gaze, the subject is confronted again with its most existential fear—the fear of castration.[38] The object *petit a,* which seems to be the shifter in this mirroring of subject and Other, testifies to the fact that there is and was castration, and makes this knowledge phantasmatically accessible to the subject.

Moving from the scopic to the invocatory object—or, in terms of textual material, from "The Sandman" to the Akedah, Lacan introduces the voice as a "fallen" object, the remainder of the Other. The Other is the place at which "it speaks," from which the law or the incest taboo originates.[39] The Oedipal situation that Freud has described in his article "The Uncanny" has to be considered here in conjunction with the myth of the primordial father. In Freud's 1913 work *Totem and Taboo* (which consists of four articles previously published in the journal *Imago*), Freud conceptualized this father as animalistic, or as animal.[40] This primordial father is the precultural father before the incest taboo; it is the father as totem. In reference to Claude Lévi-Strauss, Lacan suggests that this primordial father is a totem and a name or a designation, which in turn links it more closely with the voice.[41] Enjoyment of the primordial father is pure enjoyment; in other words, pure enjoyment or boundless satisfaction is the sole domain of the primordial father.[42] If pure enjoyment or satisfaction is on the side of the primordial father, then desire as that which relates and regulates is on the side of the father *after* the incest taboo; this is the father who has already subscribed to law. Taking up Freud's last major work on the Mosaic God (1937), as well as the concept of the uncanny, Lacan develops his conceptualization of the difference between boundless satisfaction or enjoyment and desire with reference to the Akedah, the binding of Isaac by Abraham as told in the Old Testament.[43] In this way, the story of the binding of Isaac becomes a corollary to "The Sandman" story.

Rather than "interpreting" the various events of the Akedah, Lacan allows this story to "speak for itself," here through the explication of God's names. One of the names given for the *Elohim* or for God in the Hebrew Bible is *Schem*, "the name." To Moses this God says, "I am what/who I am," or, according to the Greek Septuagint, "I am the one who is," "I am being." Lacan highlights that in the Akedah one name for God is *El Shadday*; now commonly incorrectly translated as "Almighty," but in Greek appearing as *Theos*, a name that is untranslatable, and therefore equal to *Schem*. This *El Shadday* has given Abraham a son—by Sarah, who was infertile until ninety years old—and God demands the son's sacrifice. Isaac is not Abraham's only son, although this is what Abraham claims. He has also had a son with Hagar; Ishmael is his firstborn, but Isaac is the result of a miracle, a promise, in which God played a part.[44] Lacan speaks here of two fathers, the Mosaic God and Abraham. When the angel in the name of *El Shadday* demands that Abraham refrain from sacrificing his son, a ram is sacrificed instead.[45] Lacan turns here to the medieval French rabbi known as Rashi, who claims that the ram in the rabbinic tradition is considered the primordial ram, extant since the seven days of Creation.[46] The ram is the ancestor of the house of *Sem* (one of the three sons of Noah), which links Abraham to his origin. While Isaac is spared, the ram, the eponymic ancestor, the God or the incarnation of the God of Abraham's clan, is sacrificed.[47] Lacan sees the cutting by the knife as that which introduces a difference between the enjoyment of God and his desire. The symbol of this gap is the circumcision; it signifies the covenant between the people and God who has chosen them.[48] In the first instance the God of the Akedah appears to have absolute, undivided enjoyment on his side, but in the renewed covenant with Abraham a slide towards mediated desire, castration and law occurs.[49] God who might once have represented absolute enjoyment—the totemistic father God who demands the cutting or sacrifice of the son—is then moved to accept the substitute sacrifice of the ram, which, paradoxically, stands in for God himself. Unlimited pleasure or enjoyment gives way to desire, which can only be thought of in relation to castration.

RETURNING TO FREUD'S CASE IN THE LIGHT OF LACAN'S CASE

At this point Lacan's reading of the Akedah can be brought into dialogue with Freud's reading of "The Sandman," or rather, with Freud's omissions in his interpretation of Hoffmann's story. Not unlike Isaac in the Akedah, Nathanael is caught up in a net of names or designations. While we might read Nathanael's story of castration (anxiety) at the level of repetitions and recurrences, we might also find the idea of castration in the names of the fathers/God affecting the protagonists. Lacan pointed out that, not unlike Nathanael, Isaac has two fathers, God as well as Abraham, and one could add the (dual) God represented by two names. Freud had already noted that the names of the bad or castrating fathers Coppelius and Coppola point to that which they will affect, the Italian *coppo* meaning "eye socket," *coppella* a "melting crucible," and the Latin or Italian word *copula* denoting the "connection" or "relation."[50] So the eye and the relation; that is, sexual enjoyment is on the side of these fathers. The other fathers—Nathanael's biological father and Spalanzani—complement Coppelius/Coppola. The name Spalanzani is reminiscent of the Italian physiologist Lazzaro Spallanzani (1729–1799). Spallanzani experimented with transplantation, and explored the insemination of animals; he was successful in artificially inseminating a dog, and discovered the regenerative capabilities of amphibians, which are able to regenerate severed limbs. He also disproved the then current theory of spontaneous generation, or *Urzeugung*: the idea that living organisms can develop from nonliving matter. Hoffmann's Spalanzani, and by extension Nathanael's biological father, are therefore highly ambiguous, simultaneously castrating and life-giving, and imbued with sexual potency like the pair who represent the negative father imago.

Concurrently the names Nathanael and Olimpia (Olimpia the automaton, designed by Spalanzani and Coppola) point to descent from God, or the gods. The Hebrew word Nathanael means "God has given," "God's gift";

the Greek translation develops into the name Theodor (also Hoffmann's middle name, his third initial standing for Amadeus, translated as the imperative "love God!" or often understood as "loved by god"). Olimpia stands for the one "who descends from Olympus," the "heavenly" or "divine." Both Nathanael and Olimpia are clearly marked by their connection to the divine, as was Isaac, whose name stands for "God may smile (upon him)." Isaac loses his eyesight in later life, making it possible for his second-born son Jacob to surreptitiously obtain the blessing of the blind father. Meanwhile, the names of the fatherless siblings Lothar and Clara in "The Sandman" clearly denote otherness. Lothar is a name from Old High German meaning the well-known warrior or, more generically, the army (in German *Heer*, which could be heard as *Herr*, making himself "the Lord"). Clara, from Latin *clarus*, is the light one, the one who shines; the connection to the Enlightenment, to reason and clear-sightedness is apparent here. These designations and names in "The Sandman" insert another layer, another subtext, which speaks of the father's desire by bypassing the overt theme of the eyes.

As explored in Freud's reading of "The Sandman," castration is tied to the gaze and/or the eyes, and to the body that is animated by the gaze, or by the threat of losing the eyes. As explored by Lacan, through *his* reading of Freud's reading of "The Sandman," and his own reading of the Akedah, castration is invoked not only by the gaze, but also by the voice, or by designations that impact upon the subject, inasmuch as it is a subject in language. The voice of God and/or the names of the father relate to the subject in a very ominous way: on the one hand, as law or taboo it inaugurates desire where before there was pure enjoyment. With reference to the idea of deceit one might also find that the desire of the Other/the God is taken up by the subject as its own. Hence the subject appears to be constructed through the web of messages stemming from the God/Other, a net of signifiers. This net of signifiers exists prior to the subject; as such, the subject is born into it. These signifiers must be "forgotten," or rendered unconscious before they can emerge again in the form of traumatizing memory. "The Sandman" in some way reiterates the Akedah, translating "the universal" of the mythical or biblical story that inaugurates a specific understanding and commitment to law, into "the particular" of the romantic story where the law (as castrating force) engenders a traumatized response. The God of the Old Testament inscribes himself into the net of signifiers, which determine the son/Isaac as the one who is cut symbolically. The names of the father in "The Sandman" equally provide the net in which Nathanael is caught. And, as Freud points out, the uncanny feeling we experience when reading the story results from the fact that castration is the trauma we all know, all too well.

Nathanael's madness signifies the *Wiederkehr* (return) of the real. While Nathanael makes an attempt to capture the trauma of castration in his own writing, a writing that is dark, unintelligible and formless, and that shows the characteristics of psychotic writing, the trauma keeps insisting. It is, as

Lacan says, repeated in the act. This does not entail the promise of mastery, but produces the subject as mutilated, cut, or castrated. Like the cotton reel in the "fort-da" game, Nathanael, the subject of "The Sandman" story, is caught in the repetition. Moreover, in "The Sandman" the cotton reel, which represents the object *petit a* for the child in the "fort-da" game, is replaced by the artificial eyes of the telescope, which promise to regain that which is lost. The eyes—as real, as artificial, or substituted by the telescope—evoke that object *petit a* that maintains the subject's relation to castration and to that place where the subject finds himself exposed to voyeurism; where the subject is victim or sacrifice. Here again one could reference the Akedah, since the place in which Isaac is to be sacrificed and then spared is called Mount Moriah, or, in Abraham's words, "God sees." And while in this moment the Akedah inaugurates a blending of voice (God's name and/or demand, as well as the ram's horn turned into the shofar that will henceforth remind the Jewish people of the binding of Isaac) and gaze (God seeing Isaac in the place where he is supposed to be slaughtered and eventually saved), "The Sandman" also brings together gaze (the theme of the eyes) and voice (in names and designations, and in the recurring verse of the "Feuerkreis"). Gaze and voice in their relation to the phallus constitute that which phantasmatically circulates between the subject and the Other, or rather, that which the subject deems to be the Other's desire. Both gaze and voice as object *petit a* deceive the subject. They also, however, invoke a mythical place, a place where nothing is lacking, where there is pure enjoyment or complete satisfaction before the castrating cut replaces it with desire.

In conclusion one might say that literature and psychoanalysis produce a tight web in which a conversation about cases—fictional or clinical—is developed. The *Fallgeschichte* speaks of that which it designates, a story or history of a case in reference to the fall, or to be more precise, in reference to castration or a cut. It thereby inscribes psychoanalysis into literature, or literariness into the psychoanalytic case study. Literature finds an audience in psychoanalysis, and at times clinical cases are also received as literature. I would suggest that nowadays we cannot read Hoffmann's "The Sandman" without acknowledging Freud's reading, and Freud's interpretation in turn leads to Lacan's reading of another fictional or mythical—here biblical—case, the Akedah. In literary studies we might wish to neglect psychoanalysis in favor of other theoretical approaches, but it seems almost impossible to avoid psychoanalytic thought altogether, since it has thoroughly infiltrated the public sphere. The opposite is also true. I would suggest that, particularly when it comes to case studies, psychoanalysis is unable to do away with literature, and that as "psychoanalytic" readers, Freud and Lacan urge their reading publics to consider literary cases alongside clinical cases. Of course their readings highlight the problem that when psychoanalysis addresses literature, it is brought into dialogue with a highly complex, multilayered, self-reflexive artifact that might bear little or no resemblance to the voice that comes from the couch.

NOTES

1. In this instance one could possibly understand "public" with Michael War-ner as "self-organized"; "a space of discourse organized by nothing other than discourse itself. . . . It exists *by virtue of being addressed.*" (Emphasis in original.) Michael Warner, "Publics and Counterpublics," in *Publics and Counterpublics* (Brooklyn: Zone Books, 2002), 65–124.
2. E. T. A Hoffmann, "Der Sandmann," in *Nachtstücke* (Munich: Deutscher Taschenbuch Verlag, 1984), 9–41.
3. Sigmund Freud, "Das Unheimliche," in *Gesammelte Werke*, vol. 12, ed. Anna Freud et al. (Frankfurt: Fischer, 1999), 227–68.
4. See Peter-André Alt, "Einführung," in *Sigmund Freud und das Wissen der Literatur*, ed. Peter-André Alt and Thomas Anz (Berlin: Walter de Gruyter, 2008), 1–13, at 2.
5. See Alt, "Einführung," 4.
6. See Alt, "Einführung," 4.
7. See Alt, "Einführung," 6.
8. See Jochen Hörisch, "Wissen die Literatur und die Psychoanalyse dasselbe, wenn sie sich aufeinander berufen?" in *Sigmund Freud und das Wissen der Literatur*, 17–30, at 19.
9. See Hörisch, "Wissen die Literatur und die Psychoanalyse dasselbe," 19.
10. See Hörisch, "Wissen die Literatur und die Psychoanalyse dasselbe," 20.
11. See Hörisch, "Wissen die Literatur und die Psychoanalyse dasselbe," 21.
12. See Hörisch, "Wissen die Literatur und die Psychoanalyse dasselbe," 25.
13. See Hörisch, "Wissen die Literatur und die Psychoanalyse dasselbe," 28.
14. See Hörisch, "Wissen die Literatur und die Psychoanalyse dasselbe," 28.
15. Sigmund Freud, "Der Familienroman der Neurotiker," in *Gesammelte Werke*, vol. 7, ed. Anna Freud et al. (Frankfurt: Fischer, 1999), 225–31; see Gerhard Kurz, "Wie Freud interpretiert. Hermeneutische Prinzipien in 'Der Wahn und die Träume in W. Jensens "Gradiva"'," in *Sigmund Freud und das Wissen der Literatur*, 31–58, at 34.
16. For the study of Fräulein Anna O., see Sigmund Freud, "Studien über Hyste-rie," in *Gesammelte Werke*, vol. 1, ed. Anna Freud et al. (Frankfurt: Fischer, 1999), 75–312; for the study of "Dora," see Sigmund Freud, "Bruchstück einer Hysterie-Analyse," in *Gesammelte Werke*, vol. 5, ed. Anna Freud et al. (Frankfurt: Fischer, 1999), 161–286; for the study of the "Rat Man," see Sig-mund Freud, "Bemerkungen über eine Fall von Zwangneurose," in *Gesam-melte Werke*, vol. 7, 339–463; for the study of the "Wolf Man" see Sigmund Freud, "Aus der Geschichte einer infantilen Neurose," in *Gesammelte Werke*, vol. 12, 27–157; for the study of "Little Hans" see Sigmund Freud, "Anal-yse der Phobie eines fünfjährigen Knaben," in *Gesammelte Werke*, vol. 7, 241–377. The study of Schreber's memoirs is found in Sigmund Freud, "Psy-choanalytische Bemerkungen über einen autobiographisch beschriebenen Fall von Paranoia (Dementia Paranoides)," in *Gesammelte Werke*, vol. 7, 239–320; for Freud's analysis of "Gradiva," see Sigmund Freud, "Der Wahn und die Träume in W. Jensens 'Gradiva'," in *Gesammelte Werke*, vol. 7, 29–125; in connection with *The Merchant of Venice*, see Sigmund Freud, "Das Motiv der Kästchenwahl," in *Gesammelte Werke*, vol. 10, ed. Anna Freud et al. (Frankfurt: Fischer, 1999), 23–37.
17. The idea of Lacan's "return" to Freud was coined by Samuel Weber; see Samuel Weber, *Rückkehr zu Freud. Jacques Lacans Entstellung der Psycho-analyse* (Vienna: Passagen Verlag, 1990). In English translation: *Return to Freud: Jacques Lacan's Dislocation of Psychoanalysis*, trans. Michael Levine (Cambridge: Cambridge University Press, 2008).

18. Lacan delivered only the introduction to the planned seminar, on November, 20, 1963, which was at some point intended to be published as the first chapter to his Seminar XI; see Jacques Lacan, "Introduction to the Names-of-the-Father Seminar," *Television*, special issue *October* 40 (1987): 81–95.

19. Sigmund Freud, "The 'Uncanny'," in *The Penguin Freud Library*, vol. 14, *Art and Literature*, trans. and ed. James Strachey (London: Penguin Books, 1990), 339–76, at 342; 344.

20. Freud, "The 'Uncanny'," 347.

21. Ernst Jentsch, "On the Psychology of the Uncanny (1906)," trans. Roy Sellars, in *Angelaki: Journal of the Theoretical Humanities* 2, no. 1 (1997): 7–16, at 8; also, "Zur Psychologie des Unheimlichen," *Psychiatrisch-Neurologische Wochenschrift* 8, no. 22 (August 25, 1906): 195–98; also volume 8, no. 23 (September 1, 1906): 203–05.

22. "Nathaniel" in the English translation.

23. See Freud "Das 'Unheimliche'," particularly his footnote on page 244–45, in which he develops the various ideas of the father double, the feminine complex, narcissistic love, and the castration complex.

24. See Gerhard Kurz, "Wie Freud interpretiert," 36–38.

25. Freud, "Das 'Unheimliche'," 245. In Strachey's translation: "a most sensitive subject with him"; see Freud, "The 'Uncanny'," 354.

26. See Jacques Lacan, *The Four Fundamental Concepts of Psychoanalysis. Seminar XI*, ed. Jacques-Alain Miller, trans. Alan Sheridan (New York: Norton, 1988), 206.

27. Sigmund Freud, "Jenseits des Lustprinzips," in *Gesammelte Werke*, vol. 13, ed. Anna Freud et al. (Frankfurt: Fischer, 1999), 1–69.

28. See Freud, "Jenseits des Lustprinzips."

29. See Lacan, *The Four Fundamental Concepts of Psychoanalysis*, 51.

30. See Lacan, "Introduction to the Names-of-the-Father Seminar," 81–95.

31. See Lacan, "Introduction to the Names-of-the-Father Seminar," 84.

32. Lacan, "Introduction to the Names-of-the-Father Seminar," 84.

33. Here *a* is referring to *autre*; although always left untranslated it could be thought of as "object little other."

34. See Lacan, "Introduction to the Names-of-the-Father Seminar," 82. For a detailed analysis of the *objet petit a* in reference to Hoffmann's "The Sandman" see also Jacques Lacan, *Le Séminaire de Jacques Lacan. Livre X: L'Angoisse* (Paris: Editions du Seuil, 2004), particularly Chapter 1.

35. See Lacan, "Introduction to the Names-of-the-Father Seminar," 82.

36. See Lacan, "Introduction to the Names-of-the-Father Seminar," 86.

37. See Lacan, "Introduction to the Names-of-the-Father Seminar," 86.

38. See Lacan, "Introduction to the Names-of-the-Father Seminar," 86.

39. See Lacan, "Introduction to the Names-of-the-Father Seminar," 87.

40. Sigmund Freud, "Totem und Tabu," in *Gesammelte Werke*, vol. 11, ed. Anna Freud et al. (Frankfurt: Fischer, 1999).

41. See Lacan, "Introduction to the Names-of-the-Father Seminar," 88.

42. See Lacan, "Introduction to the Names-of-the-Father Seminar," 88.

43. Sigmund Freud, "Der Mann Moses und die monotheistische Religion," in *Gesammelte Werke*, vol. 16, ed. Anna Freud et al. (Frankfurt: Fischer, 1999), 101–246.

44. See Lacan, "Introduction to the Names-of-the-Father Seminar," 92.

45. See also Kalpana Seshadri-Crooks, "Being Human: Bestiality, Anthropophagy, and Law," in *Umbr(a): Ignorance of the Law*, no. 1 (2003), 97–114, at 105.

46. Rashi refers to Rabbi Schelomo Jizchaki, who was born in 1040 CE in Troyes and died in 1105 CE, also in Troyes; he was one of the most important medieval editors and commentators of the Talmud.

47. Rashi also comments that Abraham was supposedly disappointed, since he was not allowed to proceed with the sacrifice of Isaac; instead he was going to injure Isaac, to draw blood, which would delight "Elohim," God of Israel (see Lacan, "Introduction to the Names-of-the-Father Seminar," 93).

48. In his examination of God's names in the Akedah, Jürgen Ebach comes to a similar conclusion concerning the shift from one name to another (here from *Elohim* to *YHWH*). For Ebach, this is not the result of various narratives and traditions being merged into one text, but a deliberate narrative strategy to signal the two opposing aspects of God, marking both identity and difference (see Jürgen Ebach, "Theodizee—Fragen gegen die Antworten. Anmerkungen zur biblischen Erzählung von der 'Bindung Isaaks' (1 Mose 22)," in *Gott im Wort. Drei Studien zur Hemeneutik und biblischen Exegese* (Neukirchen-Vluyn: Neukirchener Verlagsgesellschaft, 1997), 1–25, at 9–10. See also Jürgen Ebach, "Gottes Name(n) oder: Wie die Bibel von Gott spricht," *Bibel und Kirche* 65, no. 2 (2010): 62–67.

49. See Lacan, "Introduction to the Names-of-the-Father Seminar," 94.

50. See Freud, "The 'Uncanny'," 352n.

12 When the Case Writer Eclipses the Case

Linda Lê's Case Study of Ingeborg Bachmann

Alexandra Kurmann

At the age of twenty, Linda Lê (1963–), a Vietnamese voluntary exile in France, discovered a French translation of the work of the self-exiled Austrian poet-turned-writer Ingeborg Bachmann (1926–73). This "découverte capitale" (major discovery) would lead Lê to make Bachmann the subject of a literary case study, and the object of a writerly case.[1] Lauren Berlant writes that the case study is different from the case, in that it produces the case as an exemplary instance.[2] In turn, I argue that the critical attention Lê pays Bachmann—a writer she considers her own literary precursor—makes clear this trajectory between case and case study.[3]

More specifically, I contend that Lê employs a purpose-made case study to eventually produce Bachmann as a case of an ethically engaged Antigone figure; that is, a figure evocative of the daughter of Oedipus in Sophocles's Theban tragedy *Antigone*. This process was inaugurated in 1989, with a brief introductory newspaper article entitled "Ingeborg Bachmann, un brasier d'énigmes" (Ingeborg Bachmann: An inferno of enigmas).[4] The article was soon followed in 1991 by an in-depth study of the writer entitled "J'écris sur la nature du feu" (I write on the nature of fire), found in the French literary journal *Critique*.[5] To highlight the pedagogic significance of this investigation, at the end of the same decade Lê retrieved this text from storage to have it reprinted simply as "Ingeborg Bachmann," in a 1999 book of literary essays entitled *Tu écriras sur le bonheur* (You will write of happiness), which Lê dedicates to the writers she considers to have been significant in her literary coming-of-age.[6] Further to this recycling, one year later Lê fictionalized her case study in her novel *Les aubes* (Dawns), which produces Bachmann as an exemplary case of a Lacanian Antigone.[7]

In the following discussion, to make my own case for Lê's case-making venture, I first reveal the exilic affinities that appear to have drawn Lê to Bachmann. It can be shown that subsequently Lê founds an imaginary mentoring relationship with her precursor. Lê's transformation of Bachmann from the subject of a case study into an objectified case of an engaged writer reveals to me an intimate project—one that has as its ultimate goal Lê's identification with Bachmann, so as to incorporate the late writer as an ethical influence into her own, contemporary work. To argue for this proposition,

I expose the ways in which Lê's case study in the essay "Ingeborg Bachmann" draws together aspects of Bachmann's biography that reflect Lê's lived experience, and that position Lê as a privileged expert on Bachmann—both as a woman and as a writer. Through further analysis of "Ingeborg Bachmann" I trace the development of Lê's construction of a Lacanian case of Antigone, before questioning the casuist aspect of the case in face of Lê's evident self-identification with her subject. Despite the self-reflexive nature of these textual relations, my examination also reveals that when Lê sincerely calls her intertextuality an "homage" to Bachmann, she is in fact repaying a literary debt.[8] For Lê provides the late German-writing Bachmann with a renewed transnational readership in the French language, exemplifying quite literally that which Michael Warner calls the "engine of translatability" of a given public.[9]

THE MAKINGS OF A CASE STUDY

As an author of Vietnamese origin who writes in French, Lê has always been reluctant to act as a spokesperson for the Vietnamese community in France.[10] Rejecting the label "Vietnamese writer," Lê insists on calling herself a "French writer born in Vietnam," although she spent the first fourteen years of her life there.[11] While the Lê family can be considered war refugees, having fled Vietnam after the Fall of Saigon, Lê was officially repatriated to France, since her maternal family had gained French citizenship in the 1930s. Lê uses this familial history to identify primarily with her European origins, an act that is commensurate with the rejection of her mother tongue, and a desire to speak French better than any autochthon.[12] Since Lê maintains her own state of self-imposed exile in France (having returned to Vietnam only three times, for family and professional reasons), her exile status is comparable to that of Bachmann.[13] The latter left Vienna voluntarily for Italy in her twenty-seventh year, in search of freedom from newly conservative sociopolitical tendencies in postwar Austria.[14]

The similarity of both writers' situation in self-exile forms the basis of Lê's affinity for Bachmann, and allows her to bring Bachmann into such familiar proximity as to enable her to compose an intimate case study of Bachmann—of the person and her work. Lê's motivation appears to be to seek a sense of belonging, which will legitimize her writerly position in self-imposed exile. From the perceived mutual feelings of alienation, Lê creates grounds for a sisterly bond, positioning herself in respect to Bachmann as a younger sibling who seeks to learn from the example of her literary "grande sœur très admirée" (greatly admired older sister).[15] During the first sixteen years of her writing career, Lê embarks on an intertextual relationship with Bachmann that instates the latter as Lê's chosen literary precursor of distinctly European descent. The present discussion considers only the exoskeleton of this relationship, made up of explicit intertextual borrowings and references to Bachmann; these, I argue, reflect the case-making process.

Strictly speaking, literary case studies are fictional adaptations of real-life medical and psychiatric cases, or instances of criminal and sexual transgression, such as those seen in the psychopathological novels of Armand Dubarry discussed by Jana Verhoeven in this volume. Although Lê's examination of Bachmann does not begin as a fictional adaptation, this is indeed how it ends, for by the time Lê has finished with her mentor in *Les aubes*, she has made of Bachmann a psychoanalytical case that, in its transgressions, is retrospectively worthy of literary representation.

For her case study in "Ingeborg Bachmann," Lê initially takes in hand, quite simply, a unique literary life. Yet through selective quotation and paraphrasing of biographical and fictional accounts of Bachmann's experience of psychological breakdown and transgressive tendencies, Lê creates a literary case study. While there are certainly case-worthy episodes in Bachmann's life, such as her high-profile, romantic relationship with the Swiss writer Max Frisch (1911–91), and the media sensationalization of her tragic and premature death, Lê refrains from entering into social discourses about her precursor.[16] Instead, she homes in on those personal aspects of the writer's life that mirror her own, and to which only those who were intimate with Bachmann would have been privy. For instance, in a scene that recalls Lê's own hospitalization after the death of her father, Lê firstly depicts Bachmann as a patient afflicted by mental illness following the dissolution of her long-term relationship with Frisch.[17] Lê closely observes the couple's last meeting, integrating excerpts of an account written by Frisch in his autobiographical novel *Montauk*:

> *Dans une clinique de Zürich*, on retrouve la même femme. *Elle s'y fait hospitaliser.* Un homme, un écrivain suisse allemande avec qui elle vit depuis quelques années, insiste pour lui rendre visite. Il entre dans sa chambre. *Il voit des fleurs près de son lit.* Elle, il ne regarde pas. *Il ne la croit pas malade.* Il se prépare à partir pour les États-Unis. Il sait qu'elle reçoit chaque jour trente-cinq roses. *De qui, il l'ignore.* Il se croit *délivré de sa sujétion, de sa jalousie amoureuse.* Il s'en va, sans regret.[18]
>
> *In a clinic in Zurich*, we find the same woman. *She has had herself hospitalised there.* A man, a Swiss-German writer with whom she has lived for a few years, insists on visiting her. He enters the room. *He sees some flowers near the bed.* He doesn't look at her. *He doesn't believe she is ill.* He is preparing to leave for the United States. He knows she receives thirty-five roses every day. *He ignores from whom.* He believes himself to be *free of his constraints, of his jealousy.* He leaves without regret).[19]

This observational passage makes Lê into a privileged eyewitness of the event. Taking sides with her precursor, Lê employs Frisch's words against him to make him accountable for the behavior that she clearly considers to have worsened Bachmann's mental health. Reproachfully reiterating an excerpt from a private letter written by Bachmann to Frisch that he reproduced in *Montauk*, Lê accuses Frisch along *with* Bachmann: "Tu n'as même pas compris que je me suis envoyé ces fleurs moi-même" (You did not even realize that I was sending those flowers to myself).[20] Lê's empathetic rendering of Bachmann's emotional experience thus establishes a unique intimacy between the two writers that positions Lê as a knowledgeable authority on the subject of her study.

Having laid the grounds for the later development of her psychoanalytical case, Lê then draws out aspects of Bachmann's self-exile and writerly mission that she considers transgressive. To support her image of Bachmann as a "femme traquée" (hunted woman), Lê's self-pronounced "enquête" (inquiry) focuses on what she sees as the writer's rebellious, nomadic existence.[21] To Lê's mind, during an almost twenty-year absence from Austria, Bachmann would live as a "fugitive" outside her homeland, residing in Switzerland, Germany, and Italy—even transgressing, according to Lê, the norms of voluntary exile. From the writings of Thomas Bernhard (1931–89), Lê borrows and attributes to Bachmann an abhorrence for Austria; nonetheless, as the case-maker, Lê insists that "toute sa vie, l'exilée prepara son retour au pays" (all of her life the exile [Bachmann] was preparing her return home).[22] However, the literature tells us that during her lifetime the real Bachmann did not make this *volte-face* (about face).[23] Again, Lê molds her version of Bachmann to reflect her own exilic sentiments. Recycling a phrase that she has used to discuss her own "impossible retour" (impossible return) to Vietnam, Lê projects her own irreconcilable regrets in self-exile onto her precursor.[24]

In terms of her literary output, Bachmann's intrepid tackling of the difficult subject of wartime atrocities committed by the Third Reich is both celebrated and held up for emulation by Lê, herself a refugee of the Vietnam War. Bachmann's naming of the fathers of the nation as the perpetrators of these crimes—a transgressive assault against the homeland's "Kriegsvergessenheit" (war oblivion) for which Lê praises Bachmann—speaks to Lê's own later denunciation of Ho Chi Minh (1890–1969) as the failed paternal protector of Vietnam.[25] Lê reads Bachmann's seditious choice of subject, as well as her comportment as a writer, as an admirable "breaking of the rules." In her case study, Lê applauds a ten-year silence during which Bachmann "refusa . . . d'exploiter la fabuleuse gloire que lui avait apportée la publication de ces premiers vers" (refused to . . . exploit the mythical glory brought to her by the publication of her first verses) before turning to prose writing.[26] As a novelist, Lê admits to her own penchant for prose; Bachmann's veritable abandonment of poetry for prose is yet another example of Lê drawing a likeness between her precursor and herself.[27] To this end, Lê inflates Bachmann's statement in which the writer says she knew she had to write her novel *Malina* from the perspective of a male narrator, by stating: "elle évoqua souvent l'urgence et la nécessité de composer un ouvrage en prose" (she [Bachmann] often evoked the urgency and necessity to write a work of prose).[28] This urgent need to become a prose writer reflects Lê's long-held desire to write "des livres" (books) in the French language more than it does a longing in Bachmann.[29]

When Bachmann is seen to go beyond writerly and exilic conventions, Lê manipulates circumstances to conform to her own personal narrative. In constructing a study that affirms her own beliefs about herself as a writer in exile, Lê provides a clear example of Bent Flyvbjerg's assertion that the interpretative case study has a bias toward verification, leading to its failure in the scientific task of objective observation.[30] To be clear, however: in her textual relations with Bachmann, Lê is never concerned with objectivity. Rather, her text falls strategically within the "ficto-narrative genre" of the case study, employing fictionality to advance the creation of a purpose-made precursor who serves as a mirror for the literary disciple.[31] In point of fact it is Lê's contravention of the genre that renders her case-making an intriguing subject for discussion.

THE MAKING OF A CASE

Lê's text "Ingeborg Bachmann" eventually comes to pose the precursor as a problem to be solved. That is, Bachmann becomes a complex "knowledge-object" ready for evaluation when she is problematized in the text by those who knew her; to Thomas Bernhard, Bachmann is an "event," while to Max Frisch she is a "narcissistic wound."[32] Both parties produce theories as to why Bachman's life came to such an early and destructive end. Bachmann died at the age of forty-seven, following a fire said to have started from a cigarette in her bed—the unsubstantiated question of suicide has often been raised.[33] Bernhard and Frisch offer their own metaphorical hypotheses. The former suggests that Bachmann's homeland had dealt her a fatal blow, while the latter holds that death was the only way for the writer to escape her personal anguish.[34] In Bachmann's defense, Lê in turn also posits her own hypothesis regarding the writer's tragic demise, a theory that entails an Antigonean self-destruction in the face of patriarchal oppression. By these accounts, Lê's study adheres to Berlant's proposition that "the case represents a problem-event that has animated some kind of judgment."[35] I consider that Lê judges her precursor in terms of feminist resistance: through this notion of resistance (in Bachmann's person and in her work), Lê constructs Bachmann as a modern Antigone figure who stands as a role model for ethically engaged contemporary writers such as Lê herself.

To make her case, in line with Bernhard, Lê declares that Bachmann "est un *événement*" (is an event).[36] The intention is to problematize Bachmann as a question in need of being solved by a privileged, like-minded case-maker. As Berlant emphasizes, it is "the expert who makes the case," and, beginning in 1989, Lê's undertaking certainly exhibits a sound knowledge of her subject.[37] However, her role as a Bachmann expert quickly supersedes its general requirements to take on a position of power over the subject that denotes proprietorship, and extensive creative rights. My contention is that Lê produces a narrative in the specific form of the case in order to capitalize on the propensity of the genre to facilitate appropriation. Berlant touches on the unique function of the case that is so significant to Lê: "When an event occurs out of which a case is constructed," she writes, "it represents a situation in which people are compelled to take its history, seek out precedent, write its narratives, adjudicate claims about it, make a judgment, and file it somewhere."[38] As a narrative that can be treated like an object, in that it can be filed and archived, what I see as the "Ingeborg Bachmann case" is consequently studied and reproduced.[39]

Indeed the case is fundamentally a pedagogical means; Lê makes no effort to hide the fact that her interest in Bachmann is driven by a desire to learn from her example, so as to emulate it.[40] Nowhere is this more evident than in her liberal appropriation of phrases from Bachmann's well-known speech regarding the societal mission of the writer, "Die Wahrheit ist dem Menschen zumutbar" (Man is expected to face the truth).[41] Citing Bachmann, Lê states: "*La tâche de l'écrivain* est d'approcher le moment *où la douleur devient féconde. Sa tâche* consiste à apprendre *aux yeux à se dessiller*, aux bouches à dénoncer" (*The writer's task* is to draw near to the moment *when pain becomes fertile ground. His/her task* consists in teaching *eyes to open*, and mouths to denounce).[42] The repeated adoption of Bachmann's "the task of the writer" as a personal refrain reads like the espousal of another writer's manifesto. Yet just as interesting to note are Lê's own additions, for nowhere in her speech did Bachmann suggest that the role of the writer is to "teach" the reader. Rather, by means of her case study, Lê—the named reader of Bachmann—is learning from Bachmann how to write in such a way as to open the eyes of Lê's own future readers.

Furthermore, it seems that Lê requires the recurrent renewal of this lesson: as well as reproducing the "Ingeborg Bachmann" essay in 1999, she reuses this same, archived material in the year 2000, to depict Bachmann as a fictional character in the novel *Les aubes*. For this textual reappropriation, Lê transforms references made to the writer in the literary essay into intra-textual allusions in the novel. Thus Lê seamlessly incorporates Bachmann as a fiction into her literature, thanks to the effort made in the former work to establish herself as an authority on the case material and its proprietor.

In *Les aubes*, Bachmann takes on the pseudonym Sola; she is a fictional author with the same biographical history and literary publications as the real Ingeborg Bachmann. The name Sola signifies uniqueness, reflecting the singularity of Sola's character. Her novels are read to the protagonist in memory of a woman who idolized Sola the writer; this woman's fascination with Sola clearly mirrors Lê's captivation with Bachmann. Beyond biographical and bibliographical cues, Sola is recognizable as the Antigone figure from "Ingeborg Bachmann" through the recycling of textual fragments. One such example is the declaration that both writer and reader "sont mortes du même désir de pureté, comme deux Antigones dressées en vain contre les vilenies de la vie et emmurées dans la même tombe" (died from the same desire for purity, like two Antigones who rebelled in vain against life's vileness and [who] were walled into in the same tomb).[43] Binding Lê as reader to Bachmann as writer, these repetitions also refer back to Lê's own, primary case, creating a circularity that contains the Antigonean precursor as an intratextual possession.[44]

A LACANIAN CASE OF ANTIGONE

The source of the above Antigonean rhetoric can be found in the essay "Ingeborg Bachmann," where Lê first reads the influence of the Greek heroine in the narrating voice of Bachmann's novel *Malina*. In the novel, an unnamed female narrator is caught between two men: the controlling Malina (with whom she lives), and Ivan, her emotionally detached lover. Separated into three chapters, the central section of the novel takes place in a dreamscape, where the I-figure is persecuted by a murderous and incestuous father who takes the guise of oppressive authority figures, such as that of a Nazi officer. Lê equates the narrator's struggle with an Antigonean confrontation with "la Loi" (the Law).[45] The capitalization alludes to Jacques Lacan's inscription of Symbolic Law instituted by the "name of the father" when the psychoanalytical subject leaves the semiotic realm shared with the mother to enter into the symbolic world of language—the world in which Law is instated by the father's name.[46]

The Antigone figure that Lê uses to portray both Bachmann and her narrator critiques the subjugation of women in Lacan's theorization of language, where their subjection to phallic Law is undifferentiated.[47] Sigrid Weigel, a prominent Bachmann scholar, blames this suppression of the female voice for the murder of the narrator in *Malina*—the narrator disappears into a wall at the end of the novel.[48] Correspondingly, Lê links this death with that of Sophocles's Antigone, who is entombed alive in a cave.[49] Lê sees the narrator of *Malina* as "celle qui refuse d'oublier les morts sans sépulture, les Polynice d'Auschwitz" (she who refuses to forget the dead who have no grave, the Polyneices of Auschwitz).[50] The allusion to the Holocaust conjures an ethical resistance that corresponds to the principled disposition attributed by Lacan to the mythological figure. Lê's interpretation reflects the three unmistakable traits of Lacan's Antigone, found in "The Essence of Tragedy: A Commentary on Sophocles' *Antigone*," part of his collected seminars of 1959–60: Antigone's desire for purity, her incorruptible resistance and, being entombed alive, her positionality between two deaths.[51] According to Terry Eagleton, Lacan maintains that acting ethically is not about conforming to the law of the state. Rather, it is acting in conformity with one's own desire, even when this desire directly contradicts the law of the state.[52] Lacan calls Antigone's desire pure for two reasons, the first being that she does not seek an object of fulfillment in the form of a reciprocating other: Antigone's desire to be reunited with her brother can never be satisfied, since the object of her affection, Polyneices, is dead. Secondly, her desire is pure to Lacan because it is both entirely subjective and incorruptible; Antigone overrides the mandates of an authoritative superego, Creon, to do what *she* believes is right, maintaining, in Eagleton's words, the "integrity of her self-hood."[53]

Lê binds Bachmann to the Lacanian precepts of Antigone's purity and integrity by describing Bachmann as "une jeune fille *maniaque de pureté*, . . . qui portait sur elle-même et sur son œuvre . . . *un regard incorruptible*" (a young woman *obsessed with purity*, who looked at herself and her work with . . . an *expression of incorruptibility*).[54] Having identified in Bachmann the qualities of purity and incorruptibility—which are certainly descriptive of Sophocles's Antigone, but by no means unique to Lacan's—Lê goes on to confirm the Lacanian aspect of her analogy by situating Bachmann, the self-exile, between two deaths: the loss of her homeland, and "l'impossible retour" (the impossible return).[55] Lacan's Antigone finds herself in a mortal double bind: she achieves her ultimate Symbolic subjectivity by following her desire to its end, yet to complete her desired duty toward her brother also means that she must face certain death at the hands of the same Symbolic Law. Similarly, in Lê's self-reflexive view, the subjectivity that Bachmann gained in long-term self-exile, far from the fathers of the nation against whom she railed in her writing, also amounted to the relinquishing of a pre-exilic self. This strongly reflects Lê's sentiments about the loss of her Vietnamese self through the loss of her mother tongue. Even so, her assumption finds a source in Bachmann's somewhat regretful realization, "ich bin besser in Wien, weil ich in Rom bin . . ." (I am better in Vienna, because I am in Rome . . .).[56] Exile, then, comes at the cost of one's home, and the death of one's primary self.

This example points again to Lê's unfailing implication of herself in her textual relations with her precursor. Once she has established Bachmann as a Lacanian case of Antigone as outlined above, Lê then takes pains to explicitly introduce herself into the textual equation. Writing that in Bachmann's *Malina* "le lecteur est le témoin . . . l'envoyé spécial sur le front d'une guerre" (the reader is the eyewitness . . . the special correspondent sent to the front), Lê promptly places herself in the privileged position of an especially chosen "witness" to the text.[57] Far from remaining a silent witness, however, Lê implies that she is in communication with Bachmann via the writer's singular "manière inimitable d'envoyer à son interlocuteur des signaux" (inimitable manner of sending signals to her interlocutor).[58] Lê intimates that these signs are decipherable only to a privileged reader or interlocutor like herself, a fellow writer-in-exile. As such, she permits herself to enter into self-reflexive dialogue with Bachmann.

CASUISTRY AS A VEIL FOR SELF-IDENTIFICATION

Antigone is known to be one of the most divisive moral figures of Greek tragedy. Her actions are either considered highly ethical, as they are by Lacan, or entirely criminal, as they are by critics such as Slavoj Žižek, who calls Antigone a "proto-totalitarian" for her blindness to rational argument and her uncompromising will to follow her own counsel.[59] The determination of Antigone's morality—or lack thereof—represents a strong opportunity for the traditional moral enquiry of casuistry; that is to say, the practice of applying general rules of morality to a highly circumstantial case "in which there appears to be a conflict of duties."[60] Antigone's duties towards her brother and the Law are obviously conflicted, as are Bachmann's loyalties to her homeland and to the victims of the Law of her fatherland. Yet, as stipulated, the case made by Lê for Bachmann to be seen as a Lacanian Antigone figure is devoid of critical questioning, while evidencing an authorial bias. In fact this highly subjective case study avoids what is essential to casuist inquiry: practical reasoning and argumentation. Consequently, what might be called Lê's "case of conscience" is simply a judgment made in advance, a case already solved.[61] The literary case of Ingeborg Bachmann stands as a means to an end. Keeping in mind that Lê is careful not to disappear from the picture, drawing attention to herself as a first person commentator in "Ingeborg Bachmann," the utilitarian purpose of the case becomes clear. While in the beginning it functions as an opportunity for Lê to legitimize her own exile position through association with Bachmann, the case has now become a means to intertextually appropriate the ethical investment found in Bachmann's work, which, at the time of writing, is lacking in the work of Lê.[62]

The aforementioned appearance of an ethically engaged double Antigone figure in *Les aubes* one year after the publication of "Ingeborg Bachmann" is evidence of the purpose-made nature of the case in question. Acquiring Bachmann's ethics as "sa propriété exclusive" (her exclusive property) in *Les aubes* appears to be the ultimate motive for which Lê employs her position of power, affirming the inversion of roles in the relationship between precursor and literary disciple.[63] Lê gains her sovereignty by virtue of the authority she accords herself in transcribing Bachmann from an individual case study into an exemplary case.[64] To use the words of Michel Foucault, Lê clearly "situates" Bachmann "in a network of writing" and "engages [her] in . . . documents that capture and fix [her]," so that Bachmann becomes an entity of critical surveillance.[65] It must be noted, however, that in contrast with usual tendencies in case-making, the precursor is neither "corrected," nor is she "normalized."[66] Rather, she is emulated and exemplified. Indeed, from the outset the making of Bachmann into a case has been a matter of reform, but reform always centered on modifying Lê. I would like to suggest that the kinship Lê fosters with Bachmann, calling her a sister, and inviting her into her home—the world of the text—shows signs of a Lacanian imaginary identification aimed at personal modification.[67]

To Žižek, such an affinity is the "identification with the image in which we appear likeable to ourselves, with the image representing 'what we would like to be'."[68] In the foregoing discussion I have revealed an abundance of instances in which Lê incorporates Bachmann into her own texts. These, I contend, can be seen to imitate Žižek's process of identification by which "external objects are taken in and become a part of the inner psychic organization."[69] The incorporation in question, however, does not take place in the psyche, but on the level of the text. Lê takes into her writing the external object of a textually produced precursor, so that Bachmann becomes an indistinguishable part of Lê's own textual organization. Lê brings into her own work the aspects of Bachmann and her prosaic oeuvre that she identifies as most admirable and desirable; she incorporates them into her writing, thereby transfusing into her texts an idealized image of and for her own works.[70]

As self-focused as this literary case-making process has been shown to be, Lê's project of narrative infusion gains for Bachmann exposure to a new and receptive public. In spite of her fame in the German-speaking world, Bachmann has remained more or less undiscovered by French readers.[71] Françoise Rétif justifies this in noting the difficulty of translating Bachmann's poetic language, while asserting that Bachmann is best appreciated when her diverse texts are considered together, for example in her original collected works published by Piper.[72] To date, such a comprehensive collection does not exist in French.[73] Although Bachmann's reappearances in Lê's texts have not yet been critically examined in any other scholarly works, they have been duly, yet briefly noted in interviews, literary magazines, and writerly and critical works.[74] This points to the partial realization of Lê's project of literary dissemination: she is indeed successful in crossing transnational and translinguistic borders to offer Bachmann to both a scholarly French-reading public and a specialized Francophone readership. In order to deal with "the experience of coming after the event"; that is, long after the demise of the admired precursor, Lê admits to a desire to "rendre hommage . . . d'exhumer, [et] de faire revivre" (pay homage . . . to exhume, [and] to revive) Bachmann for future generations of readers.[75] In this light, it is safe to say that while Lê's personal objectives can be seen to eclipse the case study of her precursor, her tribute to Bachmann compensates by becoming a veritable textual event in and of itself.[76]

NOTES

1. Alexandra Kurmann, "An Interview with Linda Lê," (November 19, 2010): 1–6, at 5; the full text of the interview is available through the School of Advanced Study, University of London—see www.igrs.sas.ac.uk/sites/default/files/files/Research%20Centres/CCWW/Linda_Le_Interview.pdf (accessed November 20, 2013). If not otherwise stated, translations from the French are my own.

2. Lauren Berlant, "On the Case," *Critical Inquiry* 33, no. 4 (2007): 663–72, at 667.
3. I borrow the term "precursor" from Harold Bloom's postulation of literary influence, which claims that a younger writer takes as an imaginary role model, a late, great wordsmith. While Bloom's theory is fraught with Oedipal struggles between a powerful father and emulating son, I see Lê as adopting Bachmann as a substitutive personal mentor to admire and imitate. See Bloom, *The Anxiety of Influence: A Theory of Poetry*, 2nd ed. (New York: Oxford University Press, 1973; 1997). Citations refer to the 1997 edition.
4. Linda Lê, "Ingeborg Bachmann, un brasier d'énigmes," *Quotidien de Paris*, October 18, 1989, 4. Translations of primary works alone are given in the text, or in endnotes.
5. Linda Lê, "'J'écris sur la nature du feu': Ingeborg Bachmann, *Malina, Requiem pour Fanny Goldmann, Franza*," *Critique* 47, no. 534 (1991): 846–54. Lê borrows the titular phrase from Bachmann's celebrated novel, *Malina*, first published in 1971: "avec la main brûlée, j'écris sur la nature du feu" (with my burned hand, I write about the nature of fire). See Ingeborg Bachmann, *Malina: A Novel*, trans. Philip Boehm (New York: Holmes and Meier, 1990), 58; *Werke 3: Todesarten: Malina und unvollendete Romane*, ed. Christine Koschel, Inge von Weidenbaum and Clemens Münster (Munich: Piper, 1978; 2010), 95; citations refer to the 2010 edition. The phrase itself is a rendering of that written by Gustave Flaubert, "Lettre à Louise Colet, 6 Juillet 1852," in *Correspondance*, ed. Jean Bruneau (Paris: Gallimard, 1998), 128.
6. Linda Lê, "Ingeborg Bachmann," in *Tu écriras sur le bonheur*, 2nd ed. (Paris: Presses Universitaires de France, 1999; Paris: Christian Bourgois, 2009), 30–43. Rather than the 1991 essay specified in note 5 above, henceforward citations refer to the Christian Bourgois edition of 2009, as this is the version most readily available to readers. In this book no mention is made of the fact that the text has been recycled, perhaps for the reason that four other essays in this publication can be traced back to articles formerly printed in *Critique* between 1990 and 1995. See Linda Lê, "La formule de l'aboulie: Henri-Frédéric Amiel, *Journal intime Tome XII*," *Critique* 51, no. 576 (1995): 323–25; "Heinrich Heine ou 'la déchirure du monde': Heinrich Heine, *De la France*; Gerhard Höhn, *Heinrich Heine, un intellectuel moderne*," *Critique* 51, no. 582 (1995): 889–91; "'Tu écriras sur le bonheur': Paul Nizon, *L'année de l'amour, Stolz, Dans le ventre de la baleine*," *Critique* 46, no. 522 (1990): 971–77; "Le voyageur d'une vie de flânerie: Natsume Sôseki, *Les herbes du chemin*," *Critique* 49, no. 550–51 (1993): 249–51.
7. Linda Lê, *Les aubes* (Paris: Christian Bourgois, 2000).
8. Kurmann, "Interview," 6.
9. Michael Warner, *Publics and Counterpublics* (New York: Zone Books, 2002), 11.
10. Catherine Argand, "Entretien: Linda Lê," *Lire* (Avril 1999): 32.
11. Tess Do, "The Vietnamese Cooking Legacy: A Cultural and Post-Colonial Exploration of Food Metaphors in Linda Lê's *Les trois Parques*," in *Essays in Modern Italian and French Literature—In Recollection of Tom O'Neill*, ed. Alastair Hurst and Tony Pagliaro (Melbourne: *Spunti e ricerche*, 2004), 40–49, at 40.
12. Kurmann, "Interview," 1.
13. Kurmann, "Interview," 2. Lê returned to Vietnam for the funeral of her father in 1995; she returned in 1999 for fifteen days, and again in late 2010. This last visit entailed visiting her homeland as a celebrated author, partaking in a nationwide tour organized specifically for her by *L'Espace-Centre Culturel Français de Hanoi* of the French Embassy in Vietnam.

14. Michael Butler, "From the 'Wiener Gruppe' to Ernst Jandl," in *Modern Austrian Writing: Literature and Society after 1945*, ed. Alan Best and Hans Wolfschültz (London: Oswald Wolff, 1980), 236–51, at 236.
15. Kurmann, "Interview," 6.
16. Heinrich Böll considered that Bachmann had been made into a myth during her lifetime by journalists and fellow writers alike, and that this had contributed to her premature death. See Böll, "Ich denke an sie wie an ein Mädchen," in *Ingeborg Bachmann: Eine Bibliographie*, ed. Otto Bareiss (Munich: Piper, 1978), xxiii. Karen Achberger called the same phenomenon "the Bachmann myth." See Achberger, *Understanding Ingeborg Bachmann* (Columbia: University of South Carolina Press, 1995), 3–4.
17. Lê describes this time as "trois mois de stupeur et de confusion—que je n'aurais pu affronter sans l'aide de quelques amis et d'un medecin" (three months of stupor and confusion that I could not have faced without the help of a few friends and a doctor): see Linda Lê, *Les trois Parques* (Paris: Christian Bourgois, 1997), postscript; *The Three Fates*, trans. Mark Polizzotti (New York: New Directions, 1997), postscript.
18. Lê, "Ingeborg Bachmann," 30. The italicized passages are all found in the French translation of *Montauk* by Max Frisch, *Montauk: Un récit*, trans. Michèle Tailleur and Jean Tailleur (Paris: Gallimard, 1978), 124.
19. Max Frisch, *Montauk*, trans. Geoffrey Skelton (New York: Harcourt Brace Jovanovich, 1976), 104–5.
20. Lê, "Ingeborg Bachmann," 30; taken word for word from Frisch, *Montauk: Un récit*, 125; *Montauk*, 105.
21. Lê, "Ingeborg Bachmann," 33, 32.
22. Lê, "Ingeborg Bachmann," 35. From Thomas Bernhard, *In der Höhe: Rettungsversuch, Unsinn* (Salzburg: Residenz Verlag, 1989), 94; *On the Mountain*, trans. Russell Stockman (London: Quartet Books, 1991), 87.
23. A decade after Bachmann's untimely death, in an interview with the Austrian writer Hilde Spiel, Karen Achberger would learn that only just prior to her death, Bachmann had made concrete plans to finally return to Austria. A return was not, then, a lifelong project as Lê suggests it was. See Achberger, *Understanding*, 9.
24. Lê, "Ingeborg Bachmann, 35. Lê writes "impossible le retour" (return is impossible) in an autobiographical story that recounts the flight of a family with young daughters from invading communist troops in Vietnam. See Linda Lê, "Les pieds nus" [Bare feet], in *Littérature vietnamienne: La part d'exil*, ed. Le Huu Khoa (Aix-en Provence: Université de Provence, 1995), 58.
25. "Kriegsvergessenheit" refers to a sociological phenomenon in German-speaking nations signifying the repression of knowledge of the World War II in the postwar period: see Dierk Spreen and Andreas Galling-Stiehler, "Kriegsvergessenheit," in *Ästhetik und Kommunikation: Kriegsvergessenheit in der Mediengesellschaft* 152 (2011): 9–16. Lê, "Ingeborg Bachmann," 37; *Parques*, 151–57; *Fates*, 98–106.
26. Lê, "Ingeborg Bachmann," 34.
27. Linda Lê, "Tangages" [Oscillations], in *Vietnam, le detin du lotus*, ed. by Alain Sancerni (Paris: Riveneuve, 2010), 20–24, at 24.
28. In connection with Bachmann's statement, see Ingeborg Bachmann, *Wir müssen wahre Sätze finden: Gespräche und Interviews* [We must find true sentences: Conversations and interviews], ed. Christine Koschel and Inge von Weidenbaum (Munich: Piper, 1983), 99–100; Monika Albrecht, "'A Man, A Woman . . .': Narrative Perspective and Gender Discourse in Ingeborg Bachmann's *Malina*," in *"If We Had the Word": Ingeborg Bachmann, Views and Reviews*, ed. Gisela Brinker-Gabler and Markus Zisselsberger

(Riverside: Ariadne, 2004), 127–49, at 129; the quotation is from Lê, "Ingeborg Bachmann," 34.

29. Kurmann, "Interview," 3.
30. Bent Flyvbjerg, "Five Misunderstandings about Case-Study Research," *Qualitative Inquiry* 12, no. 2 (2006): 219–45, at 235.
31. Berlant, "On the Case," 664.
32. Berlant, "On the Case," 672; Lê, "Ingeborg Bachmann," 33.
33. Karen Achberger reveals that the author finally succumbed in the hospital to withdrawal symptoms from unidentifiable medications that she had been taking, supposedly for insomnia and anxiety: Achberger, *Understanding*, 1–2, 8.
34. Lê, "Ingeborg Bachmann," 33. The conflation of Bachmann with her work is particularly evident in readings of her tragic death as illustrative of fiery scenes in her novel *Malina*, in which, ambiguously, the protagonist is either murdered or commits suicide. For example, at Bachmann's death, on October 17, 1973, the West German tabloid *BILD* printed the headline "Sie starb, als wär's von ihr erdacht" (She died as if she had thought it up herself): see Achberger, *Understanding*, 9.
35. Berlant, "On the Case", 663.
36. Lê, "Ingeborg Bachmann," 33 (italics in the original).
37. Berlant, "On the Case," 664.
38. Berlant, "On the Case," 670.
39. John Forrester, "If *p*, then what? Thinking in Cases," *History of the Human Sciences* 9 (1996): 1–25, at 7.
40. Berlant, "On the Case," 665.
41. Ingeborg Bachmann, "Die Wahrheit ist dem Menschen zumutbar," in *Werke 4: Essays, Reden, Vermischte Schriften, Anhang*, ed. Christine Koschel, Inge von Weidenbaum, and Clemens Münster (Munich: Piper, 1978; 2010), 275–77 (citations refer to the 2010 edition); in 1959 Bachmann won the radio play prize "Der Hörspielpreis der Kriegsblinden" for her radio play "Der gute Gott von Manhattan," which is published in *Werke 1: Gedichte, Hörspiele, Libretti, Übersetzungen*, ed. Christine Koschel, Inge von Weidenbaum, and Clemens Münster (Munich: Piper, 1978; 2010), 269–327 (citations refer to the 2010 edition); "The Good God of Manhattan," in *Three Radio Plays*, trans. Lilian Friedberg (Riversdale: Ariadne, 1999), 119–206.
42. Lê, "Ingeborg Bachmann," 42 (italics added). Italics indicate the phrases lifted directly by Lê from Bachmann's speech in translation; see Ingeborg Bachmann, "La vérité est exigible de l'homme" [Man is expected to face the truth], trans. Claude Lutz, *Les Cahiers du GRIF* 35 (1987): 62–65, at 63; *Werke 4*, 275.
43. Lê, *Les aubes*, 74.
44. The following text fragments are examples of phrases in *Les aubes* found originally in "Ingeborg Bachmann": "la poétesse en chandail noir" (the poet in black garb); "du même désir de pureté" (the same desire for purity); "une femme égarée" (a lost woman); and "son vœu profond d'écrire un ouvrage en prose" (her deep wish to write a work of prose): see Lê, *Les aubes*, 74; "Ingeborg Bachmann," 31–34.
45. Lê, "Ingeborg Bachmann," 41.
46. Jacques Lacan, *Écrits: A Selection* (London: Tavistock, 1980, 1966; London: Routledge, 2001), 50. Citations refer to the Routledge edition. Lê has admitted to employing Lacan's theory of the foreclosure of the Law of the Father in her 1998 novel *Voix: Une crise* [Voices: A crisis], an admission which supports my Lacanian reading: see Kurmann, "Interview," 5. The application of this theory to Lê's trilogy can be seen in Alexandra Kurmann,

"Foreclosed Fatherhood: A Decade of Psychoanalytical Experimentation in Linda Lê's Fiction," in *Experience and Experiment: Women's Writing in France 2000–2010*, ed. Gill Rye and Amaleena Damlé (Oxford: Peter Lang, 2013), 125–39.

47. Jacqueline Rose, "Introduction—II," in *Feminine Sexuality: Jacques Lacan and the École Freudienne*, ed. Juliet Mitchell and Jacqueline Rose (London: Macmillan, 1982), 27–57, at 28.

48. Bachmann, *Malina*, 225; Weigel, "Der schielende Blick: Thesen zur Geschichte weiblicher Schreibpraxis," in *Die verborgene Frau: Sechs Beiträge zu einer feministischen Literaturwissenschaft*, ed. Inge Stephan and Sigrid Weigel (Hamburg: Argument-Sonderband, 1988), 83–137.

49. In a battle between Antigone's brothers Eteocles and Polyneices over the throne of Thebes, each kills the other. Antigone's sense of morality motivates her to illegally bury Polyneices, an act that she refuses to deny when on trial before Creon, King of Thebes; this leads to her incarceration and suicide: Sophocles, *Antigone*, trans. Andrew Brown (Warminster: Aris and Phillips, 1987).

50. Lê, "Ingeborg Bachmann," 41. Johanna Bossinade and Doris Hildesheim, German-language Bachmann scholars, also identify Antigone in Bachmann's novel: see Johanna Bossinade, *Das Beispiel Antigone: Textsemiotische Untersuchungen zur Präsentation der Fraufigur. Von Sophokles bis Ingeborg Bachmann* (Cologne: Böhlau Verlag, 1990), 206; Doris Hildesheim, *Ingeborg Bachmann: Todesbilder: Todessehnsucht und Sprachverlust in "Malina" und "Antigone"* (Berlin: Weißensee Verlag, 2000), 177.

51. Jacques Lacan, *The Seminar of Jacques Lacan Book VII: Ethics of Psychoanalysis 1959–1960*, trans. Dennis Porter (New York: Norton, 1992), 242–83.

52. Terry Eagleton, "Lacan's Antigone," in *Interrogating Antigone in Postmodern Philosophy and Criticism*, ed. S. E. Wilmer and Audronė Žukauskaitė (New York: Oxford University Press, 2010), 101–9, at 103.

53. Eagleton, "Lacan's Antigone," 102.

54. Lê, "Ingeborg Bachmann," 34 (italics added).

55. Lê, "Ingeborg Bachmann," 34–35.

56. Bachmann, *Gespräche und Interviews*, 65.

57. Lê, "Ingeborg Bachmann," 36.

58. Lê, "Ingeborg Bachmann," 31.

59. Slavoj Žižek, *Did Somebody Say Totalitarianism? Five Interventions in the (Mis)Use of a Notion* (London: Verso, 2001), 157.

60. Albert R. Jonsen and Stephen Toulmin, *The Abuse of Casuistry: A History of Moral Reasoning* (Berkeley: University of California Press, 1988), 11.

61. Richard B. Miller, *Casuistry and Modern Ethics: A Poetics of Practical Reasoning* (Chicago: University of Chicago Press, 1996), 3–4.

62. Lê does not use the word "political" until her text of 2005 "Antigones dans un paysage de cris" [Antigones in a landscape of screams], in her discussion of the ethical engagement of writers such as Nelly Sachs, and in her short text "Étranges étrangers" [Strange strangers] in 2011. Linda Lê, "Antigones dans un paysage de cris," in *Le complexe de Caliban* (Paris: Christian Bourgois, 2005), 151–64; "Étranges étrangers," *Carnets du Viêt Nam* 28 (2011): 38–42.

63. Lê, *Les aubes*, 73. The exchange of positions also demonstrates the literary successor's agonistic struggle for power over the precursor. Bloom, *Anxiety of Influence*, xxiv; see note 3 above.

64. Michel Foucault, *Discipline and Punish: The Birth of the Prison* (New York: Vintage, 1979), 189.

65. Foucault, *Discipline and Punish*, 189.
66. Foucault, *Discipline and Punish*, 189; Berlant, "On the Case", 664.
67. See note 11 above.
68. Slavoj Žižek, *The Sublime Object of Ideology* (London: Verso, 1989; 1991), 105. Citations refer to the 1991 edition.
69. W. W Meissner, *Internalization in Psychoanalysis* (New York: International Universities Press, 1981), 15.
70. See note 11 above.
71. Françoise Rétif, "'Du côté de la mort la vie'," *Europe: Revue littéraire mensuelle: Ingeborg Bachmann* 892 (2003): 3–7, at 3.
72. Rétif, "Du côté de la mort la vie," 4; Bachmann, *Werke 1–4*, ed. Christine Koschel, Inge von Weidenbaum and Clemens Münster (Munich: Piper, 1978; 2010). Citations refer to the 2010 edition.
73. The publication in 2009 of *Oeuvres* made accessible a collection of some of Bachmann's short stories and essays that to date had not been readily available to a French-reading public; however, the complete works available in German is not matched by a French language publication. See Ingeborg Bachmann, *Oeuvres*, trans. Cécile Ladjali (Paris: Actes Sud, 2009).
74. Agrand, "Entretien: Linda Lê," 28; Michelle Bacholle-Boskovic, *Linda Lê, l'écriture du manque* (New York: Edwin Mellen Press, 2006), ii, 23; Nancy Huston, *Professeurs de désespoir* (Paris: Actes Sud, 2004), 330; Kurmann, "Interview," 1, 3–6; Linda Lê, "Ça" [That], *Littératures "une mère étrangère,"* special issue *La pensée de midi* 5–6 (2001/2), editor's foreword.
75. Graham Allen, *Intertextuality* (London: Routledge, 2000), 133; Kurmann, "Interview," 6.
76. Kurmann, "Interview," 6.

Contributors

Warwick Anderson is an ARC Laureate Fellow and professor in the Department of History and the Centre for Values, Ethics and the Law in Medicine at the University of Sydney. His books include *The Collectors of Lost Souls: Turning Kuru Scientists into Whitemen* (Baltimore: Johns Hopkins University Press, 2008). With Deborah Jenson and Richard C. Keller he edited *Unconscious Dominions: Psychoanalysis, Colonial Trauma, and Global Sovereignties* (Durham NC: Duke University Press, 2011). His most recent book (with Ian R. Mackay) is *Intolerant Bodies: A Short History of Autoimmune Disease* (Baltimore: Johns Hopkins University Press, 2014).

John Cash is an Honorary Fellow in the School of Social and Political Sciences at the University of Melbourne, where he was formerly deputy director of the Ashworth Program in Social Theory. His research interests are in the fields of social and political theory, psychoanalytic studies, and the analysis of contemporary subjectivities. His publications include *Identity, Ideology and Conflict: The Structuration of Politics in Northern Ireland* (Cambridge: Cambridge University Press: 1996, 2010) and, most recently, "Ideology and Social and Cultural Theory" in *Routledge Handbook of Social and Cultural Theory*, ed. Anthony Elliott (Abingdon: Routledge, 2014). He is an editor of *Journal of Postcolonial Studies*.

Joy Damousi is professor of history in the School of Historical and Philosophical Studies at the University of Melbourne. She has published widely in the fields of cultural history, feminist history, the history of emotions, war and memory, and the history of psychoanalysis. Her recent publications include *Freud in the Antipodes: A Cultural History of Psychoanalysis in Australia* (Sydney: University of New South Wales Press, 2005) and, co-edited with Mariano Plotkin, *Psychoanalysis and Politics: Histories of Psychoanalysis Under Conditions of Restricted Political Freedom* (New York: Oxford University Press, 2012).

Lisa Featherstone is a senior lecturer at the University of Newcastle, Australia. Her work on sexuality, reproduction, and the history of medicine has been widely published, with key articles in *Journal of the History of Sexuality*, *Women's History Review*, and *Australian Historical Studies*. Her monograph *Let's Talk About Sex: Histories of Sexuality in Australia from Federation to the Pill* (Newcastle: Cambridge Scholars Publishing, 2011) provides a survey of multiple sexual histories. Her forthcoming work, with Amanda Kaladelfos, is on sexual crimes in the 1950s, and a monograph is currently under contract to Melbourne University Publishing.

Johanna Gehmacher is a professor at the Institute for Contemporary History, University of Vienna. Her research interests include gender and nationalism, biography, and nineteenth- and twentieth-century social movements. Among recent publications is the chapter "Narratives of Race, Constructions of Community and the Demand for Female Participation in German Nationalist Movements in Austria and the German Reich," in *The Persistence of Race From the Wilhelmine Empire to National Socialism: Re-Examining Constructions and Perceptions of Cultural Narratives of Race in German History, 1871–1945*, ed. Lara Benjamin and Oliver Haag (New York: Berghahn Books, 2014). She co-edits the journal *Österreichische Zeitschrift für Geschichtswissenschaften*.

Alexandra Kurmann is an associate lecturer in French and francophone studies at Macquarie University, Sydney. She completed her doctoral thesis at the University of Melbourne, which was entitled "'Lecteur idéal, lecteur imaginaire.' The Intertextual Relationship Fostered by Linda Lê with an Imaginary Ingeborg Bachmann." Her analysis of Linda Lê's trilogy is part of the collection *Experience and Experiment: Women's Writing in France 2000–2010*, ed. Gill Rye and Amaleena Damlé (Oxford: Peter Lang, 2013). She has articles forthcoming in *Forgotten Histories: Vietnamese Veterans in Australia*, *Mélanges pour Anne Freadman* and *Skepsi*. Her research interests include Vietnamese-francophone literature, Bachmann studies, comparative literature and intertextuality, exile writing.

Birgit Lang is senior lecturer in the School of Languages and Linguistics at the University of Melbourne. As well as the case study, her fields of research include exile and migrant literature, contemporary German and Austrian literature, and the history of sexuality. Currently she is completing the book *Making the Case: The Case Study Genre in Sexology, Psychoanalysis and Literature* with Joy Damousi and Alison Lewis (Manchester: Manchester University Press, forthcoming). She has been co-editor of *Limbus: An Australian Yearbook for German Literary and Cultural Studies* since the inception of the series in 2008.

Alison Lewis is a professor in the School of Languages and Linguistics at the University of Melbourne. She has published widely on German literature of the modern period, on German unification, women's literature, and the East German secret police. Her research interests span the fields of language study, modern literature, European studies, and Indigenous studies, as well as gender studies. Her monographs include *Die Kunst des Verrats: Der Prenzlauer Berg und die Staatssicherheit* (Würzburg: Königshausen und Neumann, 2003), and *Eine schwierige Ehe: Liebe, Geschlecht und die Geschichte der deutschen Wiedervereinigung im Spiegel der Literatur* (Freiburg: Rombach, 2009).

Katie Sutton is a lecturer in German and gender studies at the Australian National University. Previously she held an ARC Postdoctoral Fellowship at the University of Melbourne, as part of the Discovery Project team "Making the Case: The Case Study Genre in Sexology, Psychoanalysis and Literature" (led by Birgit Lang and Joy Damousi, 2010–14). Her current research focuses on the historical relationship between sexology and psychoanalysis. She is the author of *The Masculine Woman in Weimar Germany* (New York: Berghahn Books, 2011), and articles on gender history, sexual subcultures, sport, and fashion in Weimar Germany.

Jana Verhoeven completed her PhD at the University of Melbourne, and holds an MA in American History from Humboldt Universität Berlin. She currently teaches in the School of Languages and Linguistics at the University of Melbourne, specializing in nineteenth-century French cultural history as well as European cultural history. She has published on aspects of nineteenth-century French gender and cultural history; her book *Jovial Bigotry: Max O'Rell and the Debate over Manners and Morals in 19th-Century France, Britain and the United States* was published in 2012 (Newcastle: Cambridge Scholars Publishing).

Timothy Verhoeven lectures in the School of Philosophical, Historical and International Studies at Monash University, Melbourne. He has published several studies on the history of anti-Catholicism, particularly from transnational and gendered perspectives. His monograph *Transatlantic Anti-Catholicism: France and the United States in the Nineteenth Century*, appeared in 2010 (New York: Palgrave Macmillan). He has recently edited a special issue of the *Journal of Religious History* dedicated to transnational approaches to anti-Catholicism.

Christiane Weller is senior lecturer in the German Studies Program at Monash University, Melbourne. Her research interests include German travel writing and expedition reports, colonial writing, contemporary German fiction, and psychoanalytic theory. She has published on Georg Forster, Christoph Ransmayr, W. G. Sebald, Thomas Bernhard, and Wolfgang Hilbig, and on topics such as trauma, melancholia, and psychosis. She is a co-editor of *Limbus: An Australian Yearbook for German Literary and Cultural Studies* (Freiburg: Rombach, since 2008).

Index